Mixed Methods for Policy Research and Program Evaluation

We dedicate this work to our families, in grateful recognition of their continuous love and support, and to our many outstanding colleagues, students, and other collaborators (as named in the acknowledgments section of this book).

Mixed Methods for Policy Research and Program Evaluation

Patricia Burch
University of Southern California

Carolyn J. Heinrich
University of Texas at Austin

Los Angeles | London | New Delhi
Singapore | Washington DC | Boston

SAGE was founded in 1965 by Sara Miller McCune to support the dissemination of usable knowledge by publishing innovative and high-quality research and teaching content. Today, we publish more than 750 journals, including those of more than 300 learned societies, more than 800 new books per year, and a growing range of library products including archives, data, case studies, reports, conference highlights, and video. SAGE remains majority-owned by our founder, and after Sara's lifetime will become owned by a charitable trust that secures our continued independence.

Los Angeles | London | Washington DC | New Delhi | Singapore | Boston

Praise for *Mixed Methods for Policy Research and Program Evaluation*

"Drawing on their extensive experience in large scale project management, Patricia Burch and Carolyn Heinrich clearly articulate an agenda for program and policy evaluation that is designed to ensure actionable evidence of the effectiveness of a program and its implementation is generated for all stakeholders. The examples they provide, while not minimizing the challenges of employing a mixed methods approach, will convince readers of the practicality and value of iteratively integrating both qualitative and quantitative approaches throughout the entire evaluation process, from initial design through data integration and analysis to dissemination of research findings. We can all learn from their experiences, so generously shared."

—Patricia Bazeley, *Research Support Pty Limited, Australia, and President-Elect of the Mixed Methods International Research Association*

"In a time of scarce resources for social programs, wise policy requires making tough choices. To do this well, policymakers need reliable information on what works, why some approaches are more successful than others, and what can be done to improve effectiveness. This book is a vital primer on how to do that. It attacks the mistaken view that quantitative and qualitative research are alternatives, rather than essential complements that, when combined in a mix of research methods, can best provide guidance to policymakers and practitioners."

— Judith M. Gueron, *Scholar in Residence—President Emerita, MDRC*

"This rich and sophisticated book provides a wealth of insights and practical guidelines that will enhance the work of both novice and experienced researchers. Burch and Heinrich show the way to making mixed methods research more relevant and more rigorous."

— Thomas Hatch, *Teachers College Columbia University, and Co-Director, National Center for Restructuring Education, Schools, and Teaching (NCREST)*

"The gulf between qualitative and quantitative researchers is an old problem. With this useful and important new book, Burch and Heinrich help to bridge the divide, highlighting the need for a more complementary and integrated approach that can help us learn not just whether programs "work", but how and why they do."

—Douglas N. Harris, *Tulane University, and Director, Education Research Alliance for New Orleans*

"This book is just what is needed as we move into a new phase of evidence informed policy and practice. It advocates an integrated and coherent approach to policy research and program evaluation while recognizing the realities and complexities of both policy and research. It will be immensely helpful to those engaged in mixed methods research across a variety of policy fields."

—Geoff Whitty, *Director Emeritus of the London Institute of Education, Research Professor at Bath Spa University, UK and Global Innovation Chair at the University of Newcastle, Australia*

"In this book, Burch and Heinrich have successfully explained how a mixed methods approach can be applied to policy analysis and evaluation. I highly recommend it for scholars applying mixed methods to the study of public policy issues. This book should be required reading for all public policy students and researchers."

—Elizabeth A. Corley, *Arizona State University*

"This is a very useful book for researchers and evaluators contemplating or already using mixed methods in policy research and evaluation, as well as for those teaching applied evaluation courses."

— Diane Hirshberg, *University of Alaska Anchorage*

Los Angeles | London | New Delhi
Singapore | Washington DC | Boston

FOR INFORMATION:

SAGE Publications, Inc.
2455 Teller Road
Thousand Oaks, California 91320
E-mail: order@sagepub.com

SAGE Publications Ltd.
1 Oliver's Yard
55 City Road
London EC1Y 1SP
United Kingdom

SAGE Publications India Pvt. Ltd.
B 1/I 1 Mohan Cooperative Industrial Area
Mathura Road, New Delhi 110 044
India

SAGE Publications Asia-Pacific Pte. Ltd.
3 Church Street
#10-04 Samsung Hub
Singapore 049483

Printed in the United States of America

Cataloging-in-Publication Data is available for this title from the Library of Congress.

ISBN 978-1-4522-7662-5

Acquisitions Editor: Helen Salmon
Associate Editor: Katie Bierach
Editorial Assistant: Anna Villarruel
Production Editor: Kelly DeRosa
Copy Editor: Colleen Brennan
Typesetter: C&M Digitals (P) Ltd.
Proofreader: Alison Syring
Indexer: Karen Wiley
Cover Designer: Gail Buschman
Marketing Manager: Nicole Elliott

This book is printed on acid-free paper.

15 16 17 18 19 10 9 8 7 6 5 4 3 2 1

Brief Contents

Detailed Contents

List of Tables, Figures, Boxes, and Appendices

(Continued)

Acknowledgments

W̲e thank the funders of the research projects that we describe in this book:

- The Institute of Education Sciences (PR/Award number: R305A090301, Education Policy, Finance and Systems Research Program, Goal 3)
- Wisconsin Department of Public Instruction
- The Institute for Research on Poverty (IRP) and the Wisconsin Bureau of Child Support (BCS)
- The Department of Social Development (DSD), the South African Social Security Agency (SASSA), and the United Nations Children's Fund (UNICEF) South Africa

We also thank our many colleagues and collaborators in the research underlying this work:

- Chapters 1–4: Annalee Good, Robert Meyer, Rudy Acosta, Brie Chapa, Huiping Cheng, Penny Clark, Jeff Denning, Marcus Dillender, Esmeralda Garcia-Galvan, Christi Kirshbaum, Emily Kao, Julie Montgomery, Hiren Nisar, Jahni Smith, and Mary Stewart; Sandy Schroeder and staff in the Austin Independent School District (ISD), Chicago Public Schools, Dallas ISD, Los Angeles Unified School District, Milwaukee Public Schools, and Minneapolis Public Schools
- Chapter 5: Elizabeth Graue, Robert Meyer, and the WCER SAGE Evaluation Team, University of Wisconsin–Madison; Estella Bensimon, Alicia Dowd, and the Center for Urban Education, Rossier School of Education, University of Southern California
- Chapter 6: Maria Cancian, Hilary Shager, Brett Burkhardt, Steven Cook, Dawn Duren, Tom Kaplan, Dan Meyer, Ingrid Rothe, Bill Wambach, Lynn Wimer, Lara Rosen, Samuel Hall, Katie Maguire, Alan Paberz, Susan Pffeifer, Carol Chellew, Jan VanVleck, Pat Birchell-Sielaff, Karen Day, and Julie Busch
- Chapter 7: John Hoddinott, Michael Samson, Kenneth Mac Quene, Ingrid van Niekerk, Bryant Renaud, Jesse McConnell, Luca Pellerano, Nils Riemenschneider, Selwyn Jehoma, Thilde Stevens, Maureen Motepe, Thabani Buthelezi, Dibolelo Ababio, Eric Musekene, Alice Odhiambo, Rudzani Takalani, George Laryea-Adjei, Nkechi Obisie-Nmehielle, Dugan Fraser, Benjamin Davis, Ashu Handa, Jan Vorster, Linda Richter, Vuyiswa Mathambo, Lucia Knight, and Patrick Chiroro

SAGE and the authors greatly appreciate the feedback from the following reviewers: Diane Hirshberg, University of Alaska Anchorage Center for Alaska Education Policy Research; Leanne M. Kallemeyn, Loyola University Chicago; and Linda Valli, University of Maryland.

About the Authors

Patricia Burch (PhD, Stanford University) is Associate Professor at the University of Southern California. Burch's work focuses on education policy, private sector involvement in public education, mixed methods policy research, and policy theory. Burch works with practitioners, policymakers, and vendors for equitable and quality schooling in K-12 public education and out-of-school time settings. She teaches graduate-level courses in policy implementation and research methods.

Carolyn J. Heinrich (PhD, University of Chicago) is the Sid Richardson Professor of Public Affairs at the Lyndon B. Johnson School of Public Affairs, Affiliate Professor of Economics, and the director of the Center for Health and Social Policy at the University of Texas at Austin. Heinrich's research focuses on social welfare policy, workforce development, education, econometric methods for program evaluation, and public management and performance management. She regularly collaborates with government agencies and nongovernmental organizations on program evaluations and in improving program and policy design and program effectiveness. In 2004, Heinrich received the David N. Kershaw Award for distinguished contributions to the field of public policy analysis and management by a person under age 40, and in 2010, she was elected to the National Academy of Public Administration. Prior to her appointment at the University of Texas, she was the director of the La Follette School of Public Affairs at the University of Wisconsin–Madison.

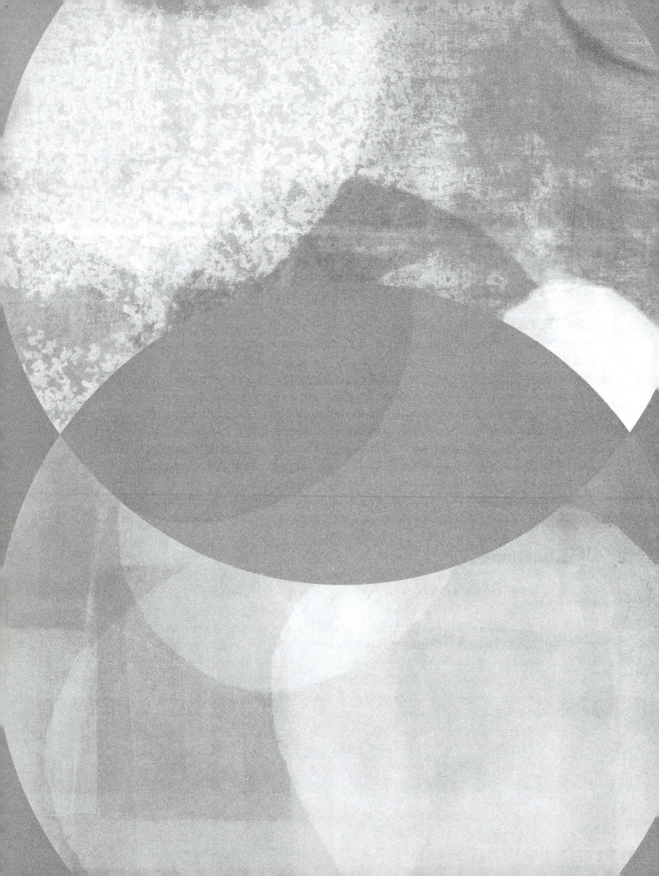

CHAPTER 1

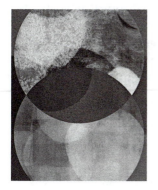

Introduction: The Demand for and Value of Fully Integrated Qualitative and Quantitative Research

The demand for more rigorous evidence of policy and program effectiveness has been building globally for more than four decades. Expanding access to data and growing expectations and capacity for measuring program performance have coincided with increasing calls by the public for greater accountability for policy and program *outcomes* and responsiveness to stakeholder interests and needs. For example, in the United States the Coalition for Evidence-Based Policy—formed in 2001 by leaders from academic and policymaking circles to promote efforts to build a knowledge base of proven interventions in social policy—argued that programs were too often implemented with little regard for evidence, costing billions of dollars while failing to address critical societal problems and needs. And in the United Kingdom, the Evidence for Policy and Practice Information and Coordinating Centre (EPPI-Centre) was created in 1993 as a social policy counterpart to the well-known, science-focused Cochrane Collaboration, to likewise promote broader use of systematic approaches to reviewing and using scientific evidence in social policymaking.

Data and methodological advances have been fundamental to, as well as spurred by, the growing demands for evidence-based policymaking. This has, in turn, stimulated ongoing debates about what constitutes rigorous and reliable evidence and how research evidence should be generated and judged. Entities such as the Cochrane Collaboration, the Campbell Collaboration, and the U.S. Department of Education's What Works Clearinghouse have established formal standards for classifying studies according to their research design and methodology, commonly assigning the highest evidence ratings to randomized controlled trials. In these forums for assessing evidence quality, qualitative research is typically considered only to the extent that it is part of an experimental or quasi-experimental study, if at all. Objections to such a rigid hierarchy for the sifting and weighing of social policy evidence have recently grown louder, however. Heinrich (2007) suggested that information on policy and program impacts is of limited use if it does not enable policymakers to attribute observed impacts to particular components of an intervention and to understand the processes that produced them. Similarly, Cook and Ludwig (2006) expressed concern that an undue focus on identifying statistically significant impacts has led to the exclusion of much policy-relevant evidence that is "concerned with basic beliefs about human nature and interactions" (p. 696).

In this context, mixed methods research (combining qualitative and quantitative methods) has attracted increasing attention as a compelling approach to identifying and explaining policy and program impacts—that is, going beyond "cause and effect" to better understand the "why" and "how" of observed effects, as we discuss in greater detail throughout this book. In this introductory chapter, we first briefly describe the importance and value of a mixed-methods approach to research in the context of the recent push for evidence-based policy, and we accordingly lay the groundwork for the case we make in this book for striving for a more fully or tightly integrated mixed methods research approach in policy and program evaluation research. We then provide readers with an overview of the contents of the book and offer some suggestions for its use in graduate courses and seminars.

THE ROLE OF MIXED METHODS RESEARCH IN MEETING THE DEMAND FOR EVIDENCED-BASED POLICY AND PRACTICE

Evidence-based policy is an approach to making informed policy decisions based principally on scientific research evidence, that is, research that achieves a high degree of internal validity as well as generalizability and replicability of its causal inferences. It has long been espoused in the medical field but has progressively extended to investigations across a range of social policy domains, including education, workforce development, poverty reduction, criminal justice, public health, and more (Sanderson, 2002). Although applied use of this term varies to some extent, it is widely seen as an attempt to move beyond the experience of the policymaker as the exclusive source of knowledge in policy design and to more deliberately, systematically, and judiciously draw on the best evidence to inform program and policy decision making. Alice Rivlin's (1971) work as scholar and practitioner was a harbinger of these efforts. She called for widespread social experimentation to improve the effectiveness of our social programs, while also recognizing that the process of developing new methods to advance this cause would be both iterative and evolving.

By many accounts, the push for evidence-based policymaking has achieved important successes. Gueron and Rolston (2013) count among them the generation and use of higher-quality evidence in policymaking, as well as the creation of "learning communities" that bridge academics and practitioners and greater awareness of the value of a continuous learning process. Gueron, as president of MDRC for nearly two decades and a staunch supporter of randomized social experiments, and Rolston, who spearheaded the use of experimental evaluation techniques during his career in government, also make clear that experimental evidence was "not the only type of evidence (or even the most important) that would matter to policymakers" (p. 426). In fact, an appreciation for mixed methods research is unmistakable in the following articulation of their approach to research (Gueron & Rolston, 2013, p. 426):

> We always viewed the random assignment design as the skeleton on which to build an evaluation that used multiple techniques to address a broader range of questions—including those raised by practitioners and managers, and by researchers who used different methods to diagnose the problems and understand why people behave as they do and how social programs work in practice.... They [program funders and government partners] cared about why program participants and managers behaved as they did, why programs were or were not successfully implemented, and what could be done to improve the results.

Defining Mixed Methods Research

Creswell and Plano Clark (2011) describe how our conceptions of mixed methods research have evolved and correspondingly discuss a range of definitions that have been offered in the literature to characterize mixed methods work. The most basic definition is of a study that includes at least one quantitative method and one qualitative method. However, as they explain in their discussion, mixed methods research has progressed to a new "way of thinking or seeing," that is, involving philosophical assumptions about how methods should be mixed throughout the research process. These more recent definitions are more prescriptive about the purpose, scope, and process of mixing qualitative and quantitative methods. We similarly argue in this book for a fuller, more tightly integrated approach to mixing methods throughout all phases of the research process (from research design to research dissemination), with the goal to increase the rigor, relevance, and influence of policy evaluation and research findings. Our own and others' research experiences suggest that the data and findings generated from a more fully integrated mixed method approach provide the kinds of rich information and insights that are essential to supporting evidence-based policy and practice.

Recognizing that the mixed methods research community is a sprawling "family," varying widely in terms of foci, strategy, and process, we spend time in Chapter 2 describing some of the frameworks or design typologies commonly associated with mixed methods research. The intent of this review is not to be comprehensive, which would be beyond the scope of this chapter given the expansiveness of this literature. We describe how we build on important strands of this work and the specific design strategies that we employ in striving toward fuller integration of qualitative and quantitative methods. We also elaborate in Chapter 2 on our own conceptualization of a more fully integrated mixed methods research approach and its application toward strengthening evidence for policy and program decision making. We describe our approach as

> a research process by which researchers interact regularly and intensively—with each other and their research partners—to draw on and combine the strengths of qualitative and quantitative methods, from the starting point of defining research objectives to the ending point of achieving those goals. In the context of applied policy and evaluation studies, research goals are defined in terms of the organizations' or policymakers' improvement goals or desired ends, and the research design is directly linked to organizational, policy, or program goals and may evolve with the policy or program landscape. The full integration of qualitative and quantitative methods contributes to both the understanding of processes for achieving outcomes or goals and, through the application of best practices in research within methodologies, the achievement of those ends.

In effect, we are describing here the end point toward which we strive in our own mixed methods research. In Chapter 2 and throughout the various chapters of this book, we will demonstrate our application of this approach and the key elements, strategies, and activities on which it turns. But we first briefly consider here the question of how researchers can gauge their progress toward the goal of a fully integrated mixed method approach. Below, we offer four basic benchmarks, which we describe in greater detail in Chapter 2 and then illustrate with practical applications and case studies throughout this book. We argue that fully integrated mixed methods research is more likely to be achieved when the follow things happen:

- Integration or mixing of methods follows through the entire cycle of the research process, from planning to inquiry, to data collection and analysis, to dissemination and redesign.
- Qualitative and quantitative methods are conducted from the start and simultaneously in ways that are interactive and iterative, in the sense that every step of the process proceeds dynamically from interaction of the two, with instrumentation and interpretation, for example, growing out of that interaction.
- Qualitative and quantitative methods are employed so as to leverage the strengths of each and provide a wider and richer range of ways to understand complex phenomena around a variety of problems and outcomes.
- The mixing of qualitative and quantitative methods is designed in ways that involve diverse stakeholders in articulating the research questions and theory of change, identifying process and outcome measures, and interpreting and disseminating the research evidence with the goal of supporting policy and program improvements.

WHAT DISTINGUISHES THIS BOOK IN THE MIXED METHODS LITERATURE

This book is not a traditional "textbook treatment" of mixed methods research. It assumes that readers have basic knowledge of what types of research methods are typically classified as quantitative versus qualitative and an understanding of the principles of causal inference, as well as the importance of situational and structural context in qualitative work. For example, as reflected in the previous discussion, the randomized controlled experiment is widely considered to be the strongest method for causal identification, yet social experiments rarely achieve the kind of controlled conditions a laboratory allows and inevitably rest on important assumptions about statistical equivalence of the treatment and control groups that require verification.

In addition, the existing mixed methods literature provides a thorough exposition of the various approaches to and classifications of mixed methods designs. Important works by Tashakkori and Teddlie (1998, 2003, 2009),

Creswell (1999), Creswell and coauthors (2003, 2011), Greene (2007), and Greene and coauthors (1989, 1997) individually and collectively offer a menu of mixed methods design options, differentiated by their attention to purpose, priority, timing, and the "how-to" and level of mixing of methods at various stages of research. Although we further discuss this prior work to a limited extent in Chapter 2, it is not our intent to provide a full appraisal of the mixed methods literature or to suggest that our own approach supplants any of these works. Rather, we view our work as building on that of these scholars, while intensifying the focus on policy and program evaluation and further probing areas of qualitative and quantitative integration that receive less attention in existing works. Here, we briefly summarize how we see our book as distinct from important works in the current mixed methods literature.

1. *Strengthening policy and program design and evaluation research*: We argue for greater use of mixed methods research to inform policy and program design and bridge the gap between the production of research evidence and the capacity of policymakers to translate findings into program and policy improvements. Mixed methods research in the disciplines typically concentrates on the use of methods to build theory and general knowledge about a given problem. Discussions are more likely to focus primarily on conceptual frameworks driving the research and arguments for its validity in the academic research community. In research that involves policy and program evaluation, research objectives are broadened to include developing evidence and insights that will serve as a key source of practical knowledge for policymakers and practitioners working in a given area. In a tightly integrated mixed methods approach to policy and program evaluation, the quality of information generated derives not only from the application of scientific methods but also from how well the data represent both specific (e.g., local) manifestations and observations of the general problem. It also requires a grounding *in* the data that captures the complexity of social phenomena and real-world policy and organizational problems.

2. *Striving for full integration and explicating the "know-how" of a fully integrated mixed methods approach*: The basic logic or "step-by-step" process for undertaking both quantitative and qualitative research is more similar than many researchers probably realize, which allows for tighter integration across the various phases or steps of the research process. These steps include defining a research problem or question,

developing a theory of change, designing instrumentation, collecting data, analyzing data and interpreting the findings, and reporting and disseminating the research results. Intensifying integration across this sequence of steps can be a very powerful strategy for ultimately increasing the validity and reliability of the results. As described in Chapters 2 and 3 and illustrated throughout the case study chapters, moving toward fully integrated mixed methods research involves developing and using knowledge in one phase of integration to inform another, that is, building feedback loops not only between qualitative and quantitative but also across the research phases to support hypothesis induction, deduction, and verification. The examples presented in this book emphasize the need for simultaneous work and coordination of that work across all aspects of the research process and offer practical insights on the "how-to" of this approach.

3. *Creating mechanisms for collaboration and coordination that also support a dynamic approach to research:* Policy and program evaluation rarely take place with a "textbook" stable intervention or within an unchanging environment that would allow for more definitive conclusions about a policy or program's effectiveness. If researchers are to generate findings that inform our understanding of a policy or program's implementation and impacts—for example, the efficacy of tax credits and tuition vouchers in increasing low-income students' participation in charter schools—then the research approach needs to have the capacity to adapt to and manage the often considerable uncertainty in the environment and intervention being studied. We argue that a more fully integrated mixed methods research approach is better able to accommodate these dynamics and incorporate them into the research design and implementation in ways that enhance what is learned from the research, particularly when the program or policy stakeholders are engaged in the research process. For example, what *is* the intervention in an environment in which a local government's capacity to administer or regulate the policy is declining and where there is a high turnover rate in key staff? Existing discussions of mixed methods research approaches tend to overlook not only the importance of collaboration between qualitative and quantitative researchers but also the valuable role for exchange and collaboration with policymakers and program implementers, which we show in this book both confirms and strengthens the validity of research findings.

OVERVIEW OF REMAINING CHAPTERS

Chapters 2 through 4 are intended to motivate the importance of tightly integrated, mixed methods research approaches, offer tools and guidance in integrating qualitative and quantitative methods, and help students evaluate the appropriateness of mixed methods work in the context of policy questions and program objectives. We offer a framework to support efforts to more fully integrate mixed methods approaches across the life cycle of the mixed methods research process in policy settings. Based on this framework, key objectives of mixed methods research include to increase knowledge and understanding of interventions (in theory and as implemented) and mechanisms/pathways to program impacts; explore policy issues in greater depth and detail, adding contextualization; inform construction of empirical measures, choice of methods, and specification of models; and aid and enhance interpretation and dissemination of qualitative and quantitative research findings.

Chapter 2. Conceptualizing Mixed Methods Research

Chapter 2 builds a conceptual argument for striving toward a fully integrated mixed methods approach in applied policy research and evaluation. We begin by mapping the increasing use of mixed methods approaches across different areas of social policy. We describe commonly accepted conditions necessitating or calling for mixed methods work. To support this work, scholars have developed multiple and sometimes overlapping categorization schemes for describing the design components that characterize a mixed methods study, as well as the attributes that distinguish different kinds of mixed method studies. While leveraging this work, we argue that policy and context changes (as discussed earlier) call for a more fully integrated mixed methods approach. We offer a "mini case" of what the components of such an approach look like in practice.

Chapter 3. Designing and Implementing Fully Integrated Mixed Methods Research

In Chapter 3, we extend our discussion of the implementation of integrated mixed methods work. This chapter offers step-by-step guidance in integrating qualitative and quantitative methods along key areas of integration—including research design, instrumentation design and data collection, data analysis and interpretation, and dissemination of findings—in applied research projects. It aims to fill a knowledge gap concerning the types of capacity-building that are needed to conduct this work and offers examples of the mechanics and logistics of integrating qualitative and quantitative methods in these areas. Readers should also acquire in this chapter an appreciation for thoroughly assessing the appropriateness of mixed methods research and developing a carefully conceptualized design that facilitates fully integrated qualitative and quantitative research.

Chapter 4. Practical Tools for Integrated Mixed Method Studies of Policy Implementation

This chapter offers program evaluators concrete tools for striving toward a more fully integrated mixed methods research approach that strengthens the validity, conceptual density, relevance, and applicability of research findings and increases stakeholder confidence in results. We argue that project administration and the structures and processes used to support the execution of the research (including how researchers structure collaboration with stakeholders, coordinate joint analyses, and build knowledge of a problem) are as important to research as the methods themselves. We also demonstrate how using these tools to provide formative as well as summative feedback and to identify mechanisms within a system that can be used to support continuous program improvement can ultimately improve policy or program outcomes.

Chapters 5, 6, 7. Applications of Mixed Methods

We argue that to be instructional, the rendering of the process of mixed methods work needs to be more granular and transparent than we have seen in much published work. Using comprehensive examples of social science research conducted by the authors, these chapters present the details of research efforts that strove toward a more tightly integrated, mixed methods approach. The case examples explore both the benefits and challenges of conducting this type of research in investigations and evaluations of policy and program impacts. The applications examine the value of this approach for policy studies conducted at the national policy level across multiple sites, including state and local policy evaluations, as well as those undertaken in international contexts, which often present unique cultural and political challenges to the research.

They also describe the authors' own experiences in which they grew in their learning about mixed methods work over time through the *practice* of these methods in actual program and policy settings.

Chapter 5 presents work from two different cases in which Patricia Burch was a co-principal investigator and describes how Dr. Burch and her collaborators strove toward a fully integrated, mixed methods approach, working at two different schooling levels (K-12 and higher education). Some of the tools, techniques, and processes that were developed in the K-12 (class size reduction) project were used as models and adapted for our integrated mixed methods study of supplemental educational services. The research project described in Chapter 6, in which Carolyn Heinrich was a co-principal investigator, is distinct in that the research team applied mixed methods in both the design and implementation of the program intervention itself, as well as in an impact evaluation of the program. This chapter describes how in the course of an 8-year study, the fully integrated mixed methods strategy was key to making contributions to the program's development as well as to a rich understanding of its effects. In Chapter 7, we feature an international study (conducted by a multinational team) in which Carolyn Heinrich was a co-principal investigator and where a carefully planned, well-coordinated effort overcame logistical, geographical, and cultural barriers to maintain a fairly tightly integrated mixed methods design throughout the research process. It is our goal to impart both knowledge and "know-how" through these cases so that researchers in the early stages of learning to apply mixed methods can benefit from these experiences.

We offer these cases as representations of mixed methods work that has striven toward full integration, rather than exemplars. In any research endeavor, analysts bring different experiences and lenses to the work. Their experiences (technical experiences as well as know-how) shape the approach and analysis. Rather than ignoring or downplaying that experience, we follow the social scientist maxim, "Mine your experience, there is potential gold there!" (Strauss, 2003, p.11). By offering comprehensive and detailed examinations of our own processes of mixed methods work, we hope to bring into fuller view the rich complexity and potential of more fully integrated mixed methods research.

We also recognize that the mixed methods projects we describe in these chapters were undertaken with teams of researchers—both large and small—and that not all of the tools and strategies discussed in the cases will be applicable to the individual researcher. Individual researchers with training in both qualitative and quantitative methods, however, could still apply the framework that we set forth in striving toward integration throughout the various stages of research in smaller scale projects, to the extent that resources allow.

Chapter 8. The Future of Fully Integrated Mixed Methods Research

This book treats integrated mixed method studies as an active and changing practice that is ultimately aimed at fostering improvement in public policies and programs and their outcomes. Although our work is broadly applicable, it has particular relevance for the current and next generation of interventions aimed at improving social, educational, and economic outcomes for low socio-economic and disadvantaged groups in the United States and in other parts of the world. The final chapter situates the application of tightly integrated, mixed methods in the dynamic economic and political context of increasing privatization and third-party governance, the shrinking role of the state, and heightened investments in social and educational policies in developing countries. We consider both the challenges and advantages of a mixed methods approach in light of these developments and conclude with a synthesis of the benefits of generating more rigorous and relevant policy research, including researcher credibility, stakeholder confidence, and effective use of research resources and dissemination of research findings.

RECOMMENDATIONS FOR HOW TO USE THIS BOOK

Presently, most upper-level undergraduate and graduate-level research methods course sequences offer separate courses for qualitative methods and quantitative methods. However, increasingly, researchers and those preparing for research and academic careers will need to understand and/or use both qualitative and quantitative methods (Hesse-Biber & Johnson, 2013). As instructors of research methods classes, we find it essential to supplement the quantitative or qualitative components of our courses with materials that illustrate the value and uses of mixed methods. We envision this book as being adopted in a variety of methods courses—including qualitative and quantitative methods and program evaluation courses, seminar courses, as well as potentially being used as a core textbook for mixed methods classes—to offer students and researchers a cutting-edge perspective on the value of and models for (or the "how-to" of) tightly integrating these two types of research methods in social and educational sciences and other policy research. Our book offers examples of practical applications of a tightly integrated, qualitative-quantitative methods approach and paves the way for future advances in the integration of these methods in applied research with detailed discussion of the mechanics of effectively mixing these methods. The examples traverse state and local, federal and international contexts and several different social science, education, and policy domains to appeal to a broad audience of students, academics, and researchers.

In addition, the case studies are presented in such a way to allow the reader to delve into the world of integrated mixed methods research and to see the challenges involved and strategies pursued. Although each setting is unique, the challenges and strategies described cut across the chapters rather than being unique to a particular study or setting. For example, in Chapters 5, 6, and 7, the reader/student will be encouraged to think about how the framework (or theory of change) introduced was shaped by the particular policy context and program objectives, and whether and how the findings from the study offered the reader new ideas for more efficient and effective use of research resources. Instructors can use the case studies to ground discussions of the strategies and challenges of mixed methods work and help students develop skills in reasoning and problem solving in striving for fully integrated, mixed methods design and implementation.

Finally, Chapters 2 through 7 conclude with a set of discussion questions and "how to apply this further" suggestions aimed at generating dialogue around the students' own content-based reflections and deliberation of the particular cases and interventions explored. These questions and applications should also appeal to readers' broader methodological interests and considerations about how and when to undertake mixed methods research. For active researchers, we aim to encourage immediate applications of some of the strategies we describe for more fully integrating mixed methods in research.

CHAPTER 2

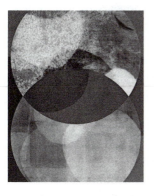

Conceptualizing Mixed Methods Research

INTRODUCTION

Research that is impactful in both informing policy and guiding practice must be both rigorous and relevant. Accordingly, the design and execution of policy research and evaluation studies invariably benefit from the articulation of an overarching framework for the research, including the conceptual linking of research and/or policy questions and goals to the methodologies that will be applied to address them. Indeed, the legwork undertaken in carefully framing a study can go a long way toward ensuring that appropriate and useful methods are applied in ways that generate desired information and illuminate new relationships and findings. Methodological design decisions should be closely connected to the study purpose and intended uses of the information generated, which, in policy and program settings, may be diverse and evolving. That is, in policy contexts, we are more often going to need to allow for flexibility in our frameworks and dynamic approaches to executing research.

This chapter builds and extends a conceptual argument for planning and striving toward a fully integrated, mixed methods approach in applied policy research and evaluation, which we suggest is more likely to provide for adaptability and accommodation of diverse stakeholder interests in these capricious research settings. We begin by considering the rationale for mixed methods research and conditions that call for it, as well as some of the challenges in its application. We then discuss the multiple and sometimes overlapping categorization schemes that are offered in the academic literature to describe the design components of a mixed methods study, as well as the attributes that distinguish different kinds of mixed method studies. While leveraging this work, we argue that evolving policy landscapes and technological advances, as described in Chapter 1, call for a fresh, orienting framework for approaching more fully integrated mixed methods work. We define the components of a fully integrated, mixed methods approach—in ideal circumstances, what it is, and what it isn't—and end with a case scenario that illustrates some of the conditions under which this approach to mixed methods research is warranted and compelling. In this context, we describe how fully mixed methods research can unfold as a process that demands ongoing engagement, assessment, and adjustment by stakeholders.

RATIONALE AND CONDITIONS FOR MIXED METHODS RESEARCH

It is easy to get the impression from academic discussions, which also spill into debates around evidence-based policy, that there is an established hierarchy of dominant research methods or a preferred method du jour at any given time. We argue that one should dispel of such preconceptions in approaching the decision of whether and how to undertake mixed methods research. There are no prevailing formulas for how best to conduct this type of work and, likewise, no one archetype for framing or organizing mixed methods research (a subject to which we return later). That said, there is considerable agreement in the existing literature on a number of compelling reasons for pursuing mixed methods research, which we think are worthwhile to synthesize here.

Rationale for Mixed Methods Research

Among the reasons most often cited for combining qualitative and quantitative methods is the opportunity to benefit from the complementary advantages of achieving greater precision and consistency in large-sample quantitative analysis and exploring phenomena in greater depth and detail, adding texture and contextualization, in qualitative research. For example, Johnson and Onwuegbuzie (2004), who have been widely cited as some of the first scholars in the social sciences to define and begin to theorize a mixed methods approach, identified the following strengths of mixed methods research:

- Words, pictures, and narratives can add meaning to numbers; numbers can be used to add precision to words, pictures, and narratives.

- Can answer a broader and more complete range of research questions because the researcher is not confined to a single method or approach.
- Can provide stronger evidence for a conclusion through convergence and corroboration of findings.
- Can be used to increase the generalizability of the results.
- Qualitative and quantitative research used together produce more complete knowledge necessary to inform theory and practice. (p. 21)

Rossman and Wilson (1985) similarly argue that mixed methods allow researchers to substantiate and strengthen research findings; elaborate (provide richness and detail); and initiate (offer new interpretations). Others refer to the importance of the phenomena under study, citing mixed methods as demanded by complex problems requiring multilevel analysis and complex perspectives (Baum, 1995; Clarke & Yaros, 1988; Driscoll, Appiah-Yeboah, Salib, & Rupert, 2007; Happ, 2009; Morgan, 1998; Steckler, McLeroy, Goodman, Bird, & McCormick, 1992). In their synthesis of empirical work across 57 mixed methods evaluations from 1980 to 1988, Greene, Caracelli, and Graham (1989) identified five purposes for mixed methods evaluations that underscore the consensus around these advantages: (1) "triangulation" that "seeks convergence, corroboration, and correspondence of results from the different methods"; (2) "complementarity" in elaborating, enhancing, illustrating, and clarifying results from different methods; (3) "development" in sampling, implementation, and measurement decisions; (4) "initiation" in the discovery of "paradox and contradiction," new perspectives or frameworks, or the reframing of research questions; and (5) "expansion" of the overall "breadth and range of inquiry" by employing different methods of inquiry (p. 259).

It is almost cliché now to hear mixed methods researchers describe their work as "opening the black box," that is, digging deeper in the research process to go beyond "cause and effect" and better understand the "why" and "how" of observed effects. In doing so, there are some very practical ways that the research process is aided by a mixed methods approach. For example, Collins, Onwuegbuzie, and Sutton (2006) draw on their work in special education to distill four practical or functional rationale for applying mixed methods, including (1) optimizing the sample for "participant enrichment," so that the most appropriate participants are included; (2) ensuring "instrument fidelity," or creating credible new instruments and assessing their appropriateness and validity; (3) assessing "treatment integrity" or fidelity of an intervention, that is, discrepancies between planned and realized implementation, and (4) enhancing significance by exploring different levels of the same phenomena, clarifying why outcomes did or did not occur, and augmenting interpretation and usefulness of findings for multiple audiences.

Later in this chapter and throughout this book, we will provide vivid examples of these types of applications, illustrating how mixed methods research can aid in the research process and generate the types of benefits described in the previous paragraphs. At the same time, we are forthcoming about the time, resources, and effort that are required to successfully engage in mixed methods work that is rigorous, relevant, and responsive to policy and program needs. That is, there may be conditions under which mixed methods research is not warranted or for which the costs of undertaking it may exceed the expected benefits.

Conditions for Methods Approaches

It is the norm in applied policy and evaluation research that resources for conducting the research will be finite, if not wanting. Therefore, there should be a clear purpose for a research strategy that employs multiple methods to avoid a situation whereby data are redundant or unlikely to shed new light on the topic of investigation (Bryman, 2006). Furthermore, the concern here is not only about inefficient use of research resources but also about the potential costs to participants' time and the possibility of generating lower-quality data and research insights if both researcher and participant resources are spread too thinly.

More fundamentally, there are some who subscribe to the notion that the qualitative and quantitative paradigms inherently study different phenomena and that these methods, therefore, cannot be combined for validation or triangulation purposes. For example, Sale, Lohfeld, and Brazil (2002) argue that "mixing research methods across paradigms, as is currently practiced, often diminishes the value of both methods" (p. 50).

However, in the practice of research, particularly policy research and evaluation, the differences between qualitative and quantitative paradigms are surely less stark than they appear in theory. For example, both qualitative and quantitative researchers frequently make context-dependent generalizations, sometimes when asserting a causal linkage between phenomena. And although qualitative and quantitative researchers may attempt value-free inquiry, they may qualify their findings in recognizing their use of value-laden measures that they cannot avert (e.g., standardized test scores in education research). Thus, we concur with other mixed methods researchers (Plowright,

2011; Teddlie & Tashakkori, 2003) who, rather than emphasizing their incompatibility, suggest the blending of these paradigmatic extremes to advance a third methodological rail—mixed methods research. That is, mixed method studies do not or should not attempt to *resolve differences* across paradigms but rather *capture or leverage the dualism* of qualitative and quantitative studies, which, in policy research, is more apt to reflect the subject of our inquiry as well.

CATEGORIZING MIXED METHODS APPROACHES

The Problem of Unnecessary Complexity

In the existing mixed methods literature, readers are likely to encounter a plethora of decision points and design choices, some of which may only be minimally motivated or developed. The researcher may be alerted about a set of choices, where once having made a choice, he or she is brought (or constrained) to another embedded set of decision points. For example, after selecting a typology to guide his or her work, an investigator may be asked to consider, among other issues, (a) the level of interaction, or the degree to which the two strands (qualitative and quantitative) are kept independent of each other; (b) priority, or the degree to which one paradigm is given precedence over the other paradigm or is treated equally; (c) timing, whether the quantitative and qualitative research will be conducted concurrently, sequentially, or in multiple phases; and (d) juncture, the point(s) at which the mixing will occur (e.g., data collection, interpretation, data analysis, etc).

After making decisions about level, priority, timing, and juncture, the investigator is typically introduced to another long list of supplementary choices that lie beneath these major issues. For example, once priority is established, how will different data sets be used within methods to illuminate relationships, and to what extent will the theoretical framework(s) serve as binding glue in the integration of the data analysis between the two methodological types? One could go on and on here, but the impression this leaves is of a field that is heavily *theorized* about the "know-what" of mixed methods research execution and yet lacking in core knowledge about the "know-how"—that is, heavy on isolated description of specific strategies along a continuum of research designs but light on guidance gleaned from mixed methods applications or instructive examples of how different approaches can be employed to achieve research and policy objectives.

Design Typologies

As opportunities and demands for mixed methods work have mounted, typologies for the design of mixed method work have proliferated. According to Creswell and Plano Clark (2011), typologies aid the researcher in choosing from among a range of well-defined options and support the researcher's use of a sound approach for addressing a research problem and forestalling and resolving challenging issues that might arise in research. The typology-based approach emphasizes the classification of useful methods and the selection and adaptation of a particular design to the study's purpose and questions. At the same time, Creswell and Plano Clark also recognize that the use of mixed methods will not always be planned at the start of the research process and/or implemented according to plan and that, in some cases, their use may be "emergent," or in response to issues that arise during the conduct of research. In fact, policy and evaluation research frequently fits a third type of design process that they describe—a dynamic approach, where various components of mixed methods research come into play interactively and are emphasized or reconsidered throughout the research process.

Creswell and Plano Clark (2011) review alternative classification schemes applied in 15 different works from a variety of disciplines, and they subsequently distill these and related classification efforts into six major mixed methods designs (or typologies) based on their level of integration, prioritization of qualitative versus quantitative methods, and timing of their application. These designs include (1) convergent parallel design, (2) explanatory sequential design, (3) exploratory sequential design, and (4) embedded design, as well as two more that bring multiple design elements together: (5) transformative design and (6) multiphase design. They then describe in detail the distinguishing features and stages of these six major design types.

For policymakers, practitioners, or students who might find these methodological details and distinctions across typologies dizzying, if not daunting, it is probably helpful to point out the commonalities among these design types that are particularly relevant to policy and evaluation research. For example, five of these major designs are described as being interactive (vs. independent) in the application of qualitative and quantitative methods, and in four of the six, either no or equal priority is given to qualitative and quantitative methods. Furthermore, we expect that for many policy and evaluation studies, they will embody more than one (or even all) of the "design purposes" that Creswell and Plano Clark identify as distinctive across these major designs. For example, it is probably more common than not for policy and evaluation studies to be interested in gaining a full understanding of a phenomenon, while also addressing program objectives and challenges and testing or explaining both qualitative and quantitative findings about a policy or program's outcomes or implementation.

In other words, those engaged in policy and evaluation work should not get stymied by these choices; indeed, Creswell and Plano Clark encourage the use of these design typologies as a guide for design choices rather than as a "cookbook recipe" for adopting a particular mixed methods approach. Competence in using mixed methods approaches is expected to build with experience, with one end goal being facility in applying a dynamic approach that allows for the mixing and matching of components across different frameworks to achieve research goals.

Design Drivers in Theory and Practice

Regardless of their disciplinary and methodological orientations, most investigators accept that knowing both the *why* and the *how* of mixed methods work is important. However, they differ in terms of how much they emphasize descriptive theoretical knowledge over practice process knowledge as drivers of design decisions and the conduct of mixed methods research. For example, education researchers Johnson and Onwuegbuzie (2004) conclude that "rather than be driven by the debate of qualitative versus quantitative, the pragmatic approach where the research question drives the choice of methods makes sense for educational research. The mixed methods approach provides the best opportunity for answering important, multi-faceted research questions with workable, practical solutions" (p. 15). They add that researchers adopting an orientation that emphasizes application and practice are more apt to see mixed methods work as "a collaborative communicative enterprise, necessitated by changing context that is becoming increasingly interdisciplinary, complex, and dynamic" (p. 15). Clearly, these are characteristics of a context in which policy and evaluation researchers are, more often than not, likely to undertake their research.

In contrast to those who view mixed methods research as an applied collaborative construct, some investigators conceptualize mixed methods research more as an epistemological tension, each embodying distinctly different ways of knowing (see, e.g., Onwuegbuzie & Leech, 2005). Investigators adopting this orientation emphasize the epistemological roots of mono-method research and the advances that come when researchers of different paradigms reach across the divide, so to speak. Scholars of this orientation acknowledge the collaborative nature of the work, but not to the extent or depth of investigators emphasizing process practice knowledge. Design decisions are consequently more likely to draw on individual attitudes and beliefs that the investigator brings when contemplating or conducting mixed methods research. For example, Madey (1982) describes mixed methods as a process that creates a sum greater than the two parts (qualitative and quantitative), with complementary effects: "In terms of methods, one plus one equals three. And what's the three? The interplay between the two types of methods; the interaction, the synergistic coming together, which creates something that never existed before" (p. 235). Similarly, in their review of 57 empirical mixed method evaluations, Greene et al. (1989, p. 259) identify a core purpose of mixed methods work as the process through which researchers using different methods corroborate and correspond around results.

Toward a More Fully Integrated Mixed Methods Approach

Finding a balance between grasping theory, or the "what" of mixed methods research, and knowing its practical application, or the "how," is important for researchers in designing and conducting highly credible mixed methods research that is useful for policymakers and practitioners. As noted earlier, there is an abundance of information about the various core and supplementary decisions (e.g., what to mix, when to mix, and models for mixing) that go into mixed methods work, yet few practice-friendly guides that can help teams consider viable or best practices in mixed methods research, obtain guidance in adapting other models and practices to their own situation and study, and see examples of the benefits of mixed methods work from other research teams.

As researchers who simultaneously collaborate actively with policymakers, finding the right balance is crucial. We want to conduct research that will stand up to rigorous peer review and be published in scholarly journals, yet we also want to cultivate a process, method, and language of mixed methods work that will generate evidence that those working *in* policy can use to inform decisions and persuade others in the face of intense political engagement. The remainder of this chapter aims to provide an overview of the definition, goals, benefits, and process of integrated mixed methods as practiced. The primary context for this overview and subsequent chapters is our own and colleagues' experiences. We begin with an orienting definition of fully integrated mixed method research and then provide interpretive guidelines and recommendations for researchers in assessing rigor and relevance of research in process.

Definitions of Mixed Methods Research: What It Is and What It Isn't

Fully integrated mixed methods research might be thought of as a member of a family of mixed methods research approaches. Mixed methods research is depicted as a sprawling family, varying widely in terms of strategy and process.

> Fully integrated, mixed methods research is a research process by which researchers interact regularly and intensively—with each other and their research partners—to draw on and combine the strengths of qualitative and quantitative methods, from the starting point of defining research objectives to the ending point of achieving those goals. In the context of applied policy and evaluation studies, research goals are defined in terms of the organizations' or policymakers' improvement goals or desired ends, and the research design is directly linked to organizational, policy, or program goals and may evolve with the policy or program landscape. The full integration of qualitative and quantitative methods contributes to both the understanding of processes for achieving outcomes or goals and, through the application of best practices in research within methodologies, the achievement of those ends.

To unpack this definition, we next offer some general guidelines of what fully integrated mixed method research is and what it is not (also summarized in Table 2.1).

A. Fully integrated mixed method research *is not* when qualitative and quantitative methods are employed in a single study but remain independent throughout data collection and analysis. Integrated mixed method research *is not* when qualitative and quantitative results are combined and corroborated after a process in which much of the inquiry and analysis has occurred separately, for example, through data collection and analysis (Caracelli & Greene, 1997).

Instead, fully integrated mixed method research occurs when integration or mixing of methods follows through the entire cycle of the research process, from planning to inquiry, to data collection and analysis, to dissemination and redesign. Designs that mix only from data collection through interpretation of results fail to leverage benefits of integrated planning and interpretation, which we view as critical to achieving research and policy objectives.

B. Fully integrated mixed method research *is not* when qualitative and quantitative methods are integrated into different phases of the work—for example, a pilot case study using qualitative methods with a quantitative study to test generalizability of findings across a large number of data points—without linking

Table 2.1 What Fully Integrated Mixed Methods Research Is Not and Is

Is Not	Is
When qualitative and quantitative methods are employed in a single study but remain independent throughout data collection and analysis	When integration or mixing of methods follows the entire cycle of the research process, from planning to inquiry, to data collection and analysis, to dissemination and redesign
When qualitative and quantitative methods are integrated into different phases of the work and linkages between them are absent	When qualitative and quantitative methods are conducted from the start and simultaneously in ways that are "interactive and iterative"
When one type of evidence (e.g., estimated effects of an intervention based on statistical analysis) is privileged over another type of evidence (e.g., narratives or life stories or rich case study data)	When qualitative and quantitative methods are employed in ways that leverage the strengths of each to provide a wider and richer range of ways to understand complex phenomena for a variety of outcomes and problems
Research driven by political agendas or epistemological preferences or trends and whose processes are invisible to outsiders	Deliberately undertaken to best address research questions and problems where processes and outcome measures will be used by diverse stakeholders and where enhancing learning and communication is an important part of the research process; processes are transparent

across those phases of the research process. Or, alternately, it is *not* present when quantitative methods are used to identify the frequency of attributes across large data sets, with qualitative research following independently to understand the conditions supporting these attributes (Teddlie & Tashakkori, 2006).

Rather, fully integrated mixed methods research is when qualitative and quantitative methods are conducted from the start, simultaneously in ways that are "interactive and iterative," so that every step of the process proceeds from interaction of the two, with instrumentation and interpretation, for example, growing out of that interaction. The emphasis in this attribute is on strategies that support a process of constant "illumination" (to use Woolley's terminology), whereby "quantitative and qualitative components can be considered 'integrated' to the extent that these components are explicitly related to each other within a single study and in such a way as to be mutually illuminating, thereby producing findings that are greater than the sum of the parts" (Woolley, 2009, p. 7).

C. Fully integrated mixed methods work *is not* when one type of evidence (e.g., estimated effects of an intervention based on statistical analysis) is privileged over another type of evidence (e.g., narratives or life stories or rich case study data).

Instead, fully integrated mixed methods work is when qualitative and quantitative methods are employed in ways that leverage the strengths of each to provide a wider and richer range of ways to understand complex phenomena for a variety of outcomes and problems (Fry, Chantavanich, & Chantavanich, 1981; Hesse-Biber & Johnson, 2013; Jang, McDougall, Pollon, Herbert, & Russell, 2008).

D. Fully integrated mixed method research *is not* research driven by political agendas or epistemological preferences or trends. This is particularly important as mixed methods work becomes increasingly popularized in the nomenclature of requests for proposals and funding priorities.

Integrated mixed method research is deliberately undertaken to best address research questions and problems where processes and outcome measures will be used by diverse stakeholders and where enhancing learning and communication is an important part of the research process.

How does fully integrated, mixed methods research fit into existing phases or models of research?

Fully integrated mixed methods research can fold into the regular cycle of research design as typically taught and applied in the social sciences. To facilitate learning and transfer, we have organized our discussion and guide to fully integrated, mixed methods research along these seven components, as shown in Table 2.2: (1) determining study objectives and foci, (2) establishing core research design elements, (3) creating supportive structures and mechanisms for mixing methods, (4) collecting data, (5) analyzing and interpreting data, (6) disseminating findings, and (7) reflecting and refining to set the agenda for future research. In addition, we have augmented the steps with design components aimed at supporting deeper engagement of research teams with other stakeholders, reducing redundancies and inefficient use of resources, and building continuous understanding of how research quality can be improved and ultimately used to achieve desired ends.

The two chapters that follow contain considerable detail on each of these components of a mixed methods research cycle and provide guidance and

Table 2.2   Components of Mixed Methods Research Cycle

Determination of study goals and foci	Agree on what to study and select research team members to support qualitative and quantitative investigation
	Identify corresponding conceptual/theoretical/logic models for research and/or evaluation
	Assess the connection or gap between research goals/questions and those of research partners (agency/program stakeholders)
Establishment of core research design elements	Select settings, sample frame, and study samples
	Design strategies for collecting data linked to research questions
	Pilot and finalize instrumentation for data collection
	Identify qualitative and quantitative methods for data analysis
	Develop processes for integrating mixed methods in each research design step and for documenting decisions and practices
Creation of supportive structures and mechanisms for mixing methods	Create mechanisms for sustaining research team member attention to full integration
	Cultivate understanding among research team leadership, members, and partners regarding the meaning and importance of mixed methods research
	Assess team members' strengths and knowledge within and across methods and delegate responsibilities accordingly; plan for professional development to build understanding and continuous improvement
Data collection	Implement integrated processes to undertake the following:
	Original data collection
	Administrative data and other secondary data extraction and documentation
	Coding and refinement of data and measures
	Cross-checking of qualitative and quantitative measures and their quality and meaning
	Identify and address process problems (e.g., timing/delays, inefficiencies, barriers to data collection) and identify strategies for improvement
Data analysis and interpretation of findings	Drawing on qualitative and quantitative methods:
	Conduct descriptive and exploratory analysis
	Analyze causal mechanisms and effects and moderating factors
	Analyze processes and implementation

	Develop feedback loops and cross-checks in the qualitative and quantitative analysis process
	Through the integrated research process, identify any unanticipated causal pathways or conditions that contribute to results (and to rigor and nuance)
	Refine analyses to explore relevant factors and relationships in greater depth (quantitatively and/or qualitatively)
Dissemination of findings	Identify target audiences for research and broad stakeholder groups.
	Develop recommendations adapted to needs of diverse audiences/ stakeholders
	Develop forums for communicating recommendations that accommodate the integrated nature of the research and diverse stakeholder interests and needs
	Monitor progress of dissemination and document demand for and use of research findings
Reflection and refinement	Assess gaps between what you planned to do in research and what actually took place (given time and resource constraints and new opportunities or explorations)
	Develop and implement changes to research plans based on assessments for subsequent stages of research and/or new projects

examples in their application to particular research projects. The importance of these components will also be further illustrated in the cases that follow in this book. Before moving on, however, we provide a brief overview of a research study in which we collaborated in pursuing a fully integrated, mixed methods approach. We will draw on and reference this work as we illustrate the various research cycle components and the importance of a planned process of mixed methods research throughout this book.

OVERVIEW OF A FULLY INTEGRATED, MIXED METHODS RESEARCH EFFORT

There are a number of reasons why we think it is valuable to highlight the mixed methods research project that we engaged in over a period of approximately 8 years. First, a central goal of this project was to evaluate the effectiveness of a publicly funded intervention that was mandated by a federal policy and affected all states and local educational agencies within them. This implies both broad policy implications and a diverse range of stakeholders for the research. Second, the research design was longitudinal, and the research questions and methods evolved over time, as did policy implementation. More often than not, this is the type of situation that policy and evaluation researchers will face. And third, we can provide an insiders' view into both the challenges and advantages of a fully integrated, mixed methods research approach, with the benefit of experience (hindsight) and candid reflections to inform future endeavors and practice.

Study Goals and Foci

Our research was funded by the Institute of Education Sciences to improve student learning and achievement by identifying successful approaches (and the variables that will increase success) in the organization and management of Supplemental Educational Services (SES) and similar supplemental educational programs within school districts, as well as effective strategies for the design and delivery of supplemental instruction by approved providers. Under the No Child Left Behind (NCLB) Act, SES is a core intervention intended to help close the achievement gap in public education. Although many school districts are in states that have now received waivers from these NCLB provisions, public schools subject to this provision (that do not make adequate yearly progress for 3 consecutive years) are required to offer children in low-income families the opportunity to receive extra academic assistance (SES), consisting of tutoring offered outside regular school day hours (delivered primarily by private sector, for-profit or nonprofit, providers.)

The NCLB Act delegated the primary responsibility for implementing SES to state and local educational entities, and it also gave parents and students in these schools unrestricted choice to serve as a key lever for ensuring the quality of supplemental instruction. States establish the specifications for SES provider applications and approval, and school districts rely on an extensive and evolving market of private sector afterschool tutoring programs to offer eligible students a range of choices for SES. Our study addressed key questions about what constitutes a high-quality SES program, what mechanisms or policy tools are available to state and local educational agencies to ensure that the most effective services are made available to and used by their eligible student populations, and the effectiveness of these programs and specific providers in improving educational outcomes and opportunities for low-income and disadvantaged students.

Throughout the study, we expanded the nature and scope of our research and strengthened the integrated qualitative-quantitative approach in the effort to increase our knowledge and understanding of these tutoring interventions *as implemented*; explore policy issues and program administration in greater depth and detail; respond to evolving policy priorities and program innovations as well as provider market changes; and support the use of our findings by federal, state, and local policymakers in improving program design, implementation, and results.

It was also an explicit goal of our project to create a forum for discussing and disseminating our study findings through what we called the Research-to-Practice Collaborative. The objective of our collaborative was to foster a professional community of practitioners and policymakers who would engage with our research teams and not only facilitate a more in-depth and meaningful investigation but also have an interest in working with our project over time to put study findings into practice and improve on the SES program components identified as contributing to student achievement. This involved the regular dissemination of our findings to local educational agencies (program administrators and other district staff), tutoring providers, parents and students making choices about SES, and the public and policymaking officials through the media, briefings, expert testimony, and other means. For example, school district officials have drawn on the results of our analyses to satisfy state reporting requirements on SES provider performance and to inform school principals, teachers, parents, and others in the district about the effectiveness of SES tutoring options available to students.

Core Research Design Elements

Our study embodied a longitudinal, mixed methods research design that integrates rigorous, nonexperimental analysis of SES program impacts on student achievement with an in-depth, comprehensive qualitative examination of the intervention—provider instructional practice in different program models and settings, the nature and quality of tutoring provided, and district-level program administration—in and across large, urban school districts. The primary settings for our research were Austin Independent School District (ISD), Chicago Public Schools, Dallas ISD, Los Angeles Unified School District, Milwaukee Public Schools, and Minneapolis Public Schools. Student demographics in these districts are generally representative of the larger, urban national population that is eligible for SES under NCLB, that is, high concentrations of economically disadvantaged students, including subgroups with higher levels of academic need/disadvantage (e.g., students with limited English proficiency and disabilities). Our study samples in each of these school districts have comprised the students eligible for SES, primarily defined as those in public schools not making adequate yearly progress for at least 3 years who were also eligible for free and reduced-price lunch. Across these school districts, there are hundreds of providers of supplemental instruction, including some with multiple locations or settings/formats for tutoring and district providers.

In terms of the mix of research methods applied in this study, qualitative components included interviews, observations, focus groups, and curriculum analysis used in examining the program and treatment in depth. Data were collected in the fieldwork using an observation instrument that was developed and refined in this study to intensively probe staffing, curricular focus, length of session, grouping of students, physical settings of tutoring, format and content of curriculum, communication formats, and other variables. Quantitative tools of analysis were used in describing treatment (SES programs and providers) and estimating the effectiveness of SES and SES providers. These included value-added, fixed effects, propensity score matching, and generalized propensity score matching models that controlled for school and student characteristics under differing assumptions.

We conducted our integrated qualitative and quantitative research in tightly linked and interactive research phases. There was no step or stage in the execution of the research that was dominated by one methodological approach or the other (i.e., qualitative or quantitative), although some sequencing of particular research tasks across the methods was warranted by the research design needs. For example, the first qualitative phase of the study defined key elements of SES program models and practices to inform the construction of treatment variables for both qualitative and quantitative analysis. The early quantitative analysis of program take-up and effects subsequently shaped the continuing qualitative research by identifying relationships that required deeper investigation, informing sample selections, and bringing to light measurement and process issues to be further explored. The qualitative and quantitative components of the research interacted regularly and continuously, facilitated by weekly exchanges and monthly team meetings in which we reviewed analytical findings from the two study components, directed additional data collection and other research activities, refined analysis plans, and prepared research papers, briefing reports, policy briefs, webinars, and so on, for disseminating to stakeholders and the academic community.

Supportive Structures and Mechanisms for Mixing Methods

The research team was formed with the explicit intention of balancing the qualitative and quantitative research components and ensuring strong connections between them. The team included researchers who specialize in qualitative or quantitative methods and those with expertise in both major types of methods, as well as one team member specifically tasked with facilitating integration of the work among team members. To support regular exchange of data and information from analyses across the qualitative and quantitative study components, a shared workspace was maintained that was segmented for the qualitative and quantitative study components and included folders for each study site. All research team members were able to post and share data, documents, and results from analyses, and access either set of folders (quantitative or qualitative) to foster unconstrained sharing of information and mixed methods analyses. As previously noted, qualitative and quantitative research team members communicated weekly, and more formally on a monthly basis, to coordinate the integrated research efforts, evaluate progress toward research goals, and refine approaches or refocus analysis and other research activities as needed.

In addition, both qualitative and quantitative research team members engaged with the study stakeholders—including school district staff who administer the programs and manage district database systems, SES provider staff, other state and local educational agency personnel (in the project sites and beyond), and community members—to keep an open line to understanding these stakeholders' questions and concerns about how the intervention was working in practice (in these urban settings) and how our study could generate the types of information they needed to inform policy and program improvements. The consistency of our own project staffing was essential to maintaining these relationships through many changes in district and provider leadership, organization, and staffing over time. Collaborative relationships such as these across our quantitative and qualitative team members *and* practitioner partners were particularly important for core research activities, such as data collection, which require substantial time investments each year by the research team and careful monitoring and oversight to ensure appropriate assembly, linking, and use of the study data.

Research Dissemination and Reflections on the Process of Mixed Methods Research

Because our research was purposely designed to provide ongoing feedback and input of the results into policy and program implementation processes, dissemination and reflection were ongoing in our study. For example, the timing of our interactions with SES program stakeholders revolved around the school year calendar and the activities involved in implementing the programs. Prior to the start of the school year, research team members stayed in close contact with district staff administering the programs, and qualitative researchers connected with tutoring providers to make them aware of our research and enlist their cooperation in the observational component of the study. In addition, our in-person research briefings and cross-district and public webinars were timed to support active use of the study findings (e.g., before the end of the school year or the start of the next school year) in policy and program planning. The research briefings emphasized the integrated nature of the qualitative and quantitative research (see Box 2.1), gave equal attention to the contributions of both methodological approaches in the discussion of findings, and revealed the richness of insights and deeper understanding that was realized from the full integration of mixed methods in this study. In fact, as we became more aware of these benefits as a team, we became ardent about ensuring that the qualitative and quantitative results would not be presented separately or in isolation of each other, lest the findings be misconstrued or a depth of understanding lost for the audience.

BOX 2.1 ILLUSTRATION OF THE FULLY INTEGRATED MIXED METHODS APPROACH

In the presentations used to brief our school district partners on the evaluation results, we always included a slide with the graphic shown below to convey the equal priority given to qualitative and quantitative methods in our investigation and the interactive, iterative approach applied in integrating them in the study. In addition, we centered the Research-to-Practice Collaborative in this graphic to depict its critical role in facilitating continuous interchange with our research stakeholders/partners throughout the research process.

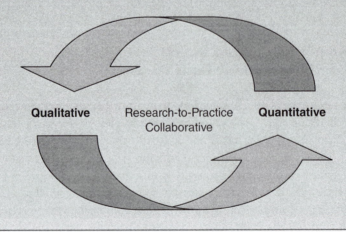

Qualitative   Research-to-Practice   **Quantitative**
                      Collaborative

For example, quantitative analyses found fewer and smaller effects of SES for students with special needs (e.g., English language learners and students with disabilities), which prompted our research team to look more closely at the nature of the intervention in practice (from awareness and registration to assessment and instruction) for these two subgroups of students in our samples. Both quantitative and qualitative analyses suggested pathways to increasing access to services for students with special needs. In addition, we uncovered unresolved issues in program implementation for these students over who was legally responsible for serving English language learners and students with disabilities. Tutoring providers depended on parents, teachers, and/or district staff to share student assessment data in order to understand student needs and have staff prepared to tailor services for them, but across our study districts, we encountered confusion and misunderstandings regarding how providers should be informed of students' English language learner or disability status. The cross-district webinars gave school district staff the opportunity to exchange ideas and strategies for improving practice in this area, and it provided researchers with a forum for interjecting evidence and documenting proposed program and policy modifications to monitor and evaluate in ongoing research.

In general, we believe that the tight integration of qualitative and quantitative methods across numerous elements of research design—from sample selection to instrumentation development to data collection and analysis—and their triangulation in interpreting and disseminating study results strengthens the credibility of our findings and their relevance for stakeholders of the research. Throughout the remaining chapters of this book, we will occasionally draw on this work (described above) to better illustrate the "know-how" of mixed methods research and offer pointers in their application.

DISCUSSION QUESTIONS

1. This chapter acknowledges a range of different typologies of mixed methods from which researchers can choose and decision points that the existing literature asks researchers to consider. How does the planning of a mixed methods study benefit from considering these different typologies and strategies for organizing the research?

2. The chapter also identifies a number of challenges to conducting fully integrated mixed methods research—what are they? How might the various stakeholders in a study (researchers, policymakers, program participants)

work together to address these challenges or determine which ones should be prioritized for resolving in the study?

3. The chapter states "mixed method studies do not or should not attempt to resolve differences across paradigms but rather capture or leverage the dualism of qualitative and quantitative studies, which, in policy research, is more apt to reflect the subject of our inquiry as well." What kinds of differences have typically been identified as unresolvable? Can you think of instances from your own research or others' work where similar tensions exist? What made them seem unresolvable?

4. The chapter stresses the importance of conducting research that will stand up to rigorous peer review and be published in scholarly journals, yet also generate evidence that those working *in* policy can use to inform decisions and persuade others in the face of intense political engagement. What in your experience, to date, have been challenges to finding this balance? And from where (structural, cultural factors) did these challenges originate?

APPLICATIONS TO YOUR OWN WORK

- For a research effort or project of your interest, describe the stakeholders you would involve and the potential benefits (and challenges) of working with them in defining research questions and a theory of action for your work.

- If you were to emulate the Research-to-Practice Collaborative in your own research project, what mechanisms would you use to engage the stakeholders in discussions at different phases of the research process, including dissemination of the study findings?

- Choose a mixed methods study on a topic of interest to you. Drawing on Table 2.1, describe to what extent (or in which ways) it "is" or "is not" better characterized as a fully integrated mixed methods approach.

CHAPTER 3

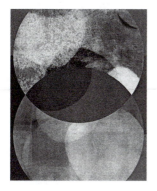

Designing and Implementing Fully Integrated Mixed Methods Research

INTRODUCTION

Policy and evaluation research are often undertaken collaboratively, with the individual researcher or research team engaging policy designers, program implementers, the target population, and other program stakeholders to understand an intervention's implementation and impacts and what drives them. In this regard, the benefits of striving toward a fully integrated mixed methods approach—in empirically investigating patterns across units to identify associations and plausible causal relationships and simultaneously digging deeper to explore the potential causal pathways and policy and contextual factors that intervene in them—seem so obvious that one might expect this approach to be ubiquitous. Yet as the literature points out, the use of mixed methods, although growing, is still limited by practical roadblocks as well as perceived barriers, which we will show in this chapter (and the chapters that follow) may be largely surmountable. In fact, a commitment on the part of the core stakeholders (in addition to researchers) to conducting mixed methods research from the earliest stages of the research process may be key to making this approach work and fully leveraging its advantages.

In this chapter, we argue the case for more tightly linking qualitative and quantitative research teams and processes from the start, that is, from the first point at which the research project begins to form. In terms of task coordination and communication, for example, qualitative and quantitative researchers are more likely to combine efforts and make accommodations along the way for research design needs or findings of the other component if they are engaged in a mixed methods process from the time that the study's objectives are first defined. Alternatively, if qualitative and quantitative contributions are initiated or enter the research process separately or at different time points, they will be less likely to "speak to each other" or to draw regularly on the contributions of the other component.

At the same time, we recognize that challenges arise in carrying out mixed methods research and that they require capacity to tackle—that is, human, social, financial, and perhaps also cultural capacity—some of which may have to be purposefully built up in the course of a project. This type of knowledge (i.e., of capacity-building strategies) is often left out of project reports and published works and may not even be fully transparent to all those engaged in a given policy research or evaluation effort. We hope to fill this knowledge gap here by describing four main areas for which researchers should strive to achieve full integration in policy research and program evaluation—research objectives and design, instrumentation design and data collection, data analysis and interpretation, and dissemination of findings— and including in our discussion examples of the mechanics and logistics of integrating qualitative and quantitative methods in these areas, as well as the benefits. In addition, the case discussions that follow this chapter further illuminate different strategies for maintaining a fully integrated mixed methods approach and addressing barriers encountered in various stages of the research process.

INTEGRATION IN RESEARCH OBJECTIVES AND DESIGN

In policy and evaluation research, there may be a number of different questions that policymakers or program designers or funders would like to address, although a core question commonly asked is: Does this policy or intervention work? Corollary questions that typically follow or that are defined as the research progresses include: If not, why not? Or if so, what are the impacts of the program, and who benefits? However, even if we assume that this is a basic objective of most policy and evaluation research, the research design decisions that follow are complex and many. What are the goals of the intervention, and how do they translate into measurable outcomes? Will all participants respond similarly to the intervention, that is, can we assume a common effect? Or does the intervention work in some settings or contexts but not others? What are the posited pathways to various outcomes, and how will our methods identify the aspects or mechanisms of the intervention that drive outcomes?

Leading With a Logic Model

Most mixed methods textbooks discuss research design as a set of choices concerning the types, priority, and sequencing of mixed methods and, accordingly, describe a menu of options for mixed methods designs (e.g., concurrent parallel, concurrent nested, explanatory or exploratory sequential, embedded, etc.; Creswell & Plano Clark, 2011; Tashakkori & Teddlie, 2003). In the context of policy and evaluation research, we suggest instead that a valuable starting point for integration in mixed methods research is with the development or fleshing out of a theory of action or conceptual model for the policy or intervention under study and its expected outcomes. For example, policy researchers might identify a logic for the intervention articulated in legislation or in a program mission or goals statement, but it may also be lacking in its conceptualization of how the intervention will achieve those goals. In some circumstances, this will be intentional, that is, leaving the details of program design and implementation to another level of government or organization, or encouraging the tailoring of policy or program features to local needs and context. The guide to logic model development of the Centers for Disease Control and Prevention (a major health sciences research institution) suggests that "the process of developing a logic model with partners and stakeholders can be as beneficial as the final [research] product" and that it promotes "ownership, commitment and support to the program" from stakeholders (Sundra, Scherer, & Anderson, 2003, pp. 7, 11).

Mixed methods primers (Morgan, 2014) have also characterized qualitative research as inductive (i.e., starting with observation to generate theory) and quantitative research as deductive (i.e., beginning with theory and evaluating it through observation). We alternatively maintain that either method can be applied inductively or deductively at different phases of research but that starting with a (deductive, visual) theory of change or conceptual model is important to making the program or policy theory and our assumptions about plausible causal linkages explicit. There is considerable guidance in the literature about how to construct a theory of change, although most discourse concurs that the following elements should constitute the core of the model: (a) research questions; (b) inputs or resources; (c) activities and interventions; (d) outputs; (e) short-, intermediate-, and/or long-term outcomes and/or impacts; (f) hypothesized causes or causal pathways to outcomes or impacts and methods for investigating them; and (g) external factors or context that can influence outcomes. Some of the benefits to constructing a theory of change include clarifying the purpose of an intervention and what is required to effect change, serving as a reference and guide for planning and executing the research activities, and monitoring progress and identifying opportunities for mid-course improvements.

Another advantage of developing a conceptual model is that it can help qualitative and quantitative researchers point to areas where tighter integration of methods will be beneficial or where one approach or the other might lead in the investigation. For example, if program implementation is expected to vary across sites or contexts in ways that will affect what is measured and how, qualitative research could provide early insights into the factors that will be important (or challenging) to capture empirically. In the first year of our study of Supplemental Educational Services (Supplemental Educational Services Integrated Qualitative and Quantitative [SESIQ^2]), our qualitative and quantitative research was launched simultaneously, and the qualitative team delivered important information to the quantitative researchers about how school districts and providers were tracking student tutoring time, which was ultimately key to developing a common empirical measure of treatment (hours tutored) across the districts.

Laying out a logic model can also help to set or clarify expectations for researchers and stakeholders about which pathways to outcomes, or the outcomes themselves, might be more effectively illuminated through qualitative or quantitative research. In the theory of change logic model shown in Chapter 7 of this book for the South African Child Support Grant program, Figure 7.1 specifies "Pathways assessed by mainly quantitative methods," "Pathways assessed by mainly qualitative methods," and "Pathways assessed by both quantitative and qualitative methods," as well as which outcomes or intervening factors would be assessed primarily by one method or the other. At the same time, we have found (based on our experiences and those of others) that it is advantageous to see the logic model as dynamic or a "living document" that can change as the research progresses or as findings/discovery pull the research in new directions or identify new pathways to outcomes. For example, in our SESIQ^2 study, qualitative researchers uncovered important variation in how digital tutoring services were being implemented by providers in school districts. This, in turn, led to the addition of a joint qualitative and quantitative effort to identify and develop measures of the key characteristics or factors believed to be driving the effectiveness of digital tutors, such as the location of the tutor, whether the curriculum was software or tutor-driven, and whether the delivery was asynchronous or synchronous.

Strengthening Validity

A fundamental research design decision in most policy or evaluation research efforts centers on whether to employ experimental or quasi-/nonexperimental methods to identify causal pathways and policy or program impacts. As the use of random assignment experiments in policy and program evaluation research has steadily expanded over the past four decades (Gueron & Rolston, 2013), the application of nonexperimental methods has also been fine-tuned and improved. Regardless of the choice (experimental or nonexperimental), researchers have increasingly recognized the value of integrating qualitative and quantitative methods into the research design, so that both play a role in strengthening the validity of inferences generated.

Experimental designs are widely regarded as the gold standard in policy and evaluation research for the primary reason that, if well-designed and implemented, they should create (through random assignment to treatment) statistically equivalent treatment and control groups that will allow for identification of policy or program impacts with a high degree of confidence that they are accurate and unbiased (i.e., internal validity is high). For this reason, experimental designs are often given priority or greater weight in evidence reviews (see, e.g., the What Works Clearinghouse *Procedures and Standards Handbook*[1]), and many recent advancements in improving quasi-/nonexperimental methods have relied on experimental data that are used to benchmark nonexperimental estimates, that is, assessing whether they closely approximate impact estimates produced by experimental analysis. At the same time, this body of work has shed greater light on the significance of the assumptions made in both experimental and nonexperimental studies and the surprising extent to which they are often not fully met. Accordingly, quantitative researchers have progressively come to appreciate the merits of building qualitative methods into both experimental and nonexperimental research designs for richer illumination of these issues, as well as for information and direction to address concerns related to empirical model specification and estimation.

One of the most critical issues to ensuring a strong research design is understanding how subjects select into, or are assigned to, treatment. Although the process of *randomly* assigning individuals or units to treatment is typically clear-cut, it is not uncommon for some assigned to treatment to fail to show up or take up the treatment; likewise, control group members sometimes cross over into the treatment group or access close substitutes for treatment. In these circumstances, it is usually critically important to understand who is not taking up treatment (or finding substitutes) and the implications for assumption of statistical equivalence. Qualitative methods, such as interviews and focus groups, used with those not in compliance with their random assignment status can generate valuable insights about the factors contributing to noncompliance. For example, in the case of the child support debt reduction

---

[1]Available at http://ies.ed.gov/ncee/wwc/documentsum.aspx?sid=19

program discussed in Chapter 6, take-up of the treatment by randomly assigned noncustodial parents was slow and selective, and focus groups with both those participating and those not participating were conducted to understand the barriers and deterrents to their enrollment. The information generated in the focus groups, along with interviews with program staff, also contributed to the specification of nonexperimental models that were estimated to adjust for the resulting differences in the treatment and controls groups in estimating impacts.

Indeed, in quasi-/nonexperimental evaluations, the ability to generate valid inferences about program impacts hinges on the ability to appropriately model (and account for factors that influence) selection into treatment. In some cases, it may be important for qualitative research to lead in the investigation and describe the processes by which individuals become aware of, and follow through on, the opportunity to receive treatment. There may also be administrative or organizational factors that limit access to treatment that can be identified through document analysis (e.g., policy directives or operations manuals) or through interviews with program administrators and staff. In the case study of the South African Child Support Grant program discussed in Chapter 7, focus groups with community members helped to generate information in advance of quantitative data collection and analysis about factors that affected grant access, such as difficulties producing required documentation or confusion about program eligibility criteria. The qualitative work also produced important information about treatment adherence (and interruptions of, or disconnections from, grant receipt) that proved to be critical in determining the most appropriate quantitative methods for estimating program impacts.

Tightly integrating qualitative and quantitative components in research design requires advance planning and possibly also training for staff so that these elements are ready to launch together at the start of an evaluation or as needed as the work unfolds. In the South African Child Support Grant program evaluation, the leading role of the qualitative research was planned from the start and was identified as an early activity in the theory of change. In the child support debt reduction program evaluation, the considerably smaller research team was staffed by researchers experienced in (or who received training in) both qualitative and quantitative methods, which enabled them to readily add a round of (unplanned) focus groups when program enrollments were unexpectedly low. In other words, choices made in staffing and staff training/preparation may be critical to achieving the full benefits of integration in this phase of research.

INTEGRATION IN INSTRUMENTATION DESIGN AND DATA COLLECTION

Starting with a logic model or theory of change in policy and evaluation research also supports our efforts to understand the properties of the phenomena (or characteristics or factors) we are trying to measure and to justify their correspondence with our choice and scale of measures. Sometimes the data and measures we employ in our research necessarily rely on existing sources—for example, administrative data, national surveys regularly conducted for a variety of uses, data from other studies, and so on—for reasons of budget or timeliness or convenience. For example, baseline data that are important to identifying individuals eligible for an intervention or controlling for differences between treatment and comparison group members are frequently collected in program application forms or other surveys or administrative databases. In these cases, qualitative methods such as documentation analysis, interviews, and focus groups may aid our appropriate use of these data by doing the following:

- Assisting in identifying errors in the data or problematic constructs (including misinterpretations or inconsistencies in respondent understandings of questions or concepts)
- Ascertaining what contributes to missing data and nonresponse and any underlying patterns in them
- Devising strategies to overcome limitations of the data or measures (e.g., identifying proxies, imputing missing values, trimming outliers, etc.)

Striving for tight integration between qualitative and quantitative researchers helps to facilitate this process of data checking, cleaning, and preparation and also enables it to proceed interactively, so that the data and measures employed in the research are in the best possible form or as accurate as possible.

Designing Instrumentation

We may also, on occasion, be presented with the opportunity to design new instrumentation—such as surveys and other tools for observation, monitoring, and measurement—and thereby collect original data for more precisely capturing and characterizing the essence of key constructs in our research. In these cases, we argue that formulating a plan to fully integrate qualitative and quantitative methods into the processes of developing instrumentation and collecting data is invaluable to ensuring the quality and accuracy of the measures. In addition, both qualitative and quantitative analysis can help to pinpoint *what* is important to measure (e.g., in the treatment and implementation process), as well as how to best measure these factors and policy or program outcomes.

To achieve integration in instrumentation design and data collection, we advise planning and coordination in the following key areas:

1. Identifying topics or constructs for which there is a need to develop or strengthen measures

2. Creating mechanisms for sharing information, insights, and data gathered in the process of instrumentation design

3. Selecting sites and determining sampling frames and strategies for piloting new instruments and (later) collecting study data

4. Establishing feedback loops for evaluating data quality and refining instrumentation following piloting

At the initial stages of determining what to measure and how, it is particularly important to bring together the perspectives of qualitative and quantitative researchers. The "deeper dive" that qualitative researchers undertake in examining how individuals view or experience an intervention or the environment around them can produce important guidance for the operationalization of constructs, that is, ensuring that essential meaning is not lost as concepts are simplified and distilled into empirical measures. For example, in the South African Child Support Grant program evaluation discussed in Chapter 7, information gathered in focus groups and key informant interviews by the qualitative research team helped to inform the design of questionnaire items that were intended to probe and identify reasons that some eligible families were not receiving the grant or were experiencing interruptions to grant receipt. A few illustrative quotes include the following:

> What you find is that these people have to spend R100 for transport (which is too much for them) to the offices. (Key informant interview, Eastern Cape)

> I am not going to reapply. This thing of coming here is time-consuming and they ask a lot of things, including documents. (Focus group participant, KwaZulu Natal)

> I did not have the right information; I didn't know where to go. (Focus group participant, Limpopo)

Besides helping to formulate specific response items to capture barriers such as high costs of transport to social welfare offices, documentation problems, and others, the qualitative research also helped to illuminate regional and temporal variation in the experiences of individuals and families, and how this variation might link to local factors or characteristics (e.g., the quality of roads or transportation, capacity of local social welfare offices), implying other variables that might be important to measure.

The case study of the South African Child Support Grant program in Chapter 7 describes one possible approach to coordinating the work of qualitative and quantitative researchers in instrumentation design. In that particularly large project, a core of eight research team members with experience in either qualitative, quantitative, or both methods established a framework and plan for pairing those with quantitative and qualitative skills (in differing substantive areas of expertise, e.g., health, education, labor, early child development) to focus on specific areas of the questionnaire design. They devised a schedule and timeline for integration points—that is, when the researchers would connect electronically, by conference line, or in person to share information essential to constructing questionnaire items and finalizing the instrumentation—prior to the target dates for pilot testing. In other projects as well, whether staffed by just a few or a larger research team, we have found that a secure project workspace or other electronic file storage location or system is an essential mechanism for facilitating regular interchanges between qualitative and quantitative researchers and ready access to the different types of information used in instrumentation design.

Continuing a fairly intensive level of integration is also important in the piloting phase so that pilot results and feedback can be effectively used to refine and finalize the instrumentation. This begins with the selection of sites or target areas/groups for the piloting, as there may be some trade-offs to getting representative samples of the intended population and assessing the validity and efficacy of survey items or other measures that are expected to be challenging or sensitive for some subgroups. Prior qualitative work and even quantitative data can help to inform these decisions. For example, are there patterns of nonresponse in existing data or known cultural barriers from qualitative sources that can point to likely problems with survey comprehension or completion? And once in the field, pilot testing can uncover problems that may need troubleshooting and retesting. To the extent that qualitative and quantitative researchers can stay engaged with each other throughout these research processes, as we see in each of the cases presented in this book, real-time feedback can be provided that can increase the efficiency of the processes and the quality of the research products and results.

Enhancing Data Collection

Making this type of concerted effort toward integration—where specific components of the process are not delegated to, or divided among, qualitative and quantitative researchers exclusively—raises the level of commitment and resources that are required for the research. However, if it results in higher-quality measures and more complete data collection, this investment will go a long way toward enhancing the accuracy and usefulness of the research findings.

Some of the key benefits of integration in the data collection phase include enhancing the ability to do the following:

- Cross-check (or triangulate) measures across different sources of qualitative and quantitative data
- Identify errors or outliers in the data that require further investigation
- Draw on administrative and other quantitative data sources to guide decisions about foci and strata for the smaller-N qualitative data collection
- Improve or refine empirical constructs or the categorization/characterization of data in defining new measures

To illustrate these benefits, we return to our experience in the SESIQ^2 study and, in particular, to our investigation of digital tutoring provided to public school students outside the school day.

The large and growing shares of public school students receiving tutoring from providers employing digital technologies spurred our deeper exploration of this tutoring option. We began simultaneously with qualitative and quantitative data collection and analysis: qualitatively extracting and synthesizing provider information about their digital services (as included in application forms to the state educational agency and in provider promotional materials) and using quantitative data in district administrative data systems to identify provider characteristics (as recorded in contracts between the districts and providers). Through integration and cross-checking of the assembled data, we identified and reconciled discrepancies in the categorization of providers across the different types/sources of data. We were also able to construct a richer categorization of provider attributes using the qualitative data, which we used in turn to develop more detailed quantitative measures of digital provider characteristics (see Box 3.1). In devising a plan for the following year of qualitative field research, the new constructs were used to define strata for digital provider data collection, and the qualitative research team also drew on the integrated data sources to refine their observation instrument for tutoring sessions, that is, adding measures specific to digital tutoring, such as the reliability of the technology in a session. As a result of the integration process, the study generated original data that shed new light on key (defining) and influential characteristics of digital providers that were subsequently linked in empirical analyses to student achievement gains from tutoring.

BOX 3.1 CONSTRUCTING A RICHER CATEGORIZATION OF DIGITAL TUTORING PROVIDERS

Based on descriptive analysis of the applications of approved tutoring providers in one school district in this study during the 2012–2013 school year, the SESIQ^2 research team developed the following categorizations that leveraged and probed deeper into digital provider characteristics first identified in the observational work.

- Tutor Location: Where does the student access the tutor?
  - Online or via the phone (remote access)
  - Face-to-face (in-person access)

- Tutor Synchronicity: How immediate is the student's communication with the tutor?
  - Asynchronous (time-delayed)
  - Synchronous (live)

- Instruction Driver: Who or what is guiding the student's learning?
  - Curriculum-based software (locally installed or delivered online)
  - Tutor actively working through curriculum-based software with the student
  - Tutor without curriculum-based software

- Curriculum Location: Where does the student access the course content?
  - Via a digital device, over the Internet
  - Via a digital device, using locally installed software
  - Via non-digital resources (e.g., books, worksheets, chalk/whiteboard, etc.)

In practice, combinations of characteristics were often observed within categories. For example, more than half of digital providers used some combination of tutor-driven and software-driven instruction drivers. These combinations were captured in the detailed measures employed in empirical analyses relating these attributes to program outcomes.

INTEGRATION IN DATA ANALYSIS
AND INTERPRETATION OF FINDINGS

As described earlier in the discussions of research and instrumentation design, the integration of qualitative and quantitative research methods and data can contribute importantly to the validity and richness of inferences and insights generated in policy and evaluation research. A rigorous, illuminating analysis is predicated on a well-specified research design and sufficient, high-quality data, but there are also critical decisions to be made in the data analysis phase that can be supported by ongoing integration of qualitative and quantitative research methods and data.

One of the most important research tasks in the analysis of data is the specification of the model(s) for estimating policy or program impacts or effectiveness. Understanding how treatment is assigned or how individuals or units select (or are selected into) treatment is of fundamental importance to the analysis. Not only can qualitative research generate rich, contextual information about the factors that determine access or treatment status, but can descriptive analysis of those data and available quantitative information can point to patterns in participation or subgroup variation that can drive heterogeneity in responses to and effects of treatment. For example, in the South African Child Support Grant program evaluation, problems experienced by grant recipients with late connections, interruptions, and disconnections from grant receipt led to substantial variation in the timing and length of grant receipt that ultimately allowed for an alternative methodological approach to the analysis. As there were fewer cases in the sample without any grant receipt, the core of the analysis shifted from a focus on comparing treatment to no-treatment cases to one that characterized treatment by the age of the child at its start and the number of months of grant receipt. Both qualitative and quantitative data analysis contributed importantly to the specification of models of selection into different treatment "dosages" and the analyses of program impacts.

The analysis of process or program implementation is another area where insights and applications are strengthened by the integration of qualitative and quantitative methods. In many policy and program evaluation studies, the implementation of policies or interventions occurs in multiple sites, sometimes in contexts that vary widely in administrative procedures, organizational capacities, personnel and monetary resources, target population characteristics, environmental constraints, and more. If researchers are to understand pathways to policy and program impacts and the factors that impede or support policy or program effectiveness, then accounting for these intervening variables in the analysis and/or interpretation of results is imperative. In early policy and evaluation research studies (and across fields), it was more common for implementation and impact studies to be conducted separately and to be integrated only in the discussion of the research findings. In the past two decades, however, it has increasingly been recognized that drawing the data and methods together earlier, and particularly in the analysis phase, can yield information that is more valuable to policymakers and program administrators.

For example, in the SESIQ² study, the quantitative research team analyzed student-level data to estimate the effects of Supplemental Educational Services on student achievement. The student-level data were also linked to information on the tutoring providers that served them, which allowed for the estimation of the average effects of specific providers on student achievement. This information was of particular interest to school district staff, who each year arranged contracts with tutoring providers to deliver services to students in the districts. However, equally (if not more) important to district staff administering these programs was to understand *why* some tutoring providers were more effective than others. The integration of qualitative and quantitative methods in the analysis was essential to addressing this question in the study.

The qualitative research team identified in their field research some key factors that their observations suggested could influence tutoring effectiveness, including (to name just a few) the following:

- What size groupings (e.g., student-to-teacher ratio) were used in delivering tutoring?
- How much instructional time was included in an invoiced hour of services?
- What were the qualifications and experience of the tutors?
- Were tutoring services offered on-site at the day school the student attended (vs. off-site or in homes)?

Where the quantitative analysis findings failed to show an association between student-to-teacher ratios reported by the providers (and recorded in district administrative data), the qualitative analysis found that the presence of a tutor in the classroom did not necessarily ensure his or her role in instruction. Thus, a provider recorded as having a 5:1 student-to-tutor ratio because it paired 10 students with 2 tutors might have an *effective* ratio of 10:1 if only one tutor is instructing while the other is doing paperwork at a desk. The qualitative observations of tutoring sessions also found that the amount of instructional time in an invoiced hour of tutoring varied considerably by the tutoring format and location, which led the quantitative team to further analyze provider effects by tutoring formats and location. Thus, although there is clearly some sequencing in the process by which the qualitative and quantitative work interacts, we argue that the feedback loops created in the tight integration of the qualitative and quantitative data analyses ultimately helped to generate evidence that was highly valued by stakeholders. In this particular case, the research findings guided district policy changes, such as improvements in monitoring tools and in how space at schools for on-site services was allocated to tutoring providers.

If integration of qualitative and quantitative methods is planned at the outset of a study and carried through the research design and data construction/collection stages, the mechanisms for integration in data analysis are usually well established by this point. Primarily, there needs to be some type of infrastructure for sharing data and the results of analyses (e.g., a project workspace, data storage site); a system or schedule for regular interchange between qualitative and quantitative researchers to discuss progress and findings; and a cultural openness to receiving feedback and acuity in applying it to enrich the analysis and interpretation of both qualitative and quantitative data. In the SESIQ^2 study, we designated one research team member to participate in all qualitative research team meetings (conducted by Skype to accommodate field researchers based in different locations) and to also interface regularly with the quantitative research team. This facilitated ongoing transmission of findings in the respective analyses and supported shared decision making and direction of the subsequent analyses; challenges that were encountered by one team or the other could be worked out together in joint meetings.

Finally, although qualitative methods are frequently lauded for their strength in drawing out nuance and quantitative methods are recognized for their rigor, we find that when combined in analysis, both achieve a greater level of rigor and generate more nuanced and constructive findings for improving policies and programs. For example, as described earlier, data collected in the qualitative fieldwork of the South African Child Support Grant program evaluation documented the challenges caregivers experienced in getting access to the grant (i.e., long waits at social welfare offices, document requirements, transportation costs, etc.). This information guided the development of household questionnaire items to gather data for understanding these administrative burdens and their implications for household access to the grant and program outcomes. In the analysis of these data, we were able to quantify administrative burdens and show in logistic regressions which problems and constraints most affected access to the grant (Heinrich & Brill, 2014). One of these findings showed that individuals who reported having problems producing the required documentation had approximately 1,000% higher odds of being disconnected from the program (with no grant restart) and about 340% greater odds of having their grant receipt interrupted. Furthermore, the empirical analyses were able to ascertain how months of cash transfers lost because of administrative burden diminished the positive impacts of the program on adolescent outcomes. The qualitative data, in turn, provided a richer understanding of how document requirements created these burdens and also how they might be unevenly experienced by eligible households, such as shown in the following focus group excerpt:

> Sometimes they ask you to provide proof of residence, or electricity or water. If you are unemployed or staying in RDP houses you cannot have these things, because we do not pay for water and do not use metered electricity.

This information provides clear guidance for policymakers on how these burdens might be reduced. In the concluding section of this chapter, we describe how integration in the dissemination of research findings can also promote confidence in, and active use of, the results and recommendations by policy and program stakeholders.

INTEGRATION IN DISSEMINATION OF RESEARCH FINDINGS

We have long known that simply having data and evidence available does not ensure that they will be used. Information needs to be seen as relevant, that is, accessed and interpreted in ways that have significance within a particular context or setting (Kowalski, 2009). Furthermore, policymakers and practitioners need to see it as credible from the lens of their own professional norms and training and their existing knowledge base and rules for evidence (Tseng, 2012). And perhaps most importantly, stakeholders need to see the link between the research findings and tangible actions they can take to improve or respond to challenges in the status quo.

The previously mentioned points are all strong reasons for maintaining a tight level of integration between qualitative and quantitative study components as research findings are disseminated to various target audiences or stakeholders. First, qualitative work is often a key source of the rich, contextual information that helps those on the receiving end to process the findings and relate them to their own settings. To the extent that researchers can tailor research dissemination to particular stakeholder groups or contexts and in language that relates to their personal or professional context, the findings are more likely to be consumed and applied. And as there is frequently a time lag in access to quantitative data (i.e., due to preparation required in cleaning, checking, and securely storing data), qualitative information may be essential to speak to the current policy or program context or to the most immediate challenges facing the prospective users of the research evidence.

In the Research-to-Practice Collaborative that we created in the SESIQ² study (discussed in greater detail in Chapter 4), research briefings were conducted each year by both qualitative and quantitative team members together at the school districts to engage district staff in a discussion of the research findings and relate them to ongoing experiences in the district with policy and program implementation. The qualitative researchers had in many cases established relationships with district staff (as needed to conduct the research) and often had encountered similar challenges and experiences in the field that the staff could relate to in the discussions. The research briefings were structured to allow the qualitative and quantitative findings to interact in the presentation—for example, sometimes illustrating an empirical finding with a specific case example, vignette, or quote—and to the extent possible, empirical findings were presented graphically as well as numerically to help the audience visualize the results in a way that was meaningful to them. For example, in presenting the study findings on the effects of specific tutoring providers on student achievement, the results were displayed graphically along with the provider "market shares" of students so that stakeholders could see the correspondence (or lack thereof) between provider effectiveness and the number of students served (and how it changed over time). Both the researchers and the district staff could contribute additional information about the providers—as observed and interviewed by the qualitative team or as encountered in program management by the district staff—that enhanced the ensuing discussion about patterns in the results and what they implied for policy and program administration.

One of the SESIQ² Research-to-Practice Collaborative elements that gained considerable momentum during the study was the cross-district webinar and follow-up exchanges that were fostered to promote peer-to-peer interactions around the study findings. In conducting our research in six large urban school districts, we sometimes observed districts trying different approaches to solve common problems (e.g., how to increase student attendance at tutoring sessions) or managing the same task (e.g., registering students for services) in different ways that impacted access and service efficacy. The networks and tools we created in the collaborative for facilitating peer-to-peer discussion of the real-time challenges they were facing and how the cross-site research evidence could inform policy and program changes were among the most appreciated by the research stakeholders. We also arranged for the cross-district webinars and communications to take place before each new school year got under way, timing them with the district calendar for these types of policy discussions. Conveying his enthusiasm for how the study findings were shared in both the research briefings and the cross-district webinars, one district official remarked, "We're just going to eat up anything you can give to us." For any given research project, the types of tools or formats for disseminating research findings in ways that promote their active use may vary, and we suggest that this is an important place to seek stakeholder input.

We also suggest that in determining the tools or approaches to disseminating research findings, it is sometimes valuable to let one component (i.e., qualitative or quantitative) lead in designing the product or approach. Some target audiences might be more receptive to information produced in qualitative (or quantitative) research or may be more interested in some aspects of findings than others. In most cases, we have found that some combination of qualitative and quantitative is most effective in espousing the credibility and persuasiveness of the research findings, even if one component dominates the other. For example, in developing a guide for parents to understand and apply the SESIQ^2 research findings (e.g., in choosing tutoring providers), the qualitative research team that had been interacting with parents in focus groups and tutoring settings drafted the parent brief and then worked with the quantitative team to appropriately incorporate the empirical findings. The guide uses simple language and there are no graphic or numerical presentations of the quantitative analysis findings.

Similarly, we worked with one of our school districts to package the results on tutoring provider effectiveness in booklets that were distributed to school principals who made decisions about providers' use of space on their campuses and to parents making choices about tutoring providers for their children. The booklet included a page that described the research methodology and general findings, followed by a chart that listed provider names, hours of tutoring provided, and whether they had significant positive effects on students' math and/or reading achievement. Rather than reporting provider effect sizes (numerically), we indicated whether a positive impact was identified and if that positive impact was higher than the average impact. Although we did not directly observe parents' and principals' use of this information, we did see over time in our empirical analyses that providers consistently identified as effective gained or maintained student market share in this district, whereas those not found to be effective sometimes saw substantial drops in their market share from one year to the next or diminishing market share over time. This insight deepened our district partner's interest in and commitment to disseminating the study results in this practical way.

Depending on a given study's research goals, timeline, resources, context, and stakeholders (to name a few factors), there are many different strategies and approaches that can be used to communicate study findings in ways that will be accessible and beneficial to target audiences. We have argued in this chapter that tightly linking qualitative and quantitative research activities from the start—from the research design through to the dissemination phase—will help to maximize the usefulness and relevance of the findings for those who can put them into practice or draw on them to support policy and program improvements. Recognizing, however, that policy and program improvement is a continuous process for most organizations, we also recommend returning to the logic model or framework that was used to set expectations for the research effort at the end of the study to assess what was learned or where knowledge is still lacking. Were the expected causal pathways to outcomes confirmed, or were some left unexplored because of limitations of the data, measures, or methods? Was evidence generated that points to clear policy or program changes that can be made to improve outcomes? What directions should future investigations take to build on the existing evidence and guide future policy and program design and developments?

DISCUSSION QUESTIONS

1. In this chapter, we describe a number of elements that are commonly included in a theory of change or conceptual model for guiding a research effort. Are there other elements or types of components that might be included in a theory of change?

2. Search the literature for a theory of change that is relevant to your research interests. How could a mixed methods approach be used to explore the causal and non-causal pathways it depicts?

3. How and why is the role of a mixed methods approach important in characterizing the treatment or intervention that is being studied in evaluation research? Can you think of an example in which mixed methods were not used but could have benefited an evaluation if employed?

4. Often times, less attention is given to our theory or theories of measurement, and existing data or measures are taken and used at face value. How can a mixed methods approach be used to enrich the measures we develop, that is, our conceptualization and operationalization of them?

5. One of the more common ways that qualitative and quantitative data have been used together is to aid in the interpretation of research findings, typically with qualitative data providing context for the empirical results. How does a more fully integrated mixed methods approach make greater use of qualitative and quantitative methods in the analysis and interpretation phases of the research, and how does this contribute to the credibility of the research findings?

6. The cases discussed in this book provide examples of mechanisms or forums through which research findings could be disseminated. What other types of information or formats or tools for their dissemination might be used in this phase of research? How can researchers work with their stakeholders to determine the most useful tools in a given context?

APPLICATIONS TO YOUR OWN WORK

- Think about the implicit theory of action in a study that you might design in an area of your interest. Drawing on any relevant literature, develop a logic model to guide your research effort.

- Choose an empirical measure that is relevant to a topic of interest in your research. What theories have been used to argue for specific approaches to its conceptualization or operationalization? What qualitative and quantitative data have been used to justify its construction? What do you find lacking in terms of theoretical or practical support for the measure as defined and constructed?

- You are asked in a grant proposal to develop a plan for the dissemination of your research findings. For a research project of your own (current or future), describe how you will engage the stakeholders of the research, particularly those in positions to use the findings for policy or program improvement, in your plan/strategies for dissemination.

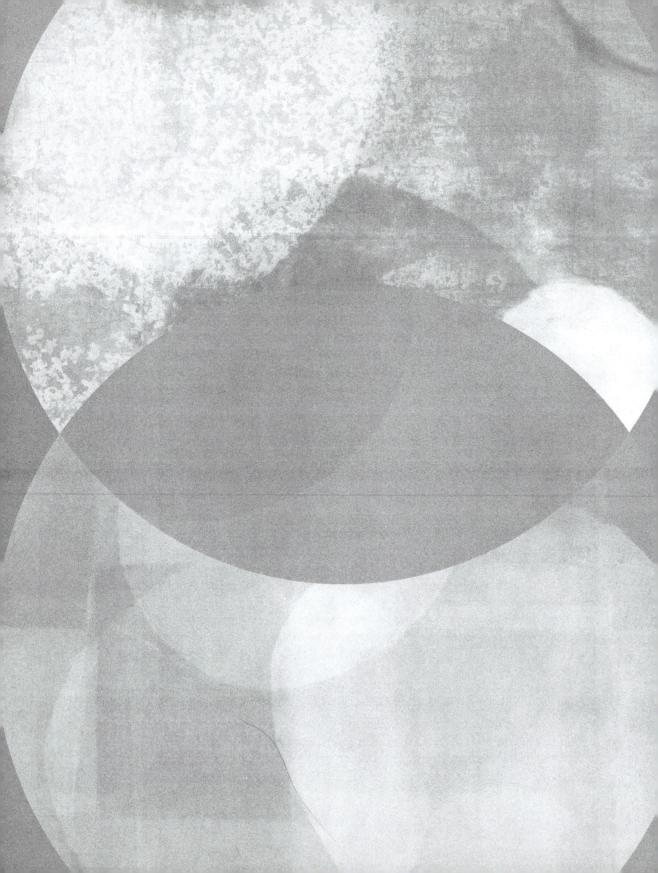

CHAPTER 4

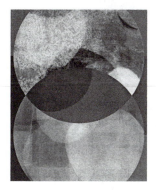

Practical Tools for Integrated Mixed Methods Studies of Policy Implementation

INTRODUCTION

Implementing a mixed methods study, similar to implementing complex policies, depends not only on research design but also on how various stakeholders and staff involved in the study (from principal investigator to field-worker to data analyst) interpret the objectives of the study and act on these interpretations. Fully integrated, mixed methods research is like policy implementation in that it is context-specific and is shaped as it is executed. For example, the value, interpretation, and responses to a common set of research findings may vary depending on the entity (e.g., the history and reform priorities of a school district) and in terms of a stakeholder's formal position or responsibility (district director of assessment or school principal). In our experience, mixed methods research is very well suited for policy studies that aim to provide stakeholders with aggregate findings (national level or local level), while also attending to site-specific differences that add nuance to these findings.

The purpose of this chapter is to offer the reader further guidance in the *how-to* of integrated mixed methods work, drawing on our study of the implementation and impact of Supplemental Educational Services (SES). We focus this discussion on the practical tools that emerged around three central objectives in our integrated design, two of which were articulated as part of our study design and one of which (district and vendor capacity) emerged as an objective as new policy developments offered districts more flexibility in designing their own afterschool programs. These objectives are the following:

- Providing formative rather than exclusively summative feedback to support continuous program improvement
- Identifying the characteristics and mechanisms at multiple levels of a system that can support high-quality programming or service delivery (from district administrators, to tutoring vendors, to classroom teachers and tutors)
- Building district and vendor capacity to design and sustain afterschool programs that have measurable impact on student achievement for any student in the district

For each of these objectives, striving for a fully integrated mixed methods approach proved critical. In what follows, we describe the central tools we developed (in-house) as part of the study in order to pursue these objectives. We illuminate how both objectives and strategies evolved over time, informed by conversations with stakeholders as well as by insights generated with the study data. We also identify the ways in which the structure and organization of the study facilitated the work, the dilemmas we faced as researchers, and any missteps in our process from which others can learn. We include samples of all of the tools that we reference in this discussion for possible use and adaptation by other researchers.

MIXED METHODS INTEGRATION STRATEGY #1: BRIDGING RESEARCH INSTRUMENTS FOR QUALITATIVE AND QUANTITATIVE INTEGRATION

The initial design of the study included a highly specified model for estimating program effects and identifying program characteristics linked to effects. The qualitative work was semi-structured in the sense that we had clear sampling strategies and general constructs of interest that would guide interviews and observations while allowing for iterations and evolution of instrumentation as we learned from the field. Over the course of the study, one research instrument in particular became a touchstone for rich dialogue around the analysis, interpretation of the data, and dissemination of both qualitative and quantitative research. In this regard, rather than having quantitative and qualitative data collection develop on parallel tracks, or having one type of data be more privileged in our analysis than another, the two teams came together around a shared (data) point of interest: the instructional setting. Shared exchanges around what we were learning about instructional setting strengthened the reliability and sensitivity of the observation tool and brought qualitative and quantitative data into close conversation, contributing to greater specificity and richness of findings.

Implementation Phase

We described in Chapters 2 and 3 the multiphase iterative process that we followed in developing and testing the research-based observation instrument for use in all observations of SES tutoring sessions across the study sites. We began with a review of existing scholarly literature on conducting qualitative observations of afterschool programs, and because there was no preexisting instrument designed specifically for use in SES tutoring programs, we built on the most salient aspects of existing observation instruments and combined these with our own materials derived from earlier pilot studies of SES. After the observation instrument was developed to capture detailed facets and the theory of action behind SES provision in the qualitative fieldwork in a standardized framework, we circulated the observation instrument for review by our own team and by outside research experts in qualitative evaluations of afterschool programming. In piloting the instrument in multiple locations and settings, we made minor revisions and then conducted multiple inter-rater reliability trainings with the entire qualitative research staff. We also created a detailed manual for use of the observation instrument, as well as an explanation of the research rationale for its use.

The observation instrument that we created allowed us to assess the quality of the tutoring program using three "sections": tutoring context, tutoring observation coding, and an instructional vignette. The tutoring context section included duration of instructional time, activity type, activity focus, grouping patterns, staffing patterns, type of space, instructional resources available, and administrative tools (e.g., attendance rosters). The tutoring observation coding section included three subsections: opportunities for skill-building and mastery—curriculum; opportunities for skill-building and mastery—instruction; and interactions/engagement. Rating indicators in the coding section were constructed on a scale of 0 to 2: The observer marked a 0 when an indicator was possible to observe but not present at any time or with any students;

1 when an indicator occasionally was present, or with only some students; and 2 when an indicator was predominant. An indicator was "predominant" when it occurred more than once during the time period and/or was so pronounced and persistent that it contributed to the overall social/emotional climate and/or learning environment. An observer rated an indicator with a 2 when it could be considered characteristic of a best practice.

The use of a 3-point rating scale in the observation instrument assisted in organizing, standardizing, and comparing observations across sites. Rather than employing a rating scale with many points, we used a comments section—that is, an instructional vignette using thick, narrative description—and follow-up conversations with tutors to better address the gradations of possible outcomes for each indicator. A 3-point scale allowed us to focus our observations with more specificity, while still basing observations on the in-depth narrative description endemic to qualitative fieldwork.

Opportunities and Dilemmas

As planned, our qualitative research team refined the observation instrument for the 2012–2013 data collection year, based on ongoing reliability trainings and emergent data and interpretation. For example, quantitative data on student participation and attendance started to show that online providers were gaining significant market share. Our initial sampling for the qualitative sample did not account for this format because at the time of the pilot studies, online providers had yet to gain much of a presence. As digital providers gained market share, in part spurred by policy developments, we sought ways to include more online indicators in our research design in order for us to keep findings relevant to district partners.

The observation instrument emerged as a central strategy in this work. The most significant changes to the observation instrument were designed to better capture elements of tutoring instruction specific to the digital context. For example, the previous instrument framed many of the indicators in terms of the tutor actions, some of which were not applicable to digital tutoring sessions without a tutor (i.e., software-based/driven). In regularly scheduled meetings, team members met to identify indicators to better respond to digital settings without a live tutor (e.g., instructional software adapts to student's instructional needs), as well as to better describe how technology is used toward better instruction (e.g., use of technology to employ higher-order thinking skills) and address issues around access (e.g., technology used is reliable and accessible to all students). We also made changes to specify multimodal instruction and the application of higher-order thinking skills, as well as to clarify language in particular indicators and broaden how we capture instructional elements specific to students with disabilities (see Figure 4.1).

Figure 4.1 Digital Observation Instrument

Evaluating the Quality of Learning Opportunities in Digital and Blended Instructional Settings

Draft Observation Instrument

Overview

- The ultimate goal of this instrument is to evaluate the quality of learning opportunities for students *within the instructional core*. Each indicator (or row) represents an element the research base suggests is critical to quality instruction. The rubric evaluates the extent to which the instructional session—through each of these areas or indicators—facilitates quality learning opportunities for students. This instrument is less focused on how well the material is learned because presumably that is the job of quantitative analysis. Instead, this instrument is evaluating the quality of learning *opportunity in implementation*.
- The instrument is fully qualitative in nature, mapping instruction in a way that is more nuanced than more prescribed tools (i.e., Quality Matters rubric, etc.) and lets the particularities of the setting and session inform this process. Yet, this instrument still integrates well with quantitative work, both in design in that it speaks to the coding schemes of the quantitative classification process of digital programs, and in analyses through the possibility of connecting findings around programs providing quality learning opportunities with those showing greater impact on statistical measures. In addition, there are certain items within each indicator that could be tallied or quantified in the coding process (e.g., skill focus, role of the instructor, etc.).
- We try to strike a balance between being open and flexible enough to capture the setting (especially the digital setting that is widely varied and constantly changing) while being discrete and particular enough to compare easily across settings and offer quantifiable ratings and averages.
- The idea is to rate or evaluate the entire learning experience, that is, the actual opportunities a student is getting. Therefore, a blended "session" would need to include both online and face-to-face elements, possibly sampled around a particular lesson or concept. In addition, it may be possible that this instrument be used in fully face-to-face sessions, especially in an evaluation project comparing digital to traditional face-to-face models.

(Continued)

Figure 4.1 (Continued)

- This instrument addresses an important hole in evaluating digital instruction in practice because it focuses on K-12 (as opposed to higher education), the entire instructional setting and core (as opposed to auditing, or focused on just teacher ability, integration of technology, or alignment to a particular set of standards), and opportunities to learn *in practice* (implementation as opposed to course design or impact).

Instructions:

I. For each indicator (row), comment on the extent to which the following are present *and* contributing to the quality of learning opportunities:

A. Environment or setting: how and where students access the instructional setting, what or who else is there, who else is interacting with instruction/technology

B. Access: how does student access instruction, accommodations for students with disabilities, language barriers, technology is safe and operable

C. Curricular content: skill focus, clear objectives, rigor, relevance, alignment to learning objectives, structure, who developed it, where it is located, ability of curriculum to adapt to student need

D. Instructional model: role of instructor, student-to-instructor ratio, role of software in instruction, instructional driver, purpose or target of instruction (e.g., supplemental, course replacement, day school), course design and format, multimodal, ability of model to adapt to student need or setting

E. What student is being asked to do and is doing: listen, recite, demonstrate, think critically, apply, problem-solve, evaluate, use various resources, use technology (for communication, retrieval, application, evaluation, etc.)

F. Interaction and engagement: positive or negative between instructors/students/ instruction, how much actual interaction with a live person, student self-regulation, persistence, instructor and student engagement (and if so, passive or active), level of community within instructional setting

G. Integration and alignment: standards alignment, alignment to other instructional settings for students (e.g., day school for out-of-school time [OST] programs), integration with other aspects of the instructional model (e.g., if blended), alignment to learning objectives

H. Assessment/evaluation: individualized, continuous, relevant, accurate, who controls it, what form the data are in

I. Narrative vignette: describe the instruction taking place over a 10-minute time period during the session — addressing how, what, who, and where of learning opportunities.

J. Miscellaneous notes: record other information important to understanding the quality of learning opportunities

II. Once the instructional session is complete and you have written comments under each of the indicators, assign a rating of 0 to 4 to each, writing it in the space provided in the left column.

Observation Instrument

Date _____ Location _____

Provider _____ Rater _____

Total observation time _____ - _____

Instructional time _____ - _____

Students: Total _____ Female_____ Male _____ Ethnicity _____
Language status _____ Disability status _____

Instructors: Total _____ Female _____ Male _____ Ethnicity _____
Professional background _____

Instructional format: ___ All face-to-face ___ All digital ____ Blended ____ Synchronous ____ Asynchronous

Technology in use by instructor _____

Functional Y/Sometimes/N (explain): _____

Technology in use by student _____

Functional Y/Sometimes/N (explain): _____

	3	2	1	0
_____ A. **Environment or setting**	The environment facilitates quality learning opportunities throughout the session.	The environment does not get in the way of quality learning opportunities, but does not contribute to them.	The environment presents occasional or partial barriers to quality learning opportunities.	The environment is a significant barrier to quality learning opportunities.
	Comments:			

Figure 4.1 (Continued)

	3	2	1	0
_____ B. **Access**	All students have full access to the instructional setting throughout the session.	Most students have access to the instructional setting throughout the session.	Most students had multiple problems accessing the instructional setting throughout the session.	Students were not able to access the instructional setting.
	Comments:			

	3	2	1	0
_____ C. **Curricular content**	Curricular content is designed and used to create quality learning opportunities throughout the session.	Curricular content is designed and/or used to create quality learning opportunities occasionally during the session.	Curricular content neither creates nor inhibits quality learning opportunities.	Curricular content inhibits quality learning opportunities throughout the session.
	Comments:			

	3	2	1	0
_____ D. **Instructional model**	The instructional model consistently facilitates quality learning opportunities and adapts to apparent (or known) student needs.	The instructional model occasionally facilitates quality learning opportunities that adapt to apparent (or known) student needs.	The instructional model rarely facilitates quality learning opportunities that rarely adapt to apparent (or known) student needs.	The instructional model does not facilitate quality learning opportunities and does not adapt to apparent (or known) student needs.
	Comments:			

	3	2	1	0
_____ E. **What student is being asked to do and is doing**	All student tasks contribute to quality learning opportunities.	Most student tasks contribute to quality learning opportunities.	Few student tasks contribute to quality learning opportunities.	No student tasks lead to quality learning opportunities.
	Comments:			

	3	2	1	0
_____ F. **Interaction and engagement**	All students and instructors have positive interaction with	Most students and instructors have positive interaction with	Students and instructors have little interaction with one	Students or instructors have no or negative interaction with
	one another and full engagement in instruction.	one another and/or are mostly engaged in instruction.	another and/ or are rarely engaged in instruction.	one another and/or are not engaged in instruction.
	Comments (probes: alignment to standards; alignment to other settings/ components, including day school, online, etc.; alignment to stated learning objectives)			

	3	2	1	0
_____ G. **Integration and alignment**	Learning opportunities are fully integrated and aligned.	Learning opportunities are partly integrated and aligned.	Learning opportunities are either integrated or aligned for portions of the session.	Learning opportunities lack integration or alignment.
	Comments:			

	3	2	1	0
_____ H. **Assessment and evaluation**	Student learning is assessed frequently in constructive ways.	Student learning is assessed frequently but is not constructive.	Student learning is assessed once during the session.	Student learning is not assessed during the session.
	Comments:			

(Continued)

Figure 4.1   (Continued)

I. *Narrative vignette*	
J. *Miscellaneous notes*	

Resources consulted in development process

- Articles we have collected in identifying basic principles of quality online instruction
- Our own mixed methods multisite longitudinal evaluation of digital tutoring
- SREB (Southern Regional Education Board) standards and checklist for evaluating online courses (http://publications.sreb.org/2006/06T05_Standards_quality_online _courses.pdf) (http://publications.sreb.org/2006/06T06_Checklist_for_Evaluating -Online-Courses.pdf)
- California State University, Chico, Rubric for Online Instruction (http://www.csuchico .edu/roi/the_rubric.shtml)
- Technology Integration Observation Instrument from TPACK (http://elvistheteacher .wikispaces.com/file/view/TPACKObservationInstrument.pdf)
- CLASS observation instrument for student-teacher interactions (http://www .teachstone.org/about-the-class/)
- Framework for 21st Century Learning (www.p21.org/our-work/p21-framework)
- Quality Matters K-12 online rubric of standards, focuses on online course *design* (http://www.uwex.edu/disted/conference/Resource_library/proceedings/29483_10.pdf)
- iNACOL standards for online courses (http://www.inacol.org/resources/publications/ national-quality-standards/)
- Smythe (2012). *Toward a framework for evaluating blended learning* (use of rubrics in blended learning environments; http://www.editlib.org/p/42695/)
- Laumakis et al. (2009). The Sloan-C pillars and boundary objects as a framework for evaluating blended learning. *Journal Asynchronous Learning Networks* (use of Sloan Consortium including access, blended learning in context of higher education; http:// bartfennemore.com/edt6040/images/9/99/Laumakis_1.pdf)

Validity and Reliability

Hill et al. (2012). Validating arguments for observational instruments: Attending to multiple sources of variation. *Educational Assessment, 17,* 1–19.

Pianta, R., & Hamre, B. (2009). Conceptualization, measurement, and improvement of classroom processes: Standardized observation can leverage capacity. *Educational Researcher, 38*(2), 109–119.

Supporting Mechanism

The observation instrument became a vehicle for integration of qualitative and quantitative data and for effectively disseminating this type of data to multiple stakeholders. As noted earlier, in the implementation phase of study, we established separate teams and meeting times for qualitative and quantitative researchers but also established mechanisms for ensuring sharing of data and interpretation of those data across the two teams. Rather than trying to share everything with everybody, we looked for "bridging" data points central to the objectives of both qualitative and quantitative work. After the meetings, one of the participants wrote up summary notes and memos of the thrust of the meeting and shared them with other team members, to check for accuracy and common understandings. This kind of discussion can even take place between an individual researcher and an advising colleague or peer (Strauss, 1987, pp. 130–131).

One such type of data was the characteristics of the instructional setting. The quantitative team was interested in these data to better specify variables at the classroom level that might explain the presence or lack of statistically significant effects that their analyses showed to be associated with some tutoring providers and not others. From larger research bases on school-level characteristics influencing student achievement, we knew that teachers'—or in this instance, tutors'—classroom practices were a critical factor in whether an intervention affected student achievement, suggesting that the classroom-level variables merited further scrutiny. In this regard, the study was designed in a way to leverage the unique capabilities of qualitative work to look inside the instructional black box. The qualitative team's observations of classroom practice would probe patterns in tutor practices in a small sample of providers that could help us see what tutors were doing and whether and how these practices varied by provider type and district context. The qualitative team was interested in the instructional setting as a specific context where the full picture of tutoring could be gathered, as well as an understanding of elements interacting in that context (e.g., how the physical setting of tutoring and organization of classrooms allowed or inhibited tutors from engaging in specific practices such as higher-order thinking).

For both teams to engage in rich conversation about the data, the quantitative data needed interpretation and the qualitative data needed quantification. To help the quantitative team leverage qualitative data, the project created an Excel sheet (see Figure 4.2) for better displaying observation data to the quantitative group. Specifically, the observation spreadsheet was set up to more easily analyze certain aspects of the observation instrument, particularly quantifiable elements such as ratings, number of participants, time, and other aspects. The qualitative team members identified as possessing the strongest quantitative skill sets took the lead for the development of this instrument. Each indicator was listed on the left-hand side of the spreadsheet and each observation date listed across the top. Because of the number of observations, they needed to be split up among sheets, so the "base sheets" (the ones the researcher worked from and linked to all of the other sheets) were organized by site. Then, for the other areas of analysis (year, format, location, etc.) the researcher linked the two columns of each observation.

At the end of each row, she included a few calculations that translated the 0–2 rating scale into a 0–1 scale. The first of these columns summed the total ratings (e.g., =SUM(3A:6A)). The second column counted the observable cells (any cell without an n/a or a —) in order to create a denominator that reflected which indicators were observable (e.g., =COUNT(3A:6A)). The third column multiplied the second column by 2, to reflect that each indicator had a possible maximum rating of 2 (e.g., =2×8A, with 8A being the second column's cell in that row). The final column was the actual sum of ratings divided by the actual possible ratings (first column divided by third column, e.g., =7A/9A).

As reflected in Figure 4.2, in addition to the numeric indicators, the researcher included rows for advertised time, observed time, difference between advertised and observed time, number of tutors in observation points A and B, number of students in observation points A and B, tutor-to-student ratio in A and B. Also included were some of the comment sections (e.g., on staffing) in order to more quickly view which sessions had information about tutors for English language learners and students with special needs. This simple organizing system allowed the qualitative team to conduct basic calculations that quantified very rich qualitative data on classroom practices, while still retaining the context for that data, for example, through vignettes. Excerpts from the field notes were included in the Excel sheet. These vignettes helped the qualitative team keep the indicators *in context* in conversations with the quantitative team.

In turn, the quantitative team organized its data in ways that supported and facilitated interpretation by qualitative team members who had little or no experience with the complex value-added modeling used by the team. For example, the principal investigator highlighted (in charts and graphs displaying data) the findings that deserved probing, sometimes because of their statistical significance (or lack thereof). We organized full team meetings that included substantive discussion of "integrated" issues. This included how much to explain quantitative modeling in a paper that also included qualitative data

Figure 4.2 Snapshots of Excel Sheet for Quantifying Qualitative Data (One District)

	A	B	C	D	E	F	G	H	I	J
2	Description	Indicator #	AUAI1A	AUAI1B	AUAI2A	AUAI2B	AUAI3A	AUAI3B	AUCO1A	AUCO1B
3	Date	1.7.1	100210		100211		91210		91210	
4	Researcher/Full Nvivo Code		IO_AA20101013pburch2 28-30		IO_AA20101013pburch2 30-32		IO_AA20101013pburch2 41-41		IO_AC20101013pburch2 06-16	
5	3-Digit Nvivo Identifier		228		230		241		206	
6	Format	1.3	home		school		school		school	school
7	Location	1.3	home		school		school		school	school
8	Grouping Patterns	2.1.4(a)/5(b)	1 to 1	1 to 1	1 to 1	1 to 1	1 to 1	1 to 1	1 to 3	1 to 3
9	Instructional Minutes	2.1.3	45		75		90		60	
10	Advertised Time	2.1.1	75		60		60		60	
11	Revised advertised time		60		60		60		60	
12	Advertised - Instructional		15		-15		-30		0	
13	Focus	2.1.6								
14	Total number of students	3.1.5	1	1	1	1	1	1	5	5
15	Number of staff	3.1.2	1	1	1	1	1	1	5	5
16	Staff/student ratio		1.00	1.00	1.00	1.00	1.00	1.00	1	1
17	Staffing description	2.2.0	1M AA	1M AA	1M	1M	1F, W	1F, W	5M	5M
18	Notes on staffing	2.2.1	She is a college student - very bubbly - met her in library first		The space for tutoring is tutor's own classroom. It is a nice room, good view, good layout tables arranged in fours. Teacher can make reference and use the math aids in his		Very low energy, mid-40s. Has special ed degree.		Director also present, distracted for part of the time.	

	A	B	C	D	E	F	G	H	I	J
1			District Y1		District Y1		District Y1		District Y1	
19	Special Ed staff	3.1.3	0	0	0	0	1	1	1	1
20	ELL/bilingual staff	3.1.4	0	0	0	0	0	0	1	1
21	ELL students	2.3	0	0	0	0	1 - spanish	1 - spanish	0	0
22	Students with Disabilities	2.3	0	0	0	0	0	0	0	0
23	Indicate skill focus	3.2.2	2	2	2	2	2	2	2	2
24	Indicate goal as homework or tutoring	3.2.3	2	2	2	2	0	0	2	2
25	Provide additional materials for home	3.2.4	0	0	0	0	1	1	0	0
26	Include cognitive/enrichment	3.2.5	2	2	2	2	0	0	1	1
27	Provide artistic or physical recreation linked to	3.2.6	0	0	0	0	0	0	0	0
28	Provide multi-modal	3.2.6a	x	x	x	x	x	x	x	x
29	Provide community or family-linked activities	3.2.7	0	0	0	0	0	0	0	0
30	Use materials toward the goal of instruction m/rla	3.2.8	2	2	2	2	2	2	2	2

(and whether readers that might require this explanation), how to manage coauthorship of papers that integrated qualitative and quantitative data, and how to develop a product that fully integrated the data while being responsive to districts' immediate needs.

In our integrated discussion of data, such as components of instructional setting, the approach we used was similar to that used in qualitative analysis, where a participant selects an artifact (e.g., student work or a district memorandum), and researchers use that artifact as the basis of an interview, with the goal of authentic and rich discussion around the question or topic of value to the participant. Thus, in the mixed methods study, the qualitative and quantitative teams worked individually on preliminary analysis of data, for example, compiling observation data including vignettes embedded in the observation. Members of the team leading this work would then prepare analysis for a full team meeting, organized around variables where the data was the richest or particularly puzzling. The document would be shared with all members of the team as pre-meeting materials. Typically, meetings would begin with lead researchers succinctly describing findings and data used in support of these findings. Following this presentation, there would be a question-and-answer period, with lead researchers taking questions from the rest of the team. These discussions (about which detailed notes were taken and then shared) helped build a shared and rich interpretation of both qualitative and quantitative data among researchers with differing areas of expertise. The meeting would end with agreement on next steps in the analysis and data collection and meeting notes that captured the integrated analysis.

Here again, it is important to acknowledge that the process (as with policy-making process) was not linear or conflict free. Several instances arose when one or another team member worried about the direction of the study and how data were being interpreted and used. For example, as the integration of data progressed, the qualitative team grew cognizant that its number of observations was relatively limited, particularly as compared to the observation points in quantitative data. When we presented the data at district briefings, the suggestion was that we increase the number of observations and include more observations that were unannounced. Districts did not have the time or capacity for these walk-throughs and wanted data that could help them track vendors' practices month-by-month. This presented us with a dilemma. We had to make the choice between structuring observation data to include fewer observations of entire tutoring sessions or, with the objective of "increasing our n," scheduling more observations, spot checks, or walk-throughs. The qualitative team carefully discussed these two alternatives in its group meetings and with the quantitative team. The team decided against increasing the number of observations by provider but did structure the observation instrument so that we were able to obtain two observation points (at different points of tutoring sessions) within each observation. The deciding factor was our commitment to leveraging the unique strengths of qualitative work in our mixed methods approach, rather than designing a study that compromised those strengths. We chose the former so we could get a full picture of the instructional experience of students. The addition of two observation points allowed us to increase our "*n*" without compromising the objective of getting rich data on instructional setting.

MIXED METHODS INTEGRATION STRATEGY #2: MIXED METHODS CODING AND ANALYSIS MEMOING

There were other points in the project where we burrowed in qualitative ways into quantitative data. We asked questions about the numbers and trends that others had tabulated and that we required for our own investigation of effects. These were particularly exciting moments in our mixed methods work—when we felt freed by boundaries of paradigms and worked fluidly to build meaning from very different kinds of data. However, this work also had its bumps. We felt cautious about counting separate dimensions of observation data for fear of extracting too much context. Similarly, quantitative researchers sometimes felt like they were moving too far into the realm of fieldwork as they worked qualitatively with quantitative data.

Supporting Mechanism

The central activity in this work involved a kind of mixed methods coding (Saldaña, 2013). In this instance, the texts being coded were state provider applications. Our objective for analyzing these texts was as a starting point to differentiate digital and non-digital providers. In the first round of coding, we used codes based on external classification schemes used by state providers required by law to share information on tutoring providers offering services in the state. In close reading of the text as part of the coding process, we found these categories to be too general, including terms such as *digital*, *online*, and *blended learning*. These categories clumped together the very data points that our study, in its focus on instructional method, was trying to unpack—what was being taught and how it was being taught. Consistent with iterative processes of coding and analysis (Stake, 2012), we refined our codes by going back to the text (state provider applications) and reread them based on our initial reactions to the coding process and refined the coding scheme based on this work. The researcher leading this work memoed to the mixed methods team about the process. The memorandum (see Figure 4.3) demonstrates the careful documentation of process necessary for any good research but particularly for fully integrated mixed methods research whereby quantitatively trained researchers work with qualitative data and qualitative researchers work with quantitative data.

Figure 4.3   Mixed Methods Memoing Coding and Analysis

A New Taxonomy for Digital Tutoring

Initial attempts at SES provider classification ran aground when we discovered that existing taxonomies—which lump tutoring services into vague and reductive categories like "digital," "online," and "blended"—could not fully capture the variability between tutoring programs evidenced by Texas SES provider applications. Specifically, we found the existing categories conflated (1) the location of the tutor relative to the student with (2) the location of the curriculum relative to the student with (3) the entity driving the instruction with (4) the synchronicity of the tutor's communication with the student. These four dimensions of tutoring services are distinct, and each can vary independently from the other dimensions.

If a tutoring program did not appear to be digital based on a quick scan of the Texas SES provider application, we nevertheless read through the entire 20-page document to make sure we did not misjudge. For example, a few providers' applications made mention of websites, but close reading indicated that only the tutors (and not the students) access these websites, just to gather curricular materials. Such programs we logged as non-digital because the students did not interact with digital technology directly. We also recorded any comments but did not evaluate these non-digital provider applications against our digital tutoring taxonomy.

If a tutoring program appeared to be digital, the application analysis was more intensive. The easiest digital provider applications to analyze were those that clearly indicated their programs' characteristics in our four major taxonomic dimensions: Tutor Location, Tutor Synchronicity, Instruction Driver, and Curriculum Location. Applications that made all four obvious were rare, but even those that did make them obvious required substantial work. For every digital provider application, we not only read the full document and recorded the most appropriate classification for each of the four dimensions, but we also logged all the excerpts of the application text that justified each of our four dimension classifications. In fact, determining just what application text was relevant to which dimensions of the tutoring programs was one of the most time-consumptive elements of this work. For each application, we also recorded comments about any judgment calls we made in its analysis, any observations about bigger research questions or issues they raised, and a handful of miscellaneous notes (affiliated providers and provider pseudonyms, application period, etc.).

When a digital provider application did not clearly indicate its program characteristics in the four major dimensions of our taxonomy, the analysis and classification work was considerably more difficult. Among the applications we analyzed, there were a number of reasons why a tutoring program's characteristics might have been hard to discern from the Texas SES provider application. These classification challenges included the following:

- Inadequately framed/specified application questions, including AND/OR ambiguity
- Vague information, including passive-voice ambiguity, in provider responses
- Insufficient details about program characteristics in provider responses
- Conflicting details about program characteristics in provider responses

---

- Inconsistent degree of detail on different modes of tutoring in provider responses, when provider offers multiple tutoring modes

In these cases, we not only had to iteratively refine our taxonomy while simultaneously classifying providers' tutoring programs according to that taxonomy, but also had to iteratively assess each tutoring program's true characteristics for classification while simultaneously determining which application text excerpts were relevant to and accurately depicted the program's true characteristics to justify those classifications. For example, it was not uncommon for a short passage on, say, the fifteenth page of a provider's application to throw suddenly into question three of the four classifications we thought we had pinned down. At that point, we would have to go back and revisit all the text excerpts we had already logged, as well as application passages we had perhaps earlier deemed irrelevant, to try to assess which way or ways the tutoring program actually operated. (Frequently, it seemed, this phenomenon followed the pattern of an application giving an initial impression of high tutor involvement that eventually gave way to doubts and questions about how much the students were really just left on their own to complete software-based drills.) And because these applications so frequently ended up contradicting themselves in often subtle but portentous ways or offering such vague language that it would have been easy to jump to any number of classification conclusions, we learned to proceed with extreme caution, a keen eye for any indication that these tutoring programs were not what they initially seemed, and a honed ear for which components and aspects of their services the providers emphasized most heavily in their applications, as well as for what the providers did *not* say.

The memorandum identified challenges encountered and key decision points (why the researcher decided to include or exclude an activity under a particular code). This was important, given collaborative nature of coding process, for inter-rater reliability. The memos also created, similar to the observation instrument, a focal point for full team discussions. The discussions emerged as a kind of informal professional development, where qualitatively trained researchers coached quantitative researchers in advanced techniques of qualitative coding and analysis. The hands-on training also created a forum for researchers to begin to identify and jointly discuss key characteristics that could be analyzed as contributing to effects.

In summary, over the course of implementation, the importance of the observation instrument and coding and memoing in our mixed methods research work deepened. The collection and interpretation of those data provided a crosswalk between the interpretive analysis central to qualitative work and the referential and causal analysis central to quantitative work. It also served as a catalyst and referent point for essential ongoing dialogue across researchers working toward the same study objectives but involved in different levels and kinds of analysis. Through discussion of data and project meetings organized around the data, integration moved from being an idea to a concrete set of strategies central to the project management and organization.

Opportunities and Dilemmas

With the advantage of experience, we now recognize the importance of other strategies and conditions that could have supported our work. For example, the integrated work would have been enriched by more training around the use of the instrument and better hosting of data on the intra-team website. Some members of the qualitative team struggled with the concept of indicators, and there was at least one observer each year that did not fully understand the rating system (i.e., some ratings given were in conflict with the comments given for that indicator). This meant that the lead in charge of quantifying the observations ended up revising some of the ratings to match the comments. The reliability trainings should have been supplemented by more training and mentoring in use of the observation instrument. In addition, we did not fully anticipate the time-intensive nature of coding state provider applications. The process proved critical in our careful work to identify characteristics of digital interventions as compared to non-digital interventions, but limited resources permitted coding of just one district in our five-district sample.

MIXED METHODS INTEGRATION STRATEGY #3: ADAPTED MONITORING TOOL AND RESEARCH REVIEWS

Under the federal regulatory guidance, districts had little ability to regulate the format or conditions of SES tutoring. They could not limit the hourly rates charged by providers, which ranged from $13.25 to $157.50 per hour over the course of our study. Because the total amount the district could spend for one student's tutoring depended on a per-pupil allotment determined by the state, hourly rates were directly associated with the total possible hours of tutoring a student could receive. In addition, districts could not put minimum requirements on tutor qualifications, the curriculum used, or the instructional format. Districts often had no choice (under federal law) about whether to enter into contracts with vendors, and they had minimal control over the terms of these agreements and little ability to enforce them. The study was designed to understand how specific elements of a policy's design supported or inhibited a district's efforts to provide high-quality instruction under SES.

Implementation Phase

In the first years of the study, large urban school districts became a magnet for preexisting and new vendors of afterschool tutoring, because of their high concentration of "failing" schools. In several of our study districts, vendors sent sales teams to the city's low-income neighborhoods to recruit students for the program. Vendors who offered incentives to parents and families for enrolling in the program grew their market share, creating a contentious atmosphere where providers competed aggressively for students and hurled accusations of malfeasance. The dynamics of vendor influence rose along with digital education. Digital vendors were able to gain market share by offering families incentives such as a free computer. The idea of tutoring at home during flexible hours often appealed to families concerned about safe transportation home from school or conflicts with other responsibilities, such as afterschool jobs and caring for younger siblings.

Research team members were an active part of the conversation that the districts were having internally about how to hold vendors more accountable. In one district, the site facilitator became a go-between that helped districts leverage the mixed methods work to support policy changes. Specifically, she collected relevant and accessible research reports from our own and larger base of afterschool work for districts to organize and consume in a steering committee charged with redesigning afterschool programs. She would share any articles or research reports that she felt were relevant to the district's implementation of SES. This led to more conversations with the SES director, during which she would ask about what the research said about best practices for a certain topic. These types of conversations also occurred during our annual or semi-annual briefings and formal meetings with district staff about our own study. When a state waiver from No Child Left Behind was granted and the district was told by the state that they had greater flexibility to redesign the program, the director (as well as the other administrators involved in redesign effort) asked her to send any research on effective programs. She sat in on the first two meetings of the redesign committee where they asked her specific questions about research-based practices, which served as its own item in the district's redesign agenda, for example, student-to-tutor ratio and minimum dosage.

The site-specific researcher (aided by the full team) helped the district redesign its own monitoring tool informed by the research and district's self-identified priorities. She helped with two different instruments—one in the SES context (A) and one in the post-waiver redesign context (B). The conversation started when, early in the study, the district looked through the study's observation instrument and asked what they could do given their limited regulatory power under the No Child Left Behind Act. When given the opportunity to redesign the program, the district wanted a more formalized way to do observations and monitoring of tutoring sessions. The community organizations involved were interested in this as well.

The researcher sat down with the director in a face-to-face meeting, looking at the observation instrument and asking what the district's needs or goals were with the instrument. The district administrator identified the following core district need: improving instruction and communication between schools and providers. So the short walk-through instrument became a way for school principals to organize their own observations of SES sessions in their buildings (which they were already doing in an informal sense), and then use the form they filled out for initiating conversations with providers about the school's expectations and standards. In this sense, it was designed more as a professional development tool than as a monitoring tool.

With the redesign process, the district wanted a tool that was more useful for monitoring the quality of sessions. So again, they looked at the observation tool used in this study, and then the site-specific researcher joined the meeting of the redesign subcommittee charged with developing a way to evaluate providers. She talked to them about the balance between creating a nuanced instrument and one that could still be used by non-educators or researcher observers, as well as the balance between breadth and depth of observations. The district leaned toward wanting more observations, so she talked them through the possible elements of a tool that had check-offs and would only require a 10- to 15-minute visit. Then the district created a draft of the monitoring tool that the site-specific researcher reviewed and provided written and verbal feedback. The tool was used by the district in two waves of observations over the course of the tutoring season.

Opportunities and Dilemmas

Soon after the steering committee was formed in 2012, the state received a waiver from the federal government, giving it the authority to terminate SES and redesign and newly regulate extended learning programs. The district used its increased authority to design tutoring programs based on local specifications and identified student needs. After receiving the waiver, the district immediately began a two-phase process of redesigning its Title I–funded tutoring programs. The task of the steering committee became to guide this. The committee members represented a number of stakeholders across the city, including community- and faith-based organizations, neighborhood centers, parents, tutoring providers, and foundations, as well as several departments within the school district.

Within the policy context of greater leverage and flexibility, one district put specific requirements into the contracts with tutoring vendors that were anchored in our research as well as feedback from the many stakeholders represented on the steering committee. For example:

- *Dosage.* The data from this study, as well as other research on out-of-school time tutoring, indicate a threshold of approximately 40 hours before students start to see positive impacts on test scores. Therefore, the district added a new requirement that providers offer a minimum of 45 hours of instruction to students at a maximum hourly rate of $35 per hour. This represented a $40 decrease in hourly rates for the district's primary digital tutoring vendor.
- *Class size.* Tutor-to-student ratios cannot be larger than 1:5.
- *Curriculum.* All providers must use curriculum explicitly aligned to that of the day school.
- *Transparency.* To allow for greater transparency, digital tutoring can only take place in school settings or online where the district can observe virtually, and monitoring is done by school staff, the Extended Learning Opportunities Office, and the school improvement team.
- *Tutor capacity.* Providers must use certified teachers as tutors, and, in the case of digital education, these tutors must have live interaction with students during the session.
- *Access.* All providers must offer services to students with disabilities and English language learners.

As expected, there was pushback from providers, who told the district they could not provide tutoring services for a lower hourly rate. The district administrator responded by showing data from our study on the comparatively lower hourly rates charged in other districts in the study and by trying to work collaboratively with the providers to ease the transition and facilitate design changes that would help to reduce their costs. For example, she arranged for the district food service to provide snacks for students in school settings and waived the cost of renting classrooms for tutoring sessions.

These program changes had specific impacts on vendors of digital tutoring. For one, it forced them to cut their hourly rates by more than half while doubling the number of instructional hours students received. In addition, the district required digital vendors to provide services in school settings to better facilitate monitoring. This proved difficult for the largest digital providers in the district, and in the first year of this redesigned program, they continued to provide services in students' homes.

Supporting Mechanism

As in the other two examples, there were specific mechanisms that we employed, in this instance, to support our work helping districts manage the political dynamics of research collaboration. Our original decision to assign a site-specific coordinator was critically important (see Figure 4.4). The site-specific coordinators were full members of the team with other research responsibilities but were designated at the beginning of the project as working with a specific school district. These individuals lived close to the setting, allowing them to make frequent or last-minute trips. They had frequent phone and e-mail conversations with district administrators, who appreciated the consistent contact and the trusting relationship that this consistency allowed them to develop. The site-specific coordinators also kept an ear to the ground on policy developments and program challenges in the district and relayed these developments to the full team where deemed necessary. This facilitated a problem-based approach in our mixed methods research and created another touchstone or bridging tool (similar to the observation instrument described earlier) around which qualitative and quantitative data could be brought into conversation. Thus, for example, the site facilitator in one district learned that district administrators were concerned about transparency and accountability among providers. The team responded by working with the district to compare the number of hours the providers were billing the district with the amount advertised. They found a significant discrepancy and shared this information with the district in one of the project briefings.

It also helped that the culture of the study was one that placed a high premium on relevance of results for the district. In the integrated work, researchers struggled with the question, "What is the boundary in my role as a researcher or consultant?" For example, the site-specific researcher described in the preceding section struggled with how many of the district redesign committee meetings to attend and how many to attend in person. She went to the first in-person and then joined two more by phone. She then had some one-to-one conversations with the research director about committee issues.

Figure 4.4a.   Project Organization Chart: Research Team and Project Support Structure

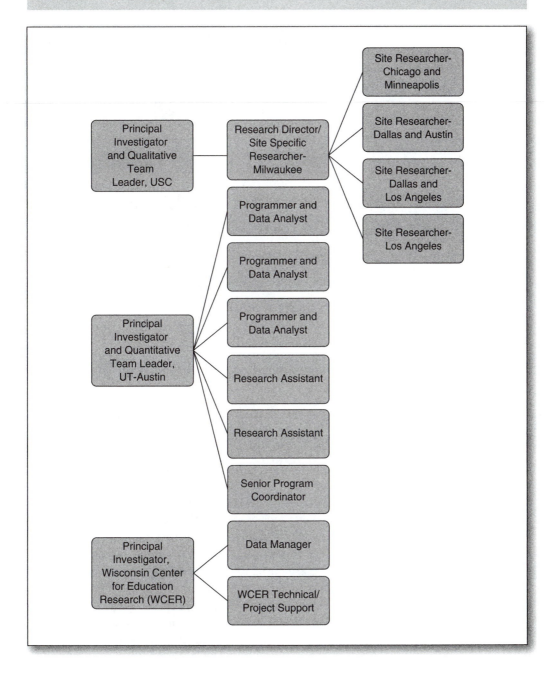

Figure 4.4b. Project Organization Chart: Site-Level (District) Structures

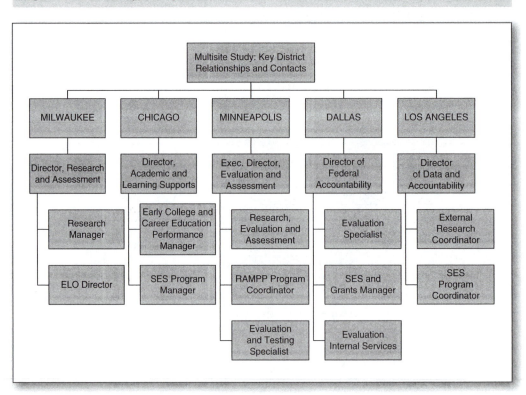

The site researchers were encouraged to have impromptu and regular contact with district administrators that went beyond regularly scheduled data collection strategies. The work would not have been possible without the active participation of districts that were research proactive and open to using multiple forms of evidence to evaluate programs. One of the districts set aside funds for evaluation in the very early years of the project, which supported a critical pilot study of mixed methods work that allowed the principal investigators to design and refine strategies of integration before going to scale with the larger five-district project.

This same district also restructured its accountability requirements for digital providers to increase transparency of the instructional setting. In particular, to remain consistent with the monitoring requirements of the school-based providers, the district asked that the primary in-home, online vendor provide the district with five recorded tutoring sessions of students from the district.

The Extended Learning Opportunities (ELO) office then compiled the data and sent it back to steering committee members as well as school and vendor administrators. The district envisioned this tool less as an evaluation instrument and more as a way to facilitate discussion among the schools and vendors about program expectations and challenges. In addition to this tool, the district sent out surveys to school-level staff and vendors about program satisfaction and areas of improvement. It also held an open house where teachers and parents could walk through and visit any tutoring session and ask questions of coordinators and vendors.

Once given the flexibility and leverage through changes in federal policy, several of the districts in our study used evidence from their own work inside the district, the research base on quality tutoring, and feedback from multiple stakeholders to make meaningful changes toward increasing learning opportunities for their low-income students. These included efforts to improve tutoring curriculum and instruction, to write these changes into contracts signed with vendors, and to create and adapt monitoring tools to facilitate accountability and transparency, including in the digital context.

In summary, over the course of implementation, the project's fully integrated mixed methods strategy benefitted from close relationships with district partners. Through the help of site-specific researchers, there was active discussion about the findings and their relevance to district-specific challenges. The role of the site-specific researchers extended beyond gathering information on districts. Site-specific researchers frequently responded to requests from the district, or even particular providers, for additional research or resources. This included gathering relevant research that made districts' positions more defensible and advising about the development of district-level tools that were informed by this study's instrumentation.

In hindsight, we now also see some of the gaps in our work. Although those administrators closest to the project were very aware of our research and asked us for other resources, we could have been better about making sure to communicate with the administrators one or two levels above them in the organization, beyond just sending an invitation to them to attend briefings. This came up when new people came into those roles and we had to reintroduce ourselves to those with ultimate decision-making power over policy changes informed by our research.

MIXED METHODS INTEGRATION STRATEGY #4: RESEARCH-TO-PRACTICE COLLABORATIVE

Our research findings were regularly disseminated through our Research-to-Practice Collaborative to local educational agencies, SES tutoring providers, parents and students, and the public and policymaking officials. These included state education officials that needed information for SES provider approval processes and for providing implementation guidance to local educational agencies and state legislators debating policy changes; school districts that were required to contract with, manage, and evaluate providers that delivered tutoring; school leadership and other district staff that made decisions about how to assign limited space on campuses for supplemental instruction and attempted to guide program and student improvements; tutoring providers that had newly entered the market or made modifications to existing programs; parents and students who required information to make appropriate choices for the types of tutoring best suited to their children's needs and the providers who could meet them; and community-based organizations and other members of the public who were attentive to the implications and effectiveness of SES. We maintained a website and toll-free number to field and respond to requests for information about our project from the broader public and to communicate our study findings in research conferences and other forums.

Implementation Phase

We wrote the Research-to-Practice Collaborative into the original design of our research. Initially, districts were very excited about the prospect of meeting face-to-face. However, as planning for the first meeting approached, we realized the logistical difficulty of hosting in-person meetings with busy district administrators who oversaw multiple projects in addition to SES. During this time, web-based technology for hosting virtual meetings and creating public websites to archive information was advancing and becoming both cheaper and user-friendly. We determined that the best approach for encouraging networking among district administrators would be to establish an information bank or common portal that both partnering districts and the public could access. We envisioned this portal as having multidirectional communication capabilities so that both researchers and participants could post information.

In developing this idea, we grew increasingly concerned about the security risks of sharing ownership rights over the website and how to design a website that would be a go-to resource for media and larger projects as well as serve the additional objective of being a vehicle for information exchange across the five districts participating in the study. We opted instead to develop a website that could serve as a resource for district partners by (a) including links to other studies and work being conducted around SES; (b) providing easy access to our reports, PowerPoint presentations, and published articles; (c) and recognizing the active participation of our district partners by identifying them on the home page and providing a calendar of upcoming events (see Figure 4.5).

In addition, rather than having district personnel travel to us to discuss research findings, we traveled to them. The two co-principal investigators, often joined by other research team members, made annual visits to each district, where we presented integrated findings to a cross-section of district staff in a 2-hour conference. To minimize surprises and political risks for the SES

Figure 4.5 Detailed Snapshot of Policy Briefs and Research Reports

---

Policy Briefs and Research Reports

Summaries of Provider Effects by District

Released November 2013: Los Angeles Unified School District

Released September 2013: Dallas Independent School District. Milwaukee and Minneapolis Public Schools; and *Chicago Public Schools*

Released September 2012: *Chicago Public Schools, Dallas ISD, Milwaukee Public Schools, Minneapolis Public Schools*

Released August 2012: Chicago Public Schools

Released August 2011: Austin ISD, Chicago Public Schools, Dallas ISD, Milwaukee Public Schools, Minneapolis Public Schools

Policy Brief: Public and Program Recommendation for Redesigning Supplemental Educational Services

Patricia Burch and Carolyn Heinrich

Policy Brief: Implementation and Effectiveness of Supplemental Educational Services for Students with Disabilities and English Language Learners

Patricia Burch and Carolyn Heinrich Mary Stewart, Annalee Good, Christi Kirshbaum & Rudy Acosta

Policy Briefs: Letter to District Administrators

Understanding Supplementary Educational Services (SES): A Guide for Parents and Guardians

Rodolfo Acosta, Particia Burch, Annalee Good, Mary Stewart, Carolyn Heinrich & Christi Kirshbaum

Comprendiendo los Servicios de Education Suplementaria (SES): Un guia para padres y guardianes

Rodolfo Acosta, Patricia Burch, Annalee Good, Mary Stewart, Carolyn Heinrich & Christi Krishbaum administrator (particularly where we planned to share findings on district challenges), we shared a draft of our findings (via PowerPoint) with the SES administrator prior to our in-person visit. We used the in-person briefings as an opportunity to maintain good rapport with district contacts that were necessary to successful data sharing agreements. We also used the briefings as opportunities to stay current on policy developments at the district, state, and national levels (e.g., executive orders allowing waivers from SES) to get a more complete picture of district-level changes that could influence our findings. For example, we learned in one in-person briefing that the district had switched to all online registration for participants, and this information helped explain the decline in participation rates for some groups; the online system was plagued with problems and was not universally accessible.

The in-person visits also were critical given high turnover in district staff over the course of the project. Every time there was a staff change, we had to reintroduce the study and its personnel. On occasions that we could not contact district staff directly by phone or e-mail, we made stop-in visits in the context of other professional travel. The turnover created enormous challenges for the quantitative work in that the point person for data access was constantly changing. The new staff often had a steeper learning curve than the principal investigator on the ins and outs of district assessment data.

We used public webinars as an additional dissemination tool for our mixed methods findings. The annual webinars were live, recorded presentations of research findings, tailored slightly (e.g., in tone and emphasis) to different stakeholders. The public webinars—attended by district and state educational agency staff, private providers, educators, academics, and community members—provided opportunities for learning about the research process we employed in the study. Participants in webinars commented (via web-based software) on the value of these webinars in terms of their understanding our research and its potential for informing their own evaluations.

Over the course of the 4 years of the study, several strategies emerged as key to a successful webinar. It was important that the platform that we used be widely accessible, especially to accommodate participants who had heard about the webinar without having received a formal invitation. Initially, our primary audience was district staff in our study sites. We broadened participation to include the interested public by developing mailing lists of potential participants (i.e., stakeholders of the intervention) via coordination with state-level partners, think tanks, and associations such as the Council for Great City Schools. As the number of participants increased, we leveraged technology such as chat forums so that participants could write in questions during the question-and-answer period, allowing us to cluster and respond to similar kinds of questions. We responded to any remaining questions in writing via a group response after the webinar and posted these responses, along with the slideshow and webinar discussion thread, on our study website.

Supporting Mechanism

The study's ability to manage challenges such as these was supported by the study's distributed approach to project implementation and dissemination (see Figure 4.4). The research director took leadership for managing the website. She worked on the design with a consultant, uploaded articles and PowerPoints, and kept the calendar up to date. Before the documents were sent out for review or published on the website, all key research staff had the opportunity to review them and suggest changes. The written work (posted on the website) became another medium through which team members collaborated in analysis that drew on both qualitative and quantitative findings. In addition, both principal investigators had at least a basic familiarity with the qualitative and quantitative data, which supported integration in the presentations and other forms of dissemination of the research findings.

The timing of our interactions with SES stakeholders revolved around the school year calendar and the activities involved in implementing these programs. Prior to the start of the school year, we stayed in close contact with district staff who administered the program (as changes in personnel occurred frequently), and the qualitative research team engaged with tutoring providers to make them aware of our research and enlist their cooperation in the observational component of the study. District support was essential to making contacts with providers and also to facilitating interviews and discussion with district and provider staff who work to enroll students and set up program activities. We kept all stakeholders informed of the data collection process for field research (see Figure 4.6), and we also made them aware of when we were releasing new research findings during the school year.

Opportunities and Dilemmas

The Research-to-Practice Collaborative created opportunities to provide formative feedback to stakeholders and the general public in real time. This feedback was critical given the constantly evolving policy context. For example, over the course of the study, districts came under increasing pressure to do

Figure 4.6 SES Multisite Evaluation Research Products (2011–2012): Project Timeline

Month Due	Product Name	Product Description
JUNE	Provider letter (CPS)	Letter to all current providers that needs to come out before or along with the provider effects coming out. Each site researcher connects with the providers in the qual sample to give them a heads-up.
JULY	AERA 2012	July 7 - Send final, 500-word description of research paper to district evaluation staff. Integrated paper between quant and qual. This paper will form basis of district briefings and for submission.
	Milwaukee district meeting	July 8 - Discussion of provider effects data with Milwaukee district
	Provider letter (MPS)	Letter to all current providers that needs to come out before or along with the provider effects coming out. Each site researcher connects with the providers in the qual sample to give them a heads-up.
	IRB Qual	Submit continuing review for IRB for qual portion of study.
AUGUST	All IRB	Early - Submit change requests for personnel changes, consent forms, etc.
	Mixed methods paper	Mixed methods design paper submitted
SEPTEMBER	District research boards	Submit applications/paperwork for renewing district research board approval on all necessary sites
OCTOBER	Parent brief	Parent brief on SES and our study completed, posted to website and sent to districts for dissemination
DECEMBER	Instructional core paper	"Instruction Matters" submitted to journal
JANUARY	Research brief	Short version of research brief completed and disseminated via website and press release
	Book chapter	"Who Benefits" chapter on equity and SES finalized for edited volume
FEBRUARY	Special needs paper	Spin-off paper from integrated analysis on issues specific to ELL and SWD submitted to journal

Chapter 4 Practical Tools for Integrated Mixed Methods   83

Month Due	Product Name	Product Description
	AERA 2012 – roundtable	"Instruction Matters: Lessons From a Mixed Methods Evaluation of Supplemental Educational Services Under No Child Left Behind" submitted
	AERA 2012 – international symposium	"Integrated Findings From a Mixed Method, Longitudinal, Multisite Evaluation of Supplemental Educational Services" submitted. Cross-site/combined site provider effects data that mixes with qual case studies.
	AERA 2012 – equity symposium	"Who Benefits? Assessing Instructional Opportunity and Quality in Market-Based Reforms: The Case of Supplemental Educational Services (SES)" submitted
MARCH	Grant report	Submit progress report to funder.
	Tech brief	Tech brief (5–7 pgs.) completed and disseminated via website and press release
APRIL	AERA 2012	Present at AERA 2012, slideshow ready
	District strategy reports	Paper that combines strategy data that other districts use to approach common issues, can use district meetings as a data collection opportunity for district strategy paper. These can become policy briefs related to the how and why of meeting challenges in SES.
MAY	All IRB	Prepare and submit all continuing review applications.
	District briefings	Integrated findings reports to all five districts
	Provider webinar	Integrated findings report to providers and other stakeholders via webinar format

more with less. States had until 2013–2014 to meet the law's mandate of having all students meet proficiency standards. Most states had intentionally set gradual proficiency cut scores, with the implications that with each year, more students and more schools became eligible for SES. Several study districts confronted the challenge of having more students eligible than they could serve, where demand for services exceeded budget resources. This required that they redesign policies in ways that would prioritize student eligibility. Districts used formative evidence on student effects to inform decisions on how to allocate funds (e.g., targeting students most likely to enroll in the program and most in need of these services).

Having a web-based presence also had its challenges. For instance, it created the possibility of strained relationships with providers in our qualitative sample and threatened the possibility of studying the same providers over time due to risk of attrition. Put simply, we could name providers in our quantitative work but ethically and by contract could not do so in our qualitative work because it would expose the providers' identity (with more detailed, program-specific information). In publications that integrated the two data sets, we identified the universe of providers in the quantitative sample. But our district partners pushed for more specificity so that they could hold providers accountable. The team resolved this issue by publishing provider-specific effects for providers with adequate numbers of students tutored to allow for statistical identification of program effects, but these effect size estimates were not linked to the qualitative (observation) data. In recruiting providers to the study in the face of attrition, we often directed them to the website, which described program goals and reported the study findings. If the providers maneuvered to the publications page and read the information, they could interpret findings (such as the implications of high hourly rates set by providers) as potentially damaging information to their business. Indeed, the CEO of one of the largest providers in Texas, on reading one of the reports, alerted us to concerns and his intent to drop out of the study for fear of loss of business.

The adverse effects of provider attrition and the importance of maintaining trusting relationships were particularly acute for the qualitative team that depended on access to providers and their employees for their data collection. At certain points in the study, districts' interests in getting more specific and immediate data on provider-level effects collided with the study's longer term pressure to get longitudinal data on tutoring practices.

There also were challenges in providing quantitative data in an accessible summary form that was easily imported into district materials for parents and principals (SES program brochures and principal handbooks). One challenge of note was getting the test score data in time to do the analysis and turn it around for use by districts in disseminating information to parents. For example, we typically did not get test score data from research and evaluation departments until early summer. The program departments needed the data by mid-summer to publish the parent information. The quantitative team had to work within these timelines and constraints (availability of data and our own interest in making data relevant and available to partners) in the context of limited staff resources.

In sum, the Research-to-Practice Collaborative emerged as a central vehicle for a key aspect of our integration (providing formative feedback to districts as a means of vetting and refining findings and gathering missing information). It also served its intended purpose of making research accessible and relevant to policymakers. There were points in the process when interest in close collaboration with district partners and a web-based presence had to be balanced against critical human subjects considerations. The website and other dissemination strategies also could have benefitted from more attention to the mechanics on how we designed the website with particular attention to making it user friendly for districts. Despite posting all of our papers (working papers, briefs, etc.) and publications (including all slideshows from webinars and provider effects data) there, we could have done more to make the website more of a collaborative space for districts. In other studies, the solution has been to create a web space that has one data set accessible only to study participants and another fully available to the public. These studies have used the intranet web space as a kind of drop box, whereby district administrators can comment on draft publications.

CONCLUSION

Similar to the policy process, policy studies have both a design and an implementation phase. In the implementation phase, how the study's design is interpreted turns on the actions of different actors and entities at various levels. How researchers working on different aspects of the study, and with varying degrees of qualitative and quantitative expertise, interpret and enact the study's objectives, helps determine whether and how the study achieves its objectives. In the examples described earlier, research staff working on the ground level furthered the objectives of fully integrated research by (a) managing websites aimed at dissemination of project materials, (b) developing the micro tools that were essential to moving integration in data analysis from an idea to a practice embedded in the organization of project, and (c) developing areas of expertise and taking the lead in addressing research problems specific to mixed methods work (e.g., developing a system for cross-checking observation data before having it shared with the quantitative team).

As in the policy process, design and implementation were hard to disentangle in the sense that the research team was continuously designing research "tools" to assist in implementation and further research objectives. These tools included things that we might expect in a mixed methods study, such as observation instruments, qualitative data analysis software, Excel sheets, data displays, coding and analysis, memoing and tools for dissemination (in this instance a web-based presence for posting publications) (Bazeley, P. and Jackson, K., 2013; Bazeley, P, 2003). It also included supporting mechanisms and tools that one might not consider major research components but proved critical for moving the principle of integration from the periphery to the mainstream of the study's practice, such as structured meetings to discuss data and practical tools that codify the idea of integration and weave it deeply into study practices, agendas that informed talk across different kinds of research, and integrated project timelines.

The work clearly did not occur without challenges, and there were situations that, in retrospect, we could have approached differently. For example, there were moments when the qualitative team worried that norms of quantitative work were subsuming principles of rich casework (depth over breadth). The quantitative team could be extremely responsive to a district's demands for data (carving out weekends to generate provider-specific effects), while the qualitative team lagged behind in the different kind of labor-intensive work based on iterative coding and inter-rater reliability (two persons coding the same data). There were tensions between integrated methods work and the study's goals of policy implementation and impact. Data sharing agreements were scheduled around when districts could provide the data, and sometimes this timing made it difficult to coordinate qualitative and quantitative work. Districts liked the quantitative and qualitative indicators in the observation instrument but struggled with ways to train their own staff to develop similar kinds of monitoring tools. Research staff went the extra mile in helping districts become producers rather than consumers of data but frequently did so on their own time and, in doing so, wrestled with balancing roles as researcher and resource for the district.

It was around these kinds of dilemmas that the structured team meetings proved so critical. Through these meetings and through joint presentations and preparation of papers, team members who might otherwise have had limited or no interactions (because they were working on different data sets) had opportunities for rich and data-focused exchanges. The regular meetings became a place where hard challenges were discussed and often resolved collectively. Absent these meetings, paradigmatic differences could have been allowed to fester (as in the case of whether to have more observations). Given scarce resources, researchers would have had less time to spend in each observation.

DISCUSSION QUESTIONS

1. In the chapter, we describe how joint work and interpretation on the part of the qualitative and quantitative teams contributed to refinement of the observation instrument to better key aspects of the intervention not identified at the outset of the study, for example, digital settings. The examples provided in this chapter are based on a large-scale study with multiple team members across several institutions. How, if at all, can an individual researcher or small group of researchers within one institution adopt and/or adapt the strategies described?

2. This chapter acknowledges tensions encountered by the team as observation data were shared with external stakeholders. How were principles of a fully integrated mixed methods approach applied in addressing these tensions?

3. This chapter offers an example of how a research team member served as a "research resource" for a steering committee formed to strengthen program accountability. How (or how not) did this activity contribute the credibility of the findings in that district? Was there a conflict of interest in the researcher assuming this role in the context of the integrated mixed methods approach?

4. This chapter identifies several supporting mechanisms (e.g., scheduled, data-focused meetings) as key to fully integrated mixed methods work. What are the problems or challenges that these tools were designed to address? How would you assess whether these tools had worked?

APPLICATIONS TO YOUR OWN WORK

- Consider a research project to which you contributed. What aspect of this work now, in retrospect, seems the most policy relevant, that is, of interest to practitioners or policymakers who desire evidence and guidance? What makes you say this? What might be an appropriate medium or practical tool for sharing these findings with this audience?

(Continued)

(Continued)

- Pick one finding and write a summary memo of the finding. Have a classmate or colleague review the memo and interview you about concepts presented in the memo and your rationale behind their order of presentation.

- You are presenting your research in class or at a professional meeting and someone in the audience asks whether you have considered quantifying your qualitative data. How do you interpret and respond to that question? Now, imagine the participant has asked about qualifying your quantitative data? Think back to discussion in Chapter 2 about what is and what isn't fully integrated mixed methods research. How do you interpret and respond to that question? What potential benefits or risks do these questions suggest for your work?

CHAPTER 5

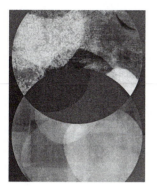

Fully Integrated Mixed Methods Research in K-12 and Higher Education in the United States

INTRODUCTION

The current generation of education policy research and evaluation is built on a somewhat more nuanced and contingent view of policies than in past decades (Honig, 2005). Relative to work done from the 1950s through the 1980s, today's education policy researchers start from the premise that policy implementation is a multilevel process involving a complex interplay of policies, places, and people. Policies made at one level are interpreted and enacted by implementers at other levels, and that interpretation can vary depending on, for example, the governance level, setting, and historical moment. Administrators in charge of getting things done once policies have been adopted may interpret their charge very differently and, through these interpretations, come to enact these policies in very different ways (Spillane, 1998).

Policy and program researchers frequently are charged with the task of explaining variation in effects, rather than trying to somehow pin down universal truths about an intervention. At the same time, practitioners and researchers in education, among other sectors, have come under increasing pressure in their work to demonstrate *what works*, specifically in terms of quantifiable outcomes. This creates a kind of paradox. On the one hand, we have reached a point where the field acknowledges the complexity of policy implementation and the problem of identifying "what works" in absolute terms. At the same time, the bottom line for most funded evaluations, and certainly the bottom line for schools and other educational agencies, is to produce evidence that the intervention is contributing in significant ways to student outcomes and is superior to other alternatives.

How should researchers manage these tensions? This chapter presents two separate cases of how an integrated mixed methods framework emerged as a superior strategy in a context in which policymakers were pressuring for outcome data. We discuss two distinct studies striving toward a fully integrated, mixed methods approach in this context, although at different schooling levels (K-12 and higher education). The first case examines an integrated mixed methods study of a statewide class size reduction policy where there was push for evidence, on the part of some policymakers, that the program contributed to improved student outcomes. The second case examines the use of integrated mixed methods as part of a larger set of studies on equity in higher education carried out by the Center for Urban Education, as colleges faced rising state and national pressure to demonstrate performance outcomes.

PROGRAM EVALUATION OF STUDENT ACHIEVEMENT GUARANTEE IN EDUCATION

Overview

The first case is a multimethod longitudinal evaluation study funded by the state of Wisconsin.[1] The study explored the implementation and outcomes of a statewide class size reduction program. Student Achievement Guarantee in Education (SAGE) is a state-supported class size reduction (CSR) program that provides funding to districts to limit class sizes to 15 students and 1 teacher in kindergarten through Grade 3 (K-3). At the time of the study (2004–2008), approximately 500 Wisconsin schools participated.

Wisconsin's SAGE legislation also requires schools to (a) provide rigorous curricula, (b) strengthen home and school links by keeping the school building open for extended hours and connecting families with community resources, and (c) enhance teacher professional development and evaluation. The theory of action behind the legislation is that improving student outcomes requires

---

[1] Patricia Burch helped lead the qualitative component of the study from 2005 through 2007.

a multipronged approach, especially in high-poverty communities. As of 2000–2001, any Wisconsin school can participate in the SAGE program. As of 2007, schools that opt to do so receive a sum of up to $2,250 per child to counterbalance implementation costs. The state legislature funded an increase in state reimbursement rate from $2,000 to $2,250 in 2007, the first increase since the program's inception in 1995. Initially an eligible school district could develop a contract for SAGE in any school that had a 30% funding rate. A 1999 bill eliminated the limits on schools per district and the poverty thresholds. One of the unique aspects of the program is that the legislation provides annual funding for program evaluation.

The research described in this chapter focuses on the period from 2004 to 2008, which includes the first project year before the lead author (Patricia Burch) joined the team. The quantitative research focused on the effects of the intervention on student achievement outcomes as measured by standardized tests. The research analyzed historical student assessment data for all Wisconsin students (in SAGE and non-SAGE schools) from the 1995 kindergarten cohort to 2007. The qualitative work involved instrumental case studies of practice in nine high-poverty schools in urban, semi-urban, and rural communities. The schools were chosen to represent a range of student achievement on statewide tests at Grades 3 and 4: high-achieving (relative to expectations), rapidly improving (20% increase across 3 years), and low-achieving schools. In 2004–2005, the research director and graduate students collected data in 27 classrooms. In 2005 and 2006, the research director and author (co-principal investigators) conducted additional data collection in the 27 classrooms. In 2006–2007, the co-principal investigators conducted data collection in nine classrooms (from three of the original schools). In the final year of the project, 2007–2008, the research director began data collection in a new sample of 12 schools.

The findings from the study were published in article format in peer-reviewed selective journals and on a project website in the form of policy briefs (see Table 5.1; see also, e.g., Burch, Theoharis, & Rauscher, 2010; Graue, Rauscher, & Sherfinski, 2009; Graue & Sherfinski, 2011). The main findings were that although prior evaluations of Wisconsin's SAGE program had found a positive and statistically significant effect of the SAGE program for students in reading, mathematics, and language arts through the end of Grades 1, 2, and 3, class size reduction alone is not a sufficient condition to produce such an effect. Class size reduction is dependent on high-quality assessments, teacher professional development, and strong partnerships with families and communities participating in the program. Class size reduction programs involve budget and instructional changes. The budget changes, in turn, involve redistribution of staffing and the school's physical resources (e.g., classroom use), and the instructional changes involve redesign of learning environments (what gets taught, how it gets taught, and how it gets assessed) in ways that support the program's vision of more individualized instruction. We elaborate on these findings later in the chapter.

Table 5.1   Representative List of SAGE Projects and Reports

Journal Articles	Burch, P., Theoharis, G., & Rauscher, E. (2009). Class size reduction in practice: Investigating the influence of the elementary school principal. *Educational Policy.* [Epub before print]
	Graue, E., Hatch, K., Rao, K., & Oen, D. (2007). The wisdom of class size reduction. *American Educational Research Journal, 44*(3), 670–700.
	Graue, E., & Rauscher, E. (2009). Researcher perspectives on class size reduction. *Educational Policy Analysis Archive, 17,* 1–23.
	Graue, E., & Rauscher, E. (2011). Reclaiming assessment through accountability that is "just right." *Teachers College Record, 113*(8), 1827–1862.
	Graue, E., Rauscher, E., & Sherfinski, M. (2009). The synergy of class size reduction and classroom quality. *Elementary School Journal, 110*(2), 178–201.
	Graue, M. E., & Oen, D. (2009). You just feed them with a long handled spoon. Family perspectives on their experiences in class size reduction. *Educational Policy, 23,* 685–713.
	Graue, M. E., & Sherfinski, M. (2011). The view from the lighted schoolhouse: Conceptualizing home-school relations within a class size reduction reform. *American Journal of Education, 117*(2), 267–297.
Policy Briefs	SAGE (Volume 1, Issue 1): General
	SAGE (Volume 1, Issue 2): How School Administrators Matter
	SAGE (Volume 1, Issue 3): Professional Development
	SAGE (Volume 1, Issue 4): How District Practices Matter
	SAGE (Volume 1, Issue 5): Lighted Schoolhouse
PowerPoints	Perspectives on Class Size Reduction
	Responsive Teaching
	The Role of Professional Development in SAGE Schools

Working Papers	Graue, E. (n.d.). *Professional development & class size reduction: Complementary resources looking for connections.*
	Graue, E., & Oen, D. (2006). *Children's perspectives on their experiences in SAGE classrooms.*
	Graue, E., Oen, D., Hatch, K., Rao, K., & Fadali, E. (2005). *Perspectives on class size reduction.*
	Graue, E., Oen, D., Rauscher, E. (2007). *"I think I learn a lot more about my kids": Understanding how class size reduction & assessment shape education experiences.*
	Graue, E., Rauscher, E., & Sherfinski, M. (2008). *SAGE implementation & classroom quality: 2006-7 student achievement guarantee in education qualitative intervention.*
	Graue, E., Rauscher, E., & Sherfinski, M. (2009). *The synergy of class size reduction and classroom quality.*
	Graue, E., Rauscher, E., Sherfinski, M., & Karch, A. (2009). *Supporting synergistic practices in SAGE schools.*
	Hassette, D. D., & Hatch, K. L. (2006). *When size matters: A hybrid theory of early literacy content and sociocultural contexts.*

For abstracts and links to full texts of these publications, see http://varc.wceruw.org/sage.

Integration in Research Design

In a piece published in 2009, the co-principal investigator and collaborators described the rationale behind the team's choice of a mixed methods approach to the SAGE program evaluation as follows:

> Class size is a structural input because it is both quantifiable and controllable. However, class size reduction is more than structural. It is about change. Implicit in the theories of why class size reduction is a strategy for improving achievement is the idea that smaller classes create opportunities that alter fundamental qualities of classroom interactions. Understanding quality in class size reduction contexts is about more than how many or how much; it is also about understanding the processes and interactions of teaching and learning. Focusing on processes and interactions makes class size reduction more complicated and more powerful—it recognizes that the number of people in a classroom is important if it changes instructional interactions. (Graue et al., 2009, p. 6)

Based on existing empirical research, the study began with the assumption that for class size reduction to have an impact on student achievement, teachers would need to change their teaching practices. These changes were viewed as much more than a sidebar or backdrop to the investigation of program effects. The team used mixed methods research to better capture the nature and effects of these changes. They couldn't even begin to look at effects until they understood what change or lack of change in teacher practice looked like, and they couldn't understand what changes in teacher practice looked like unless they made a careful examination of the schools in which change appeared to be occurring.

The core finding from the quantitative work was that better student outcomes were associated with early grade implementation and classes of 15 or fewer students. This finding was consistent with research on class size reduction in other states. The researchers were puzzled that although the literature on class size reduction was massive and rigorous, there was virtually no attention to how contextual factors inside of schools shape and contribute to positive student outcomes.

Based on these earlier findings, the principal investigators designed a multilevel study of SAGE implementation that analyzed the reciprocal relationships among teaching and administrative practices, opportunities for educators, and student outcomes. The first phase focused on pre-testing and post-testing of a sample of SAGE students, surveys of all SAGE teachers and school administrators, and case studies of successful practice in SAGE schools.

Broadly, these were the original three questions that the study sought to answer:

1. What works in SAGE schools to promote student achievement?

2. What policy, practice, or context factors appeared to contribute to better achievement in SAGE schools?

3. How can schools, districts, and teachers better use SAGE resources to promote student achievement?

The third research question was linked to the study's own theory of action about the reflective, continuous nature of school improvement. From this perspective, the role of policy research and evaluation was not to present definitive statements on what works, but rather to help educators assess the impact of the changes they were making based on the research and to allocate resources accordingly.

The team's integrated design following from these research questions outlined the following steps:

- Pre-testing of students prior to participating in SAGE (being in a SAGE classroom).

- Qualitative research to identify and document the educational practices and policies associated with exemplary teaching and learning in nine schools selected for case studies based on indicators of test scores and representativeness of urban, rural, and semi-rural populations. Compared to other SAGE schools with similar characteristics, the schools showed higher test score gains over time. Within these schools, the researchers conducted interviews and observations of teacher practice and conducted focus groups with parents in the schools where the team also was conducting observations of teachers and classroom practice.
- The development of a survey to measure educational practices and other school characteristics. More specifically, the survey was used to examine the prevalence of educational practices identified as exemplary in the qualitative research on high-performing schools. The survey also was used to gather data on patterns of teacher assistance seeking in implementation of the policy at the school level. Teachers were asked to identify who they turned to for help at the classroom, district, and state levels regarding key "resources" in the SAGE program, that is, the use of physical and financial resources, assessment practices and policy, professional development activities, curriculum, and home-school relations.

The team established regular meeting times for the qualitative group and the quantitative group as well as combined meetings. The team committed project resources from the start (e.g., including time to meet in percentages of investigators' time devoted to the project). These meetings proved critical in enabling the feedback loops in data (a member of the quantitative team sat in on meetings where qualitative analysis was discussed, offering early windows into the direction of survey development).

Integration in Data Collection

The intended design of the SAGE study also provides a good example of how built-in or predesigned integration of qualitative and quantitative methods can be used to strengthen instrumentation. In principle, qualitative and quantitative paradigms view the importance and assessment of validity and generalizability somewhat differently. Qualitative researchers are very cautious about making claims of generalizability from their work. Results are contextualized and as such are not expected to generalize to large samples. In addition, qualitative researchers talk about checking for internal validity through structured approaches to coding and data analysis and considering rival hypotheses (Clandinin & Connelly, 2004). The validity of quantitative research is likewise judged by both its internal and external validity. Typically, internal validity— that is, ensuring that results are not biased by unmeasured factors—takes precedence in study design over external validity, or generalizability of the results. Accordingly, quantitative researchers are very attentive to what they can control for in their analyses, while still striving to achieve a design that allows them to claim generalizable patterns. In practice, tests of generalizability and validity figure centrally in both qualitative and quantitative design.

In the SAGE study, claims and efforts to strengthen generalizability and reliability of findings came together in the design of survey instrumentation. The team viewed surveys as a scaled-up version of measuring educational practices and a critical variable in helping the study identify observable characteristics that operate across SAGE schools. However, the team also acknowledged that one of the major challenges to using surveys to build valid and reliable findings is that survey measures tend to incompletely capture (true) educational practices, given the brevity of questions or respondents' reluctance to answer some questions. The researchers proposed integrating qualitative fieldwork with survey construction to increase the reliability and validity of survey measures.

Qualitative research on a purposeful sample of schools in two cities was used to identify effective practices contributing to successful and unsuccessful models. These schools served similar socioeconomic populations of students and had demonstrated (from pilot data collected over 2 years) to be on a trajectory toward continuous improvement as measured by test scores. The validity of the data from the case studies was built through a common protocol using multiple data points around a single construct.

After this first phase of qualitative research and analysis, the team began survey development based on both a review of the literature and the qualitative data. For example, the team further sampled educational practices that had clear relevance for policymakers. At the district level, this included professional development programs. At the school level, the variables were indicators of how space was used. The draft surveys for principals and teachers were shared with program staff at the state Department of Education for review and comment. The team incorporated comments into a revised version of the survey and then pilot-tested the survey through debriefings with interview respondents to assess problems in how respondents interpreted the items. The team used this pilot test as the first level of assessment of reliability of surveys. The second level involved having qualitative researchers review the survey items as compared to what they observed in the field. For example, did the survey item about use of space (two separate adjoined classrooms and rotating teachers or one classroom with one teacher) reflect the range of configurations around schools' use of space as observed in fieldwork, and was the survey question framed in a way that SAGE teachers could understand?

The qualitative team's responses were then further compared with teacher and principal interview respondents to assess their reliability. In the second year of the study, the newly revised survey was administered. The team used the survey responses to refine a sample of schools in which to conduct fieldwork in year 2. In year 3, the team went back to three schools that were particularly interesting from the original sample based on multiple sources of data from the original sample of nine schools, including survey-measured observational practices.

Schools were selected on the basis of survey-measured observational practices. Through an integrated sequence of activities and feedback loops—that is, first, qualitative identification of an important educational practice; next, design of survey questions based on this work to check generalizability of practices; and following this, qualitative and quantitative processes to further measure the validity of the survey instrument—the team attempted to link qualitative and quantitative data to create more sensitive and accurate instrumentation and strengthen research conclusions.

Integration in Analysis

Qualitative and quantitative analyses were also tightly integrated. For example, in the second year of the study, the co-principal investigator and study's research director wrote a memo to the research team about her vision of how phase 2 of the fieldwork was directly informed by principles of mixed methods work, in particular, to go deeper with qualitative data and continue to collect quantitative data from the wider universe of schools on organizational practices and student outcomes. She described the purpose of the memo as generating dialogue to promote more in-depth analysis of the data generated in year 1, to get broad-based data on practice and student outcomes, and to purposefully sample school case studies based on year 1 data. In the memo, she suggested continued analysis of the fieldwork data from year 1 because it was "so rich." This would involve mapping of both assessment and professional development practice in each of the nine original case schools to get a sense of how these shaped the schools' approach to class size reduction. She also suggested linking investigation of practice to school-level analysis of student outcomes. For example, a survey of teacher and administrative practice could describe types of practice by performance type (high achieving, low achieving); by urban, rural, and semi-urban; or by density of special needs population.

To better examine how student outcomes are related to specific teacher or school practice, the investigator proposed describing student analysis at the classroom level, requiring testing of students to infer real-time effects of particular practice. The data could be used to develop a longitudinal analysis of SAGE outcomes.

The research director and co-principal investigator's memo (paraphrased earlier) reflects the iterative nature of data collection, analysis, and design in integrated mixed methods research. The principal investigators began the study with a clear and highly specified design. Their design allowed for, and indeed anticipated, the need to go back to the design drawing board as they gathered and learned from the data. The co-principal investigator leveraged this opportunity and used analysis of different kinds of data to further refine the study's design and use data formatively to sample more precisely.

Integration in Dissemination

The team also planned a structured process for communicating emergent findings in ways that were relevant for stakeholders at multiple levels (state policymakers but also district officials, school principals, and classroom teachers). Even before going into the field, the team established a timeline that combined key benchmarks in both research and communication of research (see an excerpt of this timeline in Table 5.2). For example, the timeline included the time frame for survey construction and projected data for a research briefing with the state. Over the course of 3 years, the team met five or six times with the state to communicate findings.

The project also developed a joint database where qualitative and quantitative data could be housed. A project staffer that was skilled in setting up mixed methods databases and Institutional Review Board policies set up a comprehensive and secure database and established user access restrictions that reflected this knowledge. The project manager established a database specifically designed for sharing documents with state policymakers. A separate website also became a space where the team published findings from the study. This included journal articles but also took the form of two-page research briefs on particular topics linked to the study (e.g., use of space in class size reduction, teacher professional development) that synthesized findings from quantitative and qualitative research. The team found it useful to refer to these briefs in

Table 5.2 Milestones and Deliverables in Year 1

Year 1: 2004–2005	Milestones and Deliverables
2004–2005	Research director and co-principal investigator launch first year of qualitative work in 27 classrooms
July 2005	Research team meets with DPI staff to review research timeline and procedures for contacting districts and schools
July 1, 2005	School "outliers" identified using historical assessment data and submitted to qualitative research team for use in selecting qualitative research sample
August 1, 2005	Proposal submitted to agency or foundation to raise additional research funds to support study
October 1, 2005	Paper 1 from 2004–2005 project: Children's experiences in small classes
November 2005	Biannual WCER/DPI conference on SAGE
December 1, 2005	Draft report of the research design for the longitudinal study of SAGE for review by DPI
January 15, 2006	Final report of the research design for the longitudinal study of SAGE
January 15, 2006	Paper 2 draft: Assessment and professional development in SAGE schools
February 1, 2006 (or earlier)	Letter sent to SAGE schools informing them about the new SAGE evaluation and longitudinal study
February 1, 2006	Report on the use of alternative SAGE program structures (15:1, 30:2, 15:1 pullout) based on reports submitted by all SAGE schools
March–April 2006	Survey administered to teachers and principals
March–May 2006	Sample of schools selected and recruited for cohort A of longitudinal study
April 15, 2006	Draft of papers presented at AERA on SAGE research (Parents' perspectives on class size reduction, Leadership in SAGE schools/districts)
May 2006	Biannual WCER/DPI conference on SAGE
June 1, 2006	Contract finalized to purchase assessment services

AERA, American Education Research Association; DPI, Department of Public Instruction; SAGE, Student Achievement Guarantee in Education; WCER, Wisconsin Center for Education Research.

meetings with the state to discuss the progress of research. Several of the briefs contained narrative vignettes that were designed to help policymakers see the importance of the program from the perspective of those involved in its day-to-day work, for example, teachers. In addition to briefings with policymakers, peer-reviewed journal articles, and policy briefs, the team, consistent with its original vision, sought to translate research into formats aimed at influencing school- and classroom-level practice. Over the course of the study, two SAGE summits were held during which teachers from across the state working in SAGE classrooms received professional development.

Benefits Generated by the Work

The design of the SAGE study allowed the team to study and capture the multileveled influences of embedded policy contexts (classroom, school, district, state) to deepen understanding of practices contributing to program effects. Fieldwork inside of high-performing schools and classrooms (identified through quantitative data) was used to design a survey that assessed the prevalence of potentially promising practices identified through qualitative data. Analysis of survey data informed protocol for further observations of classroom practice. Consistent and structured dialogue between qualitative and quantitative team members focused on interpreting data emerging from the study, building focus and momentum for the work. The SAGE study used feedback loops to inform sampling, to construct survey measures, and to develop and refine emerging hypotheses. Deliberate and data-focused communication with stakeholders supported the project's intent of proving rigorous summative and formative data to state-, district-, and school-level administrators for continuous program improvement.

In efforts to conduct this research, principal investigators encountered numerous challenges. Some of the challenges involved partial implementation of the study's design. Integrated meetings for the qualitative and quantitative team were scheduled months in advance and then cancelled because of unexpected schedule conflicts. This meant that the kinds of dilemmas inherent to mixed methods research and discussed in Chapter 2, such as how to integrate qualitative and quantitative findings in published work, were not fully discussed or addressed.

The project also faced the challenge, introduced in Chapter 1, of building interest and capacity on the part of policymakers for the mixed methods work. The qualitative team (in particular, the research director and graduate students) made steady progress in both collection and analysis of data and published findings in numerous venues, including peer-reviewed journals. In spite of this productivity, the project struggled to convince local policymakers of the legitimacy and contribution of the qualitative work to the study's success and impact.

RACIAL AND ETHNIC INEQUITY IN ACCESS AND SUCCESSFUL STUDENT OUTCOMES IN HIGHER EDUCATION

Overview

This next case describes an integrated set of studies supporting an overarching research agenda conducted by a group of researchers working as part of a not-for-profit research center called the Center for Urban Education (CUE), based at the Rossier School of Education at the University of Southern California. CUE designed and conducted a constellation of studies linked to this problem (see Table 5.3).

Rather than starting with a research question, CUE begins the process of study design with a research problem. In this case, the problem is well documented in both statistical and interpretive research: racial and ethnic inequities in college access, participation, and outcomes in the United States. Each study was aligned with the broader problem statement. Each study also was propelled and anchored in local manifestation of that problem. The overarching policy problem was racial inequities, and the specific problem in this constellation of studies was inequities in transfer access for community college students nationally and in particular settings, for example, Hispanic-serving organizations. Based on statistical analyses of transfer enrollment rates from 1984 to 2002, the researchers found that transfer enrollment rates at public universities tend to be much higher at public institutions than at private institutions. They also found that from 1984 to 2002, transfer enrollment rates hovered at around 20%, with some variation, for example, a decline in the late 1990s.

From this problem statement, CUE designed a broader study using the following approach: the use of Participatory Critical Action Research (PCAR) as a primary epistemology and methodology because PCAR explicitly incorporates advocacy to involve researchers and practitioners in addressing problems of educational practice.

Then, CUE selected research methods and conducted studies to illuminate and document problems of racial and ethnic inequities, producing a knowledge

Table 5.3   CUE Research Studies

Study Description	Method(s)	Contribution to Research Problem	For Further Reading
National Study of Transfer The Study of Economic, Informational, and Cultural Barriers to Community College Student Transfer Access at Selective Universities *Mixed methods study of transfer access for low-income community college students (primarily adult students and Latinos)*	Descriptive and interpretive statistics (e.g., trend lines, population estimates, point estimates, effect sizes, and confidence intervals) Instrumental case study of potential "exemplars" (pairs of community colleges and 4-year institutions with higher than expected transfer success) based on document analysis, interviews, and site visits Life history interviews with successful transfer students	Documented limited transfer access to selective colleges and universities for low-income students Described "best practices" of colleges and universities that were invested in creating a "transfer amenable" culture Provided the knowledge base for creating the Transfer Access Self-Assessment Inventory, an action research protocol Revealed the lived experience of transfer to highly selective universities for low-income community college students as "boundary crossing" and demonstrated the importance of practitioners who acted as "institutional agents" for transfer students	All methods synthesized: (Dowd Bensimon, & Gabbard, 2006) (Dowd Cheslock, & Melguizo, 2008; Dowd & Melguizo, 2008; Melguizo & Dowd, 2009) (Dowd, Pak, & Bensimon, 2013)
Equity for All *Implementation of CUE's Equity Scorecard action research process in nine California community colleges*	Action research using descriptive institutional data on enrollment, credit accumulation, degree completion, and transfer	Documented lack of transfer access to University of California campuses for community college students, especially Latino students	(Bensimon & Dowd, 2009; Bensimon & Malcom, 2012; Bensimon Polkinghorne, Bauman, & Vallejo, 2004)

Study Description	Method(s)	Contribution to Research Problem	For Further Reading
		Motivated community college practitioners to investigate root causes of low transfer rates	
		The surprising finding that 87 students who gained "transfer ready" status in only 3 years had not transferred led to the Missing 87 study	
The "Missing 87" *A study of the "transfer gap" and "choice gap"* *Action research conducted with the Equity Scorecard team and other practitioners at Long Beach Community College, as a follow-up to their Equity Scorecard findings*	The Transfer Access Self-Assessment Inventory to guide document, observational, and interview data collection and analysis by community college practitioners who researched their own transfer culture and identified practices for improvement	Produced knowledge that campus practices created barriers to transfer With greater collective agency acquired through the action research process and local ownership of the findings, the campus implemented changes to improve transfer access; e.g., a transfer academy was created and transfer options were prominently featured on the college's website	(Bensimon Dowd, Alford, & Trapp, 2007; Dowd Bishop, Bensimon, & Witham, 2012)
Pathways to STEM Bachelor's and Graduate Degrees for Hispanic Students *A mixed methods study of transfer access to STEM advanced degrees for Hispanic community college students*			(Chase Bensimon, Shieh, Jones, & Dowd, 2013; Dowd, 2012; Dowd, Sawatzky, Sawatzky, Rall, & Bensimon, 2013)

base and cultural artifacts that could change educational practice in a way that would promote equity.

By using PCAR as a way to promote local changes within educational organizations, CUE seeks to integrate research and practice in a way that can ultimately influence policy on a macro level. Taking those ideas as a starting point, the team developed a series of questions that were aligned to the research problem and then developed studies to answer those questions. For this specific set of studies, the questions revolved around the characteristics of private and public community colleges as they relate to transfer rates and the taken-for-granted practices and policies that might be impacting successful transfer by students (see Table 5.3).

Core findings from the study included that Hispanic-serving institutions (HSIs) are not awarding Latinas and Latinos an equitable share of the STEM (science, technology, engineering, mathematics) degrees granted by these institutions. Based on this research, CUE concluded that given the growth of STEM occupations and the increasing need for STEM competencies across a wide range of occupational sectors, it is clear that these inequities at HSIs need to be addressed so that Latinos can participate fully in the modern economy.

Based on this and other work, CUE recommended that in a context of economic uncertainty, where institutional budget and external funding sources have been cut, innovative models are needed. Through case studies of faculty at high-performing HSIs, CUE profiles how faculty at these institutions can act as institutional agents in using their own resources, networks, and positional authority to promote Latino student success. Based on this combined work, CUE offered concrete recommendations on how to create, support, and retain institutional agents within colleges and universities (see, e.g., Bensimon, 2007; Bensimon & Dowd, 2012; Dowd & Malcom, 2012; Dowd, Malcom, & Bensimon, 2009; Dowd, Malcom, & Macias, 2010; Malcom, Dowd, & Yu, 2010).

Integration in Design

The mixed methods study was appropriate here given the lack of research on the cultural, historical, and organizational/structural barriers that were an integral part of the kinds of outcomes policymakers were pushing community colleges to measure. The policy problem stretched across a very large student population; aggregate effects could only go so far in explaining why students in some institutions tended to have higher retention rates relative to others. The mixed methods design also was necessary given the project's objective to generate findings that could inform equity-minded policies and practices of higher education institutions as they came under pressure to demonstrate improved student-level outcomes. As in the SAGE study, the CUE researchers saw their mandate as not simply producing implementation and outcomes data but also helping those in the field interpret and use those data for program improvement.

CUE's work adopted a conceptual framework that draws from both organizational learning literature and action science literature. Researchers and students in the early stages of exploring mixed methods research tend to minimize or overlook the conceptual framework that knits together qualitative and quantitative research. In contrast, CUE's researchers, as in the case of the SAGE study, invested significant time in articulating their conceptual and theoretical framework, using their own and others' prior research on the topic in developing the framework. This theoretical/conceptual framework laid the groundwork for a better bridging of qualitative and quantitative approaches in data collection, data analysis, and data dissemination. CUE invested time and resources in articulating the theory of action and vision behind their mixed methods work and what they hoped to achieve in terms of policy impact. The research methods were selected to investigate theoretically informed dimensions of core issues or problems that might be changed to improve equity locally and nationally.

Based on active dialogue by the principal investigators on existing research and pilot studies, the concept of capacity was further defined in the study around three key concepts: (1) the importance of an asset rather than deficit perspective on the social and psychological states of low-status students, (2) the importance of institutional transfer agents in helping students leverage personal and cultural assets as well as department staff in college experience, and (3) the importance of cultural awareness in the institutional agents' ability to assist low-status students and effect change in their own colleges.

In addition to issues of capacity, the researchers were interested in better understanding the *institutional factors* that impeded and/or facilitated the access and transfer of underrepresented students in community colleges. They started with theories of organizational learning and change that identified the colleges and institutions that they were working with as embedded in a larger organizational environment. From this perspective, the colleges that they were studying did not exist in isolation but were part of a larger political, cultural, and economic environment that was dynamic and generating new demands. As in the SAGE study, researchers were interested in studying individual and organizational responses to new policy demands and measuring the relative value of practitioners' dominant adaptations of program models. What kinds of adaptations seemed more or less related to improved student outcomes, in this instance, college-going rates?

Integration in Data Collection

The researchers viewed their roles in the mixed methods study as differentiated but grounded in the principle of shared and distributed expertise. Qualitative researchers gave context to the numbers and, through life stories and fieldwork, helped the team and policymakers see the lived experience of individual students whose college-going patterns were reflected in the statistical data. Quantitative researchers helped the team look more precisely at these experiences and map the frequency of their occurrence and any possible associations to students' racial and ethnic backgrounds.

The team's explicit plan to leverage and integrate the unique advantages of qualitative and quantitative data collection is exemplified in its work with Long Beach City College. The team started its research with descriptive statistics arrayed in the "vital signs" of the Equity Scorecard to get a better sense of the scope of the problem. Trend analysis over 3 years of data helped illustrate that low transfer rates were not an anomaly and helped identify a larger number of successful transfer cases, given the low numbers in any one year.

Based on these big picture data, the CUE team could now begin to identify the sample of institutions in which it would begin to conduct its fieldwork. The research team identified eight pairs of community colleges and highly selective 4-year institutions as potential exemplars of institutions whose policies and practices supported successful transfer. The team used case studies to identify policies and practices that supported a transfer-amenable culture. For example, they found that across institutions with higher rates of transfer, there was typically an agent (often a faculty member) who performed functions that might contribute to higher transfer rates, including advising students and working to influence institutional transfer policies in areas such as curriculum, counseling and advising, financial aid, and assessment.

To better understand how this problem related to socioeconomic inequities, the team then incorporated these practices into an inventory that colleges could use to do research on their own transfer practices and policies. The institutions collaborating with CUE used the inventory to help faculty develop skills to assess problems and strengths of their own institutions and to build understanding of the challenges facing students in the transfer process and the role of institutional resources (or lack thereof) in facilitating transfer. In this manner, CUE researchers integrated and distributed expertise not only by method but also by perspective and position.

The administrators in the colleges that CUE was studying participated in the research. They helped conduct the inventories (described in more detail later) that provided a means of triangulation with case study data. By having administrators gather research on their own departments, CUE sought to increase validity of the findings. The administrators were in a position within the department to collect data that would otherwise be inaccessible or hard for external researchers to access. CUE's design leveraged unique affordances of qualitative data by integrating narrative vignettes into case studies. The narrative vignettes were designed to put words and images behind the number indicators gathered through the Self-Assessment Inventory.

Integration in Analysis

CUE's research design also leveraged the advantages of qualitative and quantitative work in analysis. For example, from a qualitative perspective, validity of data derives in part from how and how well they reflect the specific contexts in which they were gathered (Clandinin & Connelly, 2004). The qualitative researcher acknowledges that data are socially constructed and their meaning is influenced by the role of researcher in the setting. The CUE researchers' conceptual framework describes validity of data (which may look very different in different college contexts) as strengthened by a process whereby the researcher coordinates with practitioners involved in collection and interpretation of the data. Those working inside the institution possess tacit knowledge that researchers do not have. The involvement of practitioners strengthens the validity of the data because they can cross-check interpretation of data as an accurate representation of setting, and their participation in the research contributes to an understanding of setting that is multivocal.

CUE's work to build a dialogue around the qualitative and quantitative data and instrumentation generating these data was intentional and systematic. It was supported by a structure and culture whereby data were dissected and discussed with attention to the affordances (e.g., contextualized data) offered by different paradigms. The meetings were structured to support rich dialogue around the data. For example, at meetings of Equity Scorecard evidence team members, participants generated "hunches" to articulate initial assumptions about the causes of equity gaps. These hunches served as reference points as new data analyses revealed new aspects of problems of practice that had previously gone unnoticed. With data in hand, members of the evidence team brainstormed the reasons for the low number of students who were persisting and succeeding in their courses. The data were then arrayed around common categories and constructs defined by CUE's conceptual framework, including institutional policies and practices, instruction, students, and academic services and resources. The hunches exercises were not intended as an end in themselves.

The insights emerging from this dialogue were used to refine the team's priority areas for inquiry in the context of limited time and resources.

In these and other ways, CUE leveraged its integrated model to keep data collection focused and to enrich the quality of instrumentation and data collected. Structured dialogue was employed to contextualize quantitative data and help researchers see the data from the perspective of students' lived experiences. Other activities aimed at strengthening researchers' inferences and interpretations of policy changes. For example, the team organized site visits that used both a structured observation protocol and self-assessment protocol. Researchers used the observation protocol to systematically capture common indicators of program change in community colleges where transfer rates were high. Simultaneously, via the self-assessment protocol, interviews were conducted with program staff to develop a richer picture of the planning, negotiation, administration, and collaboration leading to changes captured in indicators.

Integration in Research Dissemination

Another feature of CUE's integrated work is that it leveraged an integrated mixed methods design to deepen stakeholders' understanding of research so that they could take informed action. CUE's strategy also involved continuous communication around the findings of its research, including engaging in a structured dialogue with policymakers about the meaning of research. This strategy is particularly important in mixed methods work given the multilayered nature of the data. In an interview, one of CUE's codirectors summarized the philosophy as follows: "We know data don't act on themselves. We see research as a communicative activity."

Similar to the integrated model discussed in Chapters 2 and 4, CUE also has built a sophisticated website that is aimed at helping potential consumers of research interact with its data. CUE also communicated with practitioners who are considered insider experts able to vet the relevance of the work for other practitioners. They obtained feedback on the presentation of research with regard to the racial and cultural diversity of the populations it aims to help.

CUE's integrated dissemination strategy is based on principles that data don't act on themselves. This principle extends to both the colleges that CUE works with, as well as policymakers identified as having influence on the national level. CUE's approach to communicating mixed methods research to high-level policymakers is exemplified in a series of events surrounding presentation of its research before the House Subcommittee on Research and Science

Education of the Science and Technology Committee on March 16, 2010. The committee's mandate was to investigate the issue of broadening diversity in STEM fields. This document as formally presented appears on the CUE website (http://cue.usc.edu/tools/dowd_ac_2010_broadening_participation_in_stem _testimony_before_the_house_subcommittee_on_research_an.html).

The principal investigator used findings from CUE's combined work to provide the committee with insights on the challenges of increasing the participation of Hispanic students in STEM fields. The principal investigator's testimony illustrates the ways in which mixed methods findings can be powerfully integrated to increase policy impact. In the first part of her testimony, she used statistical analysis as means for developing a problem statement aligned with the policymakers' agenda. In framing this problem statement, she drew on empirical analyses from several of CUE's nested studies. As part of the testimony, she mapped a national picture of *what kind* of institutions were serving Hispanic students, or enrollment trends, concluding that two types of institutions—community colleges and HSIs— were more likely, based on national enrollment data, to educate Hispanic students.

To interpret the relevance of their study for the committee's work, the team leveraged both qualitative and quantitative methods. Beyond enrollment rates, what were the educational characteristics of students obtaining bachelor's degrees in STEM fields among this population? Here again, using simple percentages based on inferential statistics, the researchers demonstrated to the committee that transfer students who held associate degrees were more likely to graduate from two categories of institutions (HSIs and 4-year institutions) than from academically selective institutions or research institutions. They spelled out the comparison points for policymakers in ways that helped the policymakers see the study's essential headlines and contradictions: that the institutions that provide the greatest access to graduate degrees (academically selective and research institutions) were least accessible to Latinos and Latinas.

The chair of the subcommittee asked for further clarification in a written request for information following the testimony. The principal investigator used personal correspondence to elaborate on the points made in the oral testimony. The committee member said that as a result of the presentation, the committee was convinced of the importance of the problem, in terms of both its scope and its influence on individual life chances. The committee member asked the principal investigator for recommendations about how the committee could begin to act on the research. The principal investigator responded to the request through multiple forms of correspondence, continuing to integrate qualitative and quantitative research to help the committee think concretely and with urgency about its own next steps.

Benefits Generated From Mixed Methods Work

Through dialogue, the team developed a conceptual framework that provided a road map and rationale for how they expected the mixed methods research to generate findings with impact and relevance to key decision makers. As noted, reflecting broader accountability pressures, state policymakers tend to frame student success issues as primarily an accountability problem. Colleges needed to generate more data and correct performance problems. Drawing on data across several disciplines, the CUE team reframed the problem as one of institutional and organizational capacity. It used both qualitative and quantitative research to map the scope of the problem nationally and identify institutions that seemed to be doing something right based on transfer rates. It used qualitative and quantitative data to get inside these organizations to better see the practices that might be associated with these outcomes and develop indicators that practitioners and researchers could use to assess the capacity of their institution. The team strengthened its findings by sharing data with participants and allowing participants to work further with the data through a web-based tool.

CHALLENGES AND STRATEGIES FOR ADDRESSING CHALLENGES

Integration in Distribution of Resources

Mixed methods work requires thoughtful investment of resources. Qualitative research is labor intensive and, given the nature of fieldwork, may require more personnel time in certain phases. Both case studies described in this chapter invested heavily in qualitative research, but the strength of conclusions and impacts also required adequate time and investment on the part of those with quantitative expertise. In the SAGE project, the principal investigators primarily responsible for quantitative analysis allocated a smaller percentage of their time, and they hired graduate students working on multiple studies at once. There were practical reasons for these decisions, but they also worked against the goal of integrated analysis. With quantitative personnel resources stretched thin, analyses of student-level outcomes lagged behind fieldwork and created asymmetries in the availability and specificity of quantitative and qualitative data.

Creating a Policy Climate for Mixed Methods Work

Both studies articulated a clear rationale for mixed methods research and created multiple occasions to communicate this rationale to policymakers.

There appeared to be initial buy-in on the part of policymakers and administrative leaders for the mixed methods studies; they approved it. However, over the course of both studies, policymakers came under increasing pressure to demonstrate outcomes measured numerically, for example, in terms of test score gains or increased student retention. This meant that when it came time to report findings, researchers faced the paradox of presenting complexity while offering headlines that showed what works and why. To address these challenges, both studies made sure to include organizations where things were working as part of their sample. They mapped back from this sample to build recommendations that showed policymakers different pathways to improvement. In the case of the SAGE study, the qualitative work, although successful and productive by all standards of rigorous research, continued to be seen, by some policymakers, as soft data, of limited use, even when integrated with quantitative data, in demonstrating impact. This was unfortunate. Multilayered reforms such as SAGE, aimed at addressing complex social problems, require by their very nature data and analyses that help policymakers see the bigger picture through researchers' careful and iterative analyses of different dimensions of the problem.

In both studies, broader accountability mechanisms had focused attention on outcome data and the need to generate more of it. Taking pressures seriously, both studies seized the opportunity to conduct a study that helped policymakers see the complexity of policy issues at play. Mixed methods research was used to better understand how practices and behaviors at different levels of policy and organization were associated with different outcomes and, in this way, offered policymakers leverage points for improving outcomes. Both studies invested time and resources in articulating the rationale behind their mandate (including through the use of theory) and used collaborative processes and the exchange of information to make sure that design was operationalized and improved on wherever possible.

DISCUSSION QUESTIONS

1. The cases describe a set of conditions under which a mixed methods approach is warranted. What were these conditions? Identify a mixed methods policy study or program evaluation related to your area of research. Based on the research questions and study objectives, would you say the use of mixed methods made sense? What made it a superior alternative to a purely quantitative or qualitative approach?

2. What are some common ways that mixed methods data can be used to enrich the development of instrumentation as described in the cases? What was similar or different about these activities across the two cases, as well as in different circumstances described within the cases?

3. In both of these cases, the researchers had to make a case for mixed methods approaches to their program funder. Based on the case descriptions, what objections might they anticipate in seeking continued funding for their work? How can they use examples from their studies to help address these issues?

4. Think about a time when you felt really good about the research that you were doing. What was it about the work that assigned it that value for you? How did you, or would you, communicate that value to others, for example, in a 30-second "elevator speech"?

APPLICATIONS TO YOUR OWN WORK

- This chapter discussed the importance of thoughtful use of resources in fully integrated mixed methods work, particularly given that activities such as fieldwork and cleaning data sets take time and skilled personnel. Consider a study that you plan to undertake or in which you recently participated. How should or were financial resources allocated in the study's design? Which activities might you anticipate to have higher true costs (e.g., time spent in the field, time spent cleaning data), and how might you budget for them and defend an argument for additional funds to be allocated to these activities?

- In policy evaluation and research, it can sometimes be the case, as in the SAGE example, that the government agency you are studying is the same agency funding your research. Based on your own experience, construct a list of advantages and disadvantages to this scenario from the perspective of fully integrated mixed methods research.

CHAPTER 6

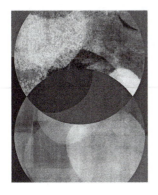

An Application of Fully Integrated Mixed Methods in Program Development and Evaluation

INTRODUCTION

Occasionally an opportunity emerges to become involved in the evaluation of a new program from its inception and design through to its implementation and the follow-up of program outcomes and impacts. From our experience, the use of integrated qualitative and quantitative methods is not only valuable in these cases but essential to successful program development and to fully understanding if and how the program is working as intended, the pathways to impacts, and the nature and significance of the results. Researchers with mixed methods skill sets are also advantageous for engaging with program implementers, data managers, those eligible for and participating in the program, and the many other potential stakeholders of a public program. In addition, as discussed in Chapter 2, a dynamic approach to the evaluation work, where different components of mixed methods research regularly interact and are refined throughout the research process, is likely to be necessary as the evaluation progresses from the design to analysis and dissemination stages.

In this chapter, we present a case study of a long-term evaluation of a publicly funded demonstration program,[1] beginning with the design of the program by the state and its evaluation partner and continuing through a multiyear, mixed methods follow-up that, in total, spanned 8 years of collaboration in program development and evaluation research. This case is distinct from the others discussed in this book in that it also shows some of the special challenges of engaging in both program and evaluation design work and the careful balance that needs to be maintained in interactions between program implementers and evaluators to ensure the objectivity and rigor of the evaluation. In this particular case, the evaluation team also provided direct support in some of the program implementation tasks, which simultaneously facilitated monitoring of the program rollout, documentation of program activities, and data collection for the evaluation.

This chapter begins with a discussion of the policy problem that motivated the development of the demonstration program—growing child support debt obligations—and the early work of the evaluation team and state program administrators in reviewing existing policy efforts in other states and devising an innovative and viable solution to this problem that could be implemented and tested in Wisconsin. The chapter goes on to describe how both qualitative and quantitative methods played central (if not always equal) roles in the initial program design and implementation stages, and how they continually interacted throughout the subsequent evaluation phases to the final analysis and reporting of program impacts. This account also shows how the richness of the insights gained in this evaluation through the application of tightly integrated qualitative and quantitative methods contributed to the generation of important knowledge about what drove program impacts, as well as challenges in program implementation that limited the program's effectiveness. This knowledge, which was disseminated in state and national conferences of practitioners and researchers and in reports and academic publications, also served as an essential resource for a program replication in another state that is currently under way.

PROGRAM AND EVALUATION MOTIVATION

In 2003, the state of Wisconsin Bureau of Child Support (BCS) and the Institute for Research on Poverty (IRP) began exploring policy options to address the problem of growing child support debt in Wisconsin. At the time of the initia-

---

[1]Carolyn Heinrich was the principal investigator of this study at the Institute for Research on Poverty, the University of Wisconsin–Madison.

tion of this project, and despite federal and state policy efforts to address non-payment of child support, national child support debt levels stood at $102 billion, and Wisconsin's portion of this total was over $2.1 billion (in Fiscal Year 2004; Heinrich, Shager, Rothe, & Cancian, 2005). Child support debt presents significant hardships for low-income noncustodial parents (NCPs) and their custodial families who are not receiving support, as well as for states that expend resources on collection and enforcement efforts and face federal performance standard consequences for non-collection (Bartfeld, 2003).

A number of studies confirm the role of poverty in contributing to the buildup of child support debt. One national study found that of the 7 million nonresident fathers who did not pay child support, approximately 36% had incomes below the poverty line (Sorensen & Zibman, 2001). Another study in nine large states found that half of the obligors reported no annual income or earnings of less than $10,000 a year, and the debt owed by these NCPs accounted for 70% of the total arrears (Sorensen, Sousa, & Schaner, 2007). Other factors contributing to the inability of NCPs to pay child support include poor job skills and employment opportunities, low levels of education, incarceration, unstable health, and a lack of assets to negotiate large, lump sum payments for conventional debt forgiveness (Pate, 2002). The custodial parents (CPs) and children in these families also bear the burdens of unpaid child support. In 2007, approximately 25% of CPs had incomes below the federal poverty level, and for those who received full payments, child support represented approximately 48% of their average income (Grall, 2009). A 2005 study of Wisconsin child support cases found that 20% of families relied on child support for more than half of their income, and only 51% of poor families received some support in at least 10 months of the year (Cancian & Meyer, 2005).

In an effort to address these problems, a number of states, including Wisconsin, began experimenting with policy and program models for reducing child support debt, also known as arrears leveraging, arrears management, or arrears forgiveness programs. Federal law allows states to accept less than full payment of *state-owed* arrearages, and it also allows compromise of *custodial-owed* arrears if both parties agree (Office of Child Support Enforcement, 2000). Child support debt owed to custodial families may be composed of unpaid current support, retroactive support, and interest. Debt owed to the government derives from a mix of policies that pass costs on to NCPs, including reimbursement for public assistance benefits paid to CPs, lying-in (medical) costs for childbirth, interest charging, and other fees associated with case processing or genetic testing (Bartfeld, 2003). With the flexibility embodied in federal law, states or other jurisdictions can allow reduced debt payments or expunge debt altogether in exchange for expected behaviors such as on-time payment of current support obligations or participation in employment or parenting programs. Another desired aim of these policy efforts is to relieve some of the financial burden associated with child support debt and thereby enable NCPs to more regularly comply with current support orders (Ovwigho, Saunders, & Born, 2007).

At the time that this program development and impact evaluation effort was launched in Wisconsin, the existing literature on child support debt reduction initiatives had identified small-scale (or pilot) debt forgiveness programs operating in a number of states, primarily at the county level (Bartfeld, 2003; Hennessey & Venohr, 2000; Pearson & Griswold, 2001). Yet despite increasing experimentation with alternative program approaches, there was little empirical evidence on the effectiveness of child support debt forgiveness programs (see Heinrich, Burkhardt, & Shager, 2011, for a more in-depth discussion of these program efforts). Only three other pilot programs had been formally evaluated, and program challenges and evaluation limitations precluded the rigorous identification of their impacts. In each of these cases, NCPs' success in meeting program requirements was correlated with their prior earnings or child support payments, making it difficult to reach definitive conclusions on whether and how such programs might have worked to reduce debt and increase formal child support payments. In Wisconsin, three counties—Pepin, Waukesha, and Milwaukee—had implemented pilot or small-scale programs to forgive state-owed interest or debt; however, there was no systematic evaluation to inform the design or understand the potential for a state-wide policy to reduce child support debt.

PILOT PROGRAM DEVELOPMENT FOR CHILD SUPPORT DEBT REDUCTION

The collaboration between IRP and the Wisconsin BCS began in early 2003 with a review of the existing knowledge base on child support debt forgiveness programs operating in Wisconsin counties and other jurisdictions to inform the design and evaluation of a new child support debt reduction program. The guiding questions in this review were jointly identified by IRP and BCS.

1. What should be the goals of the program?

2. Which parents should be targeted for participation?

3. Which types of child support debt should be forgiven?

4. How should the program be structured; for example, how much debt should be forgiven and at what rate?

5. Should debt forgiveness be contingent on the behavior of the participants?

6. Will the forgiveness of child support debt be permanent?

7. How will prospective participants be selected and notified?

Simultaneously, IRP began work with BCS officials to identify a county site for implementing the demonstration program. IRP staff first analyzed BCS administrative data to select possible sites for the implementing the program, focusing on caseload size and county characteristics and their representativeness of the target population. IRP staff subsequently traveled to four candidate counties to describe the program and evaluation plans and assess county administrative capacity for and interest in working collaboratively with IRP and BCS on the implementation and evaluation of a child support debt reduction program. Thus, from the first steps in program development, quantitative and qualitative methods were combined to make key project decisions. Racine County (in southeastern Wisconsin) was chosen as the experimental site because of the large number of cases with high levels of child support debt; its county demographics (e.g., race, income and poverty, employment rates, single-parent families), which were comparable to other large urban U.S. counties (such as Milwaukee) where arrears are concentrated; and the expectation that program administration would be less complicated in Racine than in a site such as Milwaukee County, where other child support program initiatives were being tested at the time.

Determining Demonstration Program Features and the Evaluation Design

A major advantage of very early involvement of the evaluation team in the child support reduction program's development was the ability to discuss evaluation design decisions (and corresponding evaluation requirements) with the prospective program implementers (as well as state officials). After the site selection was finalized, a meeting was arranged with state and county officials and the IRP evaluation staff to propose an experimental impact evaluation design (involving random assignment of NCPs to treatment and control groups), in combination with the qualitative study of program design, implementation, and outcomes. In that meeting and over the course of the next 6 months, IRP, BCS, and Racine County staff developed strategies and processes for determining the program design and carrying out the mixed methods evaluation in ways that would minimize burdens to the state and county program implementers. For example, a data subcommittee including IRP, BCS, and Racine County staff was formed to address issues concerning the administrative data systems and system modifications that would be necessary for the implementation of the program and the experimental evaluation (i.e., selecting and documenting experimental and control cases, tracking program participation and outcomes, and making adjustments in the arrearage amounts for participating NCPs at regular intervals). The partners also agreed to use focus groups combined with surveys of NCPs and CPs (another mixed methods strategy) to collect data to inform the child support debt reduction program design. In addition, a project timeline was developed that specified both program development and evaluation design tasks (up to the date of the program launch) and assigned primary or joint responsibility to the partners (IRP, BCS, and Racine County) for executing the tasks and making key decisions (see Appendix 6.1).

The focus groups and surveys that were conducted to gather data to inform the child support reduction program design (i.e., its major features) required the creation of scripts and questionnaires; the identification of data collection sites and a sample frame for the NCPs and CPs who would be invited; random selection of the focus group/survey invitees from administrative data; staff training for the focus group implementation and survey data collection; and other activities related to the logistics of data collection (e.g., mailing invitations to prospective participants, making reminder calls, arranging for translation and transcription, etc.). Qualitative information gathered from discussions with state and county officials and child support program managers was key to selecting an appropriate site for the data collection (other than the demonstration program site, so as not to "contaminate" the program site with speculative information about how the program might operate), whereas quantitative data allowed the team to target cases that were expected to be eligible for the debt reduction program and to assess their comparability with the Racine County target population. The focus group discussions were moderated to generate information on the following key issues:

- Demonstration program features—the rate of arrears forgiveness, forgiveness of interest on child support debt and/or principal owed, forgiveness of CP-owed and/or state-owed arrears, the timing and conditions of arrears forgiveness, termination of agreement (i.e., consequences of failure to comply) and restart terms, etc.

- Target group/enrollment criteria for the program—payment history, minimum arrears, minimum age of child support order, complex cases, etc.
- Options for program outreach (i.e., how to offer the opportunity to participate in the debt reduction program) and for random assignments to treatment and control groups

Both qualitative and quantitative analysis of the focus group and survey data (including CPs and NCPs) generated critical information for the next steps in determining the program features. For example, whereas both CPs and NCPs supported a program model where debt reduction would be gradual and conditional on NCP payments toward their current support orders or debt, CPs (not surprisingly) preferred a lower rate of debt forgiveness, for example, 50 cents on the dollar versus a more generous dollar-for-dollar rate that was preferred by NCPs. Survey responses also showed that both CPs and NCPs thought there should be a waiting period (e.g., 3 months) during which the NCP would make timely payments before any debt reduction would begin, and they also concurred in the focus group discussion that special credits should *not* be given for participation in other programs such as the Children First job readiness program. Most NCPs, as well as a number of CPs, were highly enthusiastic about the possibility of participating in child support debt reduction program, although it was also uncovered that many NCPs were apprehensive about responding to the focus group invitation, as they feared that they were being "set up" for arrest for failure to pay their child support. This insight turned out to be critical in foreshadowing a barrier to program enrollments that arose later in the demonstration program implementation.

The focus group findings were reported to the director of BCS and BCS and Racine County child support staff in an August 2004 meeting in which these findings guided decisions about the child support debt reduction program features (see the meeting summary in Appendix 6.2). In many cases, the specific decisions reflected compromise between the interests of NCPs, CPs, and those of staff who would be charged with program implementation, drawing on the focus group and survey data generated. For example, the forgiveness of debt owed to CPs as well as to the state was allowed, but the provisions specified that interest on debt would be forgiven first, and consequences were established for NCPs who missed payments. In addition, debt owed to CPs could only be forgiven if stipulated (or agreed to) by the CPs in a legal agreement. More complex (e.g., interstate, foster care, and kinship) cases were excluded to reduce administrative burdens, and the program eligibility criteria were set to identify the largest debt holders and keep the caseload manageable during the demonstration program. Issues related to program outreach and enrollment were also identified, but those final decisions were deferred pending a proposal for implementation of the experimental evaluation design.

During fall 2004 and early spring 2005, the IRP evaluation team worked closely with BCS and Racine County child support staff to establish workable procedures for random assignment of child support cases to treatment and control groups and for enrollment of those cases selected for treatment. The discussions drew on a review of recent experiences with random assignment in experiments, discussions with programmers who worked with the administrative data, and input from child support staff on how the processes would be managed in Racine. For example, administrative data could be used to identify the eligible cases (per the eligibility criteria set for the program), and the programmers would need to create a new data field flagging eligibility that would be viewed by caseworkers in Racine. It was determined that assignment to treatment and control groups could also be made in advance of the program using the eligibility flag and NCP social security numbers, but a process also had to be established for flagging and assigning newly eligible NCPs to treatment and control groups over time that would not unduly burden state and county child support staff. Another important set of decisions concerned how county child support staff would inform NCPs of their treatment or control status, and how they would handle NCPs who would find out about the program via word-of-mouth and express an interest in enrolling. It was noted, for example, that if the program model was widely adopted later (and not operated as an experiment), interest in the program would be expected to be generated by word-of-mouth or recommendations from community organizations and advocates; hence, if the experimental program were to operate more like a regular program, those who were not randomly assigned and invited to participate by letter should be given the same consideration for enrollment as those targeted for participation, as long as they met eligibility criteria. Issues raised in these exchanges between the evaluation team and program implementers also included how to inform control NCPs (or other interested but ineligible NCPs) that they would not be allowed to participate at this time and how to minimize the potential for NCPs to pressure CPs to forgive their portion of the arrears owed, both of which might have negative, unintended consequences for family relationships. Thus, it was critical for the program implementers to contribute to the evaluation or research design decisions in the same way that they had weighed in on program design decisions.

DEMONSTRATION PROGRAM ROLLOUT AND EARLY EVALUATION FOCUS

The preparations for the demonstration program rollout began in earnest during late fall 2004 and extended into the first several months of 2005, so that the initial date for the first mailing of invitations for program enrollments was pushed back from January 2005 to March 2005. A significantly more detailed project timeline was developed jointly by the IRP evaluation team and BCS and Racine County program implementers to guide the program rollout and evaluation efforts (see Appendix 6.3), including specific tasks, their goals, target deadlines, and the partner with primary responsibility for their undertaking. During this period, the evaluation staff interacted frequently with program implementers to develop a program manual and quick reference card for staff to guide program implementation; design outreach materials (e.g., posters, pamphlets) and a plan for their dissemination; make required administrative data system modifications; create consent forms for participants and secure Institutional Review Board (IRB) approval at the University of Wisconsin; design program monitoring and reporting tools; hold training and orientation sessions for Racine County child support staff; and select random samples of eligible NCPs for the first mailings of invitations to participate, followed by the preparation of those mailings to initiate program enrollment. In the majority of these tasks, the demands of program implementation and the requirements for a rigorous evaluation combined to present challenges for the research team and their partners, and qualitative methods (e.g., interviews, document review, etc.) as well as quantitative methods (e.g., analyses of administrative data to project enrollments, select random samples, etc.) were drawn on to meet those challenges. In fact, the early phase of both the program rollout and the experimental evaluation continued to bring about new hurdles that required adaptations in the program implementation plans and in the ongoing mixing of research methods to address them.

Prior to the demonstration program launch, the evaluation team also set forth with BCS and Racine County program staff a refined list of priority questions for the program process and impact evaluations to address. These included the following:

Do NCPs respond to incentives to reduce their child support debt by making child support payments? How many (or what proportion of those invited to participate) sign up for the program and make payments?

Are CPs willing to forgive the interest and/or arrears owed to them? How many (or what proportion of those asked to participate) sign stipulations and participate in the program?

Do those NCPs who participate pay more child support and pay more regularly than those randomly assigned to a control group?

How much of the child support debt owed to the state is reduced by this program (in interest and arrears)?

How much of the child support debt owed to the CPs is reduced by this program (in interest and arrears)?

Although many related questions were raised and pursued throughout the subsequent 6 years of research collaboration, these remained the core, guiding questions throughout the mixed methods evaluation.

Overcoming Obstacles to Program Implementation and Evaluation

The first major obstacle that arose after the letters of invitation were mailed to treatment and control group NCPs was a very slow response to the opportunity to enroll in the demonstration program, known as Families Forward. The lack of interest in applying was unexpected, given the enthusiasm that NCPs had communicated in the first focus groups that were held to inform the program's design. Indeed, the rollout of letters of invitations was designed to be staggered—taking 10% random samples of those eligible each month—to prevent program staff from being overwhelmed. Racine County staff taking calls from NCPs confirmed the low volume of calls but did not have additional insights as to why the response was weak.

IRP and BCS staff decided to hold a second round of focus groups (separately with NCPs and CPs) in August 2005, 5 months after the program officially started, to (1) address possible problems in implementation that might depress enrollments (e.g., Were NCPs receiving the letters of invitation, did they understand the program features and next steps required to enroll, and what factors were influencing their decision or efforts to enroll, including perceived burdens of the time or steps required to do so?); (2) assess the effectiveness of outreach efforts and materials (e.g., posters and pamphlets), including how NCPs and CPs learned about the program and whether the messages were effective in encouraging enrollment; and (3) explore early perceived effects of the program on child support payments and family relationships (see the focus group script in Appendix 6.4). These focus groups, which were not originally planned (and required an IRB modification to proceed), offer an example of the dynamic nature of the mixed methods research process. The decision to hold the focus groups was based on both quantitative analyses of program administrative data and (qualitative) interviews with demonstration program staff that together confirmed low enrollments but could not answer the "why" question or point directly to modifications needed in the program's design or implementation.

The findings of these August 2005 focus groups shaped the subsequent program implementation and the engagement of the program evaluators and implementers in important ways. First, they showed (as foreshadowed in the program design focus groups) that Racine County's effectiveness in communicating its seriousness about child support enforcement and the use of enforcement tools such as incarceration deterred NCP enrollments in two ways: (1) It made them less inclined to open or to read mail with a Racine County Child Support return address, and (2) they were fearful that the letters of invitation to participate (in the demonstration program and the focus groups) might be a set-up or sting operation that would lead to their arrest. In response to this information, BCS and IRP agreed that future mailings of invitations to participate in the program would go out with the institute's (university) return address, so that NCPs would be more likely to open the envelopes. In addition, IRP agreed to staff a toll-free information line dedicated to the program (and to include the phone number in the letters of invitation) to increase the perceived legitimacy of the program, as well as to offer NCPs an additional option for readily accessing basic information about the program and instructions on how to enroll (see Appendix 6.5 with the toll-free information flowchart that guided staffing of the line).

At the same time, the program developers and evaluators recognized the importance of limiting the direct involvement of the evaluation staff in the implementation of the program. The objective was to operate the demonstration program as similarly as it would in the absence of an evaluation. It was decided, however, that supporting outreach was an acceptable role for IRP staff, as in any future statewide effort to roll out the program, a wider range of options to increase enrollment would be available (e.g., radio or TV advertising, public forums, etc.) that would not be appropriate for an experimental program with a limited target population. In addition, the evaluation staff took advantage of the toll-free information line to collect qualitative data from callers about any problems they were having in understanding the program features or in enrolling in the program. Participants in the focus groups had also indicated that the messages in the outreach materials could be made simpler, and IRP and BCS responded by redesigning the posters, brochures, and letters of invitations and remailing them to all eligible NCPs. A program logo was created as well to brand the program and link outreach materials and invitation letters. This logo was printed on magnets with the enrollment number for NCPs and CPs.

Program Monitoring and Early Evaluation Insights

The expanded role of the evaluation team in program monitoring was also critical to the effective execution of the experimental evaluation, which required Racine County staff to adhere to specific procedures in recording calls from NCPs and their intent to enroll in the program (or declines of the invitation), for both experimental and control group members. In a training session with IRP and Racine County staff prior to the program rollout, this was conveyed with the handout shown in Appendix 6.6. However, over time, turnover in the child support staff implementing the demonstration program and changes at the agency in how calls from NCPs were fielded led to additional problems in enrolling NCPs in the program. Through quantitative analyses of state administrative data, IRP staff were able to monitor NCP inquiries about the program (as well as enrollments) and identify slowdowns or gaps in contacts between NCPs and program staff. And in qualitative analyses of information collected from the toll-free information line calls and through interviews with program staff, IRP staff explored factors potentially contributing to the program implementation problems.

For example, it was found from the interviews with county child support staff that some staff had not enrolled interested and eligible NCPs because they did not have a recent child support payment and it was assumed that these people would not be willing or able to pay. Because eligibility for the program was defined in part by a poor history of current support payments, this procedure worked to exclude individuals who should have been enrolled. In addition, in January 2006, Racine County changed its phone system so that calls to the phone number originally dedicated to the demonstration program were rerouted to a Milwaukee call center. The Milwaukee call center staff lacked specific knowledge about the program and callers had very long wait times for connections, which the evaluation staff was able to confirm with their own attempts to reach the call center, as well as from the calls that came into the IRP toll-free information line because they could not get through at the call center. Administrative delays in processing the stipulation agreements (for NCPs who were enrolling with CPs who also agreed to forgive family-owed arrears) also led to lower enrollments of child support cases that would receive forgiveness of both state-owed and family-owed debts. As both quantitative and qualitative evidence of these problems accumulated, a third round of focus groups—with program participants, eligible nonparticipant NCPs, and CPs—was held in May 2006 to shed light on the underlying issues and to identify possible solutions to the challenge of increasing enrollments.

Based on the focus group findings and other mixed methods research evidence that was being generated, the diagram in Appendix 6.7 was constructed by the evaluation team to summarize the program enrollment process and indicate the "exit points" where eligible NCPs were dropping from the enrollment process. Some of the reasons for exit related to NCP misunderstandings or lack of follow-through in the process, whereas a number of others pointed to administrative errors (i.e., failure of program staff to adhere or follow through in the process) or obstacles (e.g., bad addresses for NCPs in the administrative data system). Strategies were recommended by the evaluation team to address these issues—including more extensive outreach and education efforts, additional training sessions for county child support staff, reestablishing a dedicated phone line for the program in Racine, and increased case management and communication with enrolled NCPs—but only a subset of them were implemented. Thus, even though the period of program enrollment was extended to November 2007, enrollment totals did not reach expectations. Of the 531 NCPs (with 1,976 Title IV-D child support cases) who contacted Racine County to try to enroll in the program, 376 (71%) were randomly assigned to the experimental group, but only 120 (32%) of these NCPs successfully enrolled. Another 150 eligible NCPs who expressed an interest in participating, but did not enroll because they were randomly assigned a "control" status, formed the control group for the evaluation.

Table 6.1 (see the first two columns) shows that with regard to NCP characteristics and key measures of interest in this study—total family debt balances and state debt balances and recent payment histories at program start—the 376 willing experimental NCPs who contacted Racine County to sign up for the program were statistically equivalent to the 150 control group members who also expressed an interest in participating but did not enroll. Comparing the 376 experimental NCPs and the 150 control group members, the evaluation team could calculate the "intent to treat" impacts as the average difference in changes in outcomes between these two groups. However, as indicated earlier, all willing NCPs with experimental status did not complete all steps to enroll in the program, and those who did enroll were not statistically equivalent to willing NCPs assigned to the control group. The third column in Table 6.1 presents descriptive statistics on *actual participants* in the demonstration program. Comparing actual participants with NCPs assigned to the control group, statistically significant differences are evident

Table 6.1   Characteristics of Noncustodial Parents in the Program Evaluation

Noncustodial Parent Characteristics	Experimental (Willing to Participate) Group (n = 376)	Control (Willing to Participate) Group (n = 150)	Experimental Group and Participating (n = 120)
Age in years	37.9	38.2	40.5*
Percentage female	5.3	5.0	2.5
Percentage white	36.0	35.0	27.5
Paternity case	70.0	68.6	73.1
Unemployment insurance earnings in 2004	$4,970 (9,060)†	$5,059 (11,822)	$4,630 (8,644)
Number of children (across all cases)	3.2	3.1	3.5
State child support debt balance March 2005	$10,823 (17,875)	$9,847 (18,227)	$16,907* (17,924)
Family child support debt balance March 2005	$24,399 (24,013)	$21,087 (21,572)	$27,987* (25,502)
Percentage with no child support paid in 2004	11.4	11.3	10.8
Number of months made payment in 2004	6.2	6.1	6.6

*A t-test or chi-square test confirmed that the difference between this value for participating experimentals and the value for those in the control group was statistically significant at $p < .05$.

†Standard deviations are in parentheses below the measures of earnings and state and family debt balances.

for NCP age and for two key characteristics concerning the program intervention (family and state debt balances prior to program start). As random assignments to the treatment and control groups were made prior to the mailing of invitations to participate in Families Forward, the evaluation team was not able to make the same assumption that *participation* in the program was independent of factors influencing program outcomes. Therefore, calculating average differences in outcomes between *actual participants* ($n = 120$) and control group members would not identify the impact of "the treatment on the treated"; these estimates would have to be recovered through quasi-experimental evaluation methods.

In this regard, the fully integrated mixed methods design proved to be pivotal in preserving the integrity of the impact evaluation. The experimental "intent-to-treat" program impact estimates would necessarily be based on 376 experimental NCPs, of which only 120 (or 32%) had actually participated in the program, yielding "diluted" experimental impact estimates. However, the knowledge generated in the mixed methods evaluation about how the enrollment processes were working and why some experimental cases were not being enrolled was critical to specifying empirical models for a quasi-experimental evaluation of program impacts that would adequately adjust (statistically) for selective differences between actual program participants and eligible nonparticipants and also account for changes in program implementation. For example, because program enrollments took longer than expected (and continued over a period of 33 months), the timing of key events (e.g., NCPs' first contact with program staff and dates of program enrollment for participants) varied considerably. It was important to accurately capture this information in modeling the pre-intervention and post-treatment pattern in outcomes over time. In addition, because the participating NCPs had larger state and family debt balances prior to enrolling than those not participating, and because interest charging (on debt) affects the growth rate in these balances, it was important to account for these pre-program differences and to model expected changes in debt growth rates over time. The fact that all researchers worked jointly in the quantitative and qualitative evaluation activities (because of the small size of the evaluation team) readily facilitated the integration of such insights into the impact evaluation analyses.

IMPACT EVALUATION FINDINGS AND THEIR INTERPRETATION AND USE

The data used in producing the program impact estimates came primarily from the state child support administrative data system (the **Kids Information**

Data System [KIDS]), **which** tracks child support orders and payments. These data included information on child support orders, payments, receipts, and arrearages; the method of payment and destination of payments (family, state); and demographic information about the parents and children in the cases (i.e., birth dates, residential location of both parents, and dates of marriage, divorce, and paternity establishment). These data were merged with unemployment insurance (UI) wage record files to allow for construction of controls for the employment and earnings histories and other characteristics of parents in the quasi-experimental analysis of program impacts. The KIDS data also provided information on child support case outcomes that were central to the evaluation, including (1) changes in the *family-owed* child support debt balances, (2) changes in the *state-owed* child support debt balances, (3) changes in the *average* monthly (amount of) payments made by the NCP toward current support or debt accounts, and (4) changes in the probability that any payment was made by the NCP toward current support or debt accounts. The program impacts were measured as "differences in differences"; that is, the difference in the pre- to post-intervention changes in outcomes for program participants compared to changes in these outcomes for the control or comparison groups of nonparticipating NCPs.

As described earlier, the choices made in specifying models for program impact estimation were informed by contextual knowledge of child support program operations and our observations and insights from the mixed methods study of the implementation of this demonstration program. For example, it was gleaned from the focus groups that although we could expect the new incentives offered by the program to encourage NCPs to pay more support once enrolled, we should also anticipate possible lags in NCP responses to them, as some might hold off on making more or bigger payments until they were sure they were enrolled and getting extra credit toward their debt for each dollar paid. A possible drop-off in payments over time was anticipated as well, as participants might exhaust financial reserves, and because participation in the program was time-limited. In addition, a follow-up survey of both NCPs who participated and NCPs assigned to the experimental group who did not enroll was conducted between March 2007 and April 2008 by phone to gather more in-depth information about those eligible for the program, enrollees' experiences with the program, and potential effects of the program not identifiable in the KIDS data.[2] The follow-up survey showed that the program was

---

[2]A sample frame of 327 NCPs—68 participants, 151 willing but unenrolled experimentals, and 108 willing controls—was selected, and 97 of these (30%) completed a survey by phone. Data from KIDS and UI wage records were used to compare the surveyed NCPs with the other (nonrespondent) NCPs.

targeting a profoundly disadvantaged group of NCPs, who, in addition to their high child support debt balances, had high rates of limiting health conditions, low rates of personal assets, and considerable experience with incarceration (i.e., 84% had been incarcerated in prison or jail since they were first ordered to pay child support, with a majority of these incarcerated at some time for non-payment of child support).

Experimental and Quasi-Experimental Evaluation Findings

Here we present the highlights of the analyses of program impacts along with a brief description of the methodological approaches. (A fuller discussion of the experimental and quasi-experimental methods employed and the findings of this evaluation can be seen in Heinrich, Burkhardt, & Shager, 2011.) First, as expected, the experimental, "intent-to-treat" calculations of program impacts (comparing interested NCPs who were assigned experimental status, even if not participating, with those assigned to the control group) showed no statistically significant differences in the changes in outcomes, although for some outcomes such as state debt balances, the observed difference was in the direction expected (e.g., state debt balances of experimental NCPs declined more than those of control group NCPs by $353). In fact, the standard errors of all of the experimental differences were large, suggesting that conclusions could not be drawn about the direction of these estimated impacts. Comparing only participating NCPs with the control group, without adjusting for known differences in their characteristics, the pattern of program effects was noticeably different: The magnitude of estimated effects was larger and all were in the direction expected if the program incentives were working (i.e., NCP debt balances decreasing and payments increasing).

The quasi-experimental analyses took full advantage of the use of random assignment (as an exogenous source of variation for identification of program impacts), as well as insights from the mixed methods study of the program implementation, in specifying models to estimate program impacts. Propensity score (differences-in-differences) matching methods—both with and without random assignment as an instrumental variable for predicting treatment in the first-stage models—were estimated, along with multilevel growth curve models

---

t-Tests of differences in means showed no systematic differences between the groups in terms of their current support orders, family-owed debt balances, state-owed debt balances, amount of state- or family-owed debt reduction, total child support payments, wages, or demographic characteristics, suggesting they were representative of the larger analytic sample on these key measures.

that estimated changes in the outcome variables over time and their relationship to the timing of events (including the expression of interest in the program and the start and length of program participation), while controlling for other time-varying and stable characteristics of NCPs. These quasi-experimental analyses of the "treatment on the treated" that adjusted for pre-intervention differences between actual participants and nonparticipants found considerably larger program impacts. Specifically, the matching results showed that state-owed debt balances of participating NCPs declined by more than $2,700 more than the state-owed debt balances of nonparticipating NCPs from the month of enrollment (or first contact) to their last month of program participation (or approximately 24 months later). Similarly, family-owed debt balances of participating NCPs declined by more than $2,500 more than those of nonparticipating NCPs (again, between the month of enrollment to their last month of program participation). The matching models also found the frequency (or percentage of months that NCPs were paying) increased by 6.5% more (than nonparticipants) for any type of payment and by almost 23% more than nonparticipants for payments toward state-owed debt, compared to their rate of payments in the year prior to the program. Results of after-matching balancing tests confirmed that there were no statistically significant differences between participant and nonparticipant characteristics after matching.

The multilevel growth curve models, which allowed for modeling of some of the idiosyncratic aspects of program implementation, yielded additional insights about how the program was working to affect NCP child support payments. The results of these models, estimated for four payment outcomes (average monthly payment made, the probability of making a payment in a given month, the probability of making a payment toward state-owed debt, and the probability of making a payment toward family debt), are shown in Table 6.2. The key parameter of interest—indicating how NCP payments changed during NCPs' time of participation in the demonstration program—is highlighted in bold. Across the months NCPs were participating in the program, on average, they paid $105 more per month toward their current support or debt than NCPs who were not participating, a fairly dramatic increase. To fully interpret this key estimate, however, one also needs to assess the interactions of this variable with other measures of post-contact/enrollment growth rates and cohort indicators. For example, among the interactions with cohort indicators, only one interaction (cohort 3 participants) is statistically significant (and negative), suggesting that the impact was significantly smaller for participants who began the program in the first or second quarters of 2006. Specifically, NCPs in the third cohort paid approximately $53 more per month toward their current support or debt than NCPs in other cohorts, but the NCPs who were participating in

Table 6.2 Multilevel Longitudinal Estimates of Demonstration Program Impacts

Outcome measure	1. Monthly payment amount			2. Made *any* payment			3. Made payment on state-owed arrears			4. Made payment on family-owed arrears		
Predictor	Coef	Std error		Coef	Std error		Coef	Std error		Coef	Std error	
Intercept	−220.37	47.7432	*	−0.157	0.0676	*	−0.1574	0.03435	*	−0.090	0.053	
Growth rate before first *contact* to initiate program enrollment	2.18	0.85	*	0.0037	0.0007	*	0.003	0.001	*	0.007	0.001	*
Post-contact growth rate	1.26	0.41	*	0.001	0.000	*	0.000	0.000	*	0.002	0.000	*
First 3 months post-contact indicator	8.72	25.69		0.015	0.009		−0.005	0.007		0.006	0.012	
Second 3 months post-contact indicator	−18.82	25.84	*	−0.001	0.010		−0.012	0.007		0.012	0.012	
March–May 05	47.71	22.11	*	0.012	0.008		0.014	0.006	*	0.014	0.010	
March–May 06	37.12	22.59		0.011	0.008		0.005	0.006		0.014	0.010	
March–May 07	61.93	21.86	*	0.014	0.008		0.000	0.006		0.005	0.010	
March–May 08	46.64	21.80	*	0.005	0.008		0.002	0.006		0.004	0.010	
March–May 09	72.62	22.55	*	0.018	0.008	*	0.014	0.006	*	−0.010	0.010	
Partcipating in Families Forward	104.56	40.58	*	0.035	0.023		0.130	0.017	*	0.109	0.028	*
Participant post-contact growth rate	−2.31	1.30		0.000	0.001		−0.002	0.001	*	−0.002	0.001	*
Participant first 3 months post contact	−96.20	59.28		−0.020	0.024		−0.052	0.018	*	−0.034	0.029	
Participant second 3 months post contact	4.71	57.60		0.023	0.021		−0.002	0.016		0.000	0.027	

(Continued)

Table 6.2 (Continued)

Outcome measure	1. Monthly payment amount			2. Made *any* payment			3. Made payment on state-owed arrears			4. Made payment on family-owed arrears		
White	70.70	15.64	*	-0.017	0.023		-0.020	0.011		0.065	0.017	*
Non-white	45.33	20.79	*	-0.022	0.030		-0.021	0.015		0.008	0.023	
Male	36.31	30.08		0.030	0.043		0.048	0.022	*	0.015	0.033	
Age in years	4.13	0.85	*	0.010	0.001	*	0.004	0.001	*	0.005	0.001	*
Never married	-23.56	20.75		-0.041	0.030		-0.013	0.015		-0.041	0.023	
Log of 2004 earnings	2.53	1.12	*	-0.005	0.002	*	0.001	0.001		0.000	0.001	
Number of children	17.71	3.27	*	0.011	0.005	*	0.007	0.002	*	-0.006	0.004	*
Monthly earnings	9.64	1.00	*	0.007	0.000	*	0.003	0.000	*	0.010	0.001	*
Current support order	266.16	10.75	*	0.843	0.004	*	0.049	0.003	*	0.252	0.005	*
Cohort 2–first contact July–Dec 05	21.34	19.62		0.022	0.026		0.015	0.014		0.022	0.021	
Cohort 3–first contact Jan–July 06	52.86	20.30	*	0.013	0.027		0.013	0.014		0.030	0.022	
Cohort 4–first contact July–Dec 06	68.77	22.95	*	0.061	0.032	*	0.033	0.016	*	0.075	0.025	*
Cohort 5–first contact in 07	67.14	34.58		-0.006	0.062		0.108	0.027	*	0.136	0.044	*
Cohort 2 participants	-42.62	44.69		-0.036	0.026		-0.040	0.020	*	-0.013	0.031	
Cohort 3 participants	-94.73	45.71	*	0.043	0.030		0.041	0.022		0.037	0.035	
Cohort 4 participants	-79.67	59.57		-0.026	0.041		0.026	0.031		-0.134	0.048	*
Cohort 5 participants	-75.57	107.23		-0.085	0.073		0.108	0.053	*	0.114	0.084	

Notes: Key parameter of interest is highlighted in bold.

Italicized variables are interactions between a participant indicator and other covariate in the model. *N* = 530.

*Indicates coefficient is statistically significant at α < .05.

the demonstration program paid just $10 per month more than nonparticipants in the third cohort (i.e., $104.56 + $52.86 − $94.73 = $62.69), so the differential impact is smaller. As discussed earlier, the mixed methods evaluation revealed that the first two quarters of 2006 were besieged with the most extensive county administrative and demonstration program management problems.

The results in Table 6.2 also show that for *all* NCPs, there was no change (0% growth rate) in the probability of making a payment toward state arrears after their first contact to enroll, but the probability that *demonstration program participants* made payments toward their state-owed arrears in a given month was 13% higher during participation. Likewise, the probability of making payments toward family-owed debt was increasing by just 0.02% for all NCPs in the months following their first contact to enroll, whereas the probability that demonstration program participants made payments toward their family-owed debt was 11% higher on average (than for nonparticipants). These findings affirmed those of the matching models that showed significantly higher *frequencies* of paying debt (especially state-owed debt) among Families Forward participants.

Applications of the Mixed Methods Study Findings

The quasi-experimental results that statistically adjusted for the selective nature of program take-up among NCPs were more promising than the experimental estimates, which combined both treatment effects for participants and null effects for the 68% of experimental cases who did not participate. If program participation remained low in future program implementation efforts, then the study suggests that only about one-third of NCPs and their families might realize significant benefits from participation (i.e., debt reduction for NCPs and increased payments for families). In this regard, the mixed methods findings were particularly important in speaking to whether the types of implementation problems observed in the Racine County demonstration program would be likely to reoccur in future attempts to successfully implement this program model.

For example, it was later learned that only 5% of the Milwaukee call center calls (essential for enrolling after the switch to the call center at the end of 2005) were being answered. Significant measures were later taken by the state to remedy this problem, and it could also readily be thwarted by establishing a direct line at the implementing agency for receiving NCP calls to enroll. Another approach to increasing NCP participation would be to improve communications with NCPs, both during and after the enrollment process. The follow-up survey results showed that participants had difficulty ascertaining even if they were enrolled in demonstration program, as well as whether it was reducing their debt. The evaluation team recommended to the state that future implementations of the program should provide unambiguous notifications to NCPs when their participation begins and, once enrolled, statements showing how much credit they were receiving toward their arrears. In addition, beyond proactive communication on the part of child support agency staff, the mixed methods study of program implementation showed that promotional materials distributed throughout the community (e.g., in libraries, unemployment offices, churches, etc.) were effective not only in increasing awareness but also in substantiating the veracity of the program. Focus group findings further suggested the importance of using advertisements in media such as radio, newspapers, and the Internet, along with testimonials from parents who were in the program, to allay fears that it might be a sting operation.

To date, we are aware of one other attempt to replicate this demonstration program; this effort is ongoing in Texas, in the form of a pilot program (the Texas Payment Incentive Program). The substantial documentation that the evaluation team compiled of all activities—program development and implementation as well as research and evaluation—during the 8-year period of collaboration between IRP researchers and BCS and Racine County staff made the groundwork of launching the demonstration in Texas much lighter. That said, there were also important differences in Texas law and state program priorities that required modifications in the program design and that also shaped the program rollout in Texas. Again, the rich insights generated in applying a fully integrated, mixed methods approach to the demonstration program evaluation were essential to guide these decision-making processes, as well as in offering an exemplar for how the program implementers and evaluators might work together to produce important knowledge about the program's implementation and effectiveness.

CONCLUSION

This case study was distinctive in that the evaluation team was involved in both the design and the development of the intervention itself, as well as in the evaluation of its implementation and impacts. The integrated qualitative and quantitative methods approach proved to be crucial to understanding not only if and how the program was working, but also for troubleshooting problems in implementation and addressing their implications for the evaluation of the program's effectiveness. Unlike the case study of the Child Support Grant program impact evaluation in South Africa (see Chapter 7), the research team involved in this program evaluation was small (one principal investigator working with one research staff member and one or two graduate students part-time throughout the project), and thus, it was important for all research staff to have mixed methods training, some of which was provided during the course of the project. In addition, as shown in this chapter, the research approach was dynamic, in that qualitative and quantitative methods were often drawn in at unplanned times and nearly always simultaneously to generate knowledge as needed at the various stages of program design, implementation, and evaluation.

This case study also described a fairly intense level of engagement between the state and county program staff and program evaluators, which, given some of the problems that emerged in program implementation, was not without tension or, at times, friction among the collaborators. For example, the county child support agency did not inform the state or the evaluation team that they were discontinuing the direct phone line for the demonstration program, and it was only after calls to the university's toll-free information line came in with concerns about how to get through and enroll that the other partners became aware of this change. The switch had direct implications for the evaluation team's role in outreach, as the letters of invitations, brochures, and logo magnets included the county's direct phone number for enrollment and had to be reprinted. In addition, the phone number switch affected the decisions of how to deploy the evaluation resources (e.g., convening additional focus groups) and the methodological and modeling choices made in the evaluation. Evaluations of programs and policies operating in the real world are almost inevitably vexed with both expected and unanticipated challenges (and human error), and it is in these instances that the mixing of methods can rescue the execution and credibility of the evaluation.

DISCUSSION QUESTIONS

1. In new or pilot programs, should a theory of change or conceptual model for guiding the research be constructed deductively or inductively? How is the development of a model of program implementation potentially distinct from a theory of change that guides the overall evaluation?

2. What are the potential benefits and risks to researchers of becoming involved in program development as well as evaluation?

3. Correspondingly, what are the advantages and disadvantages of involving program staff in research design and measurement decisions? What are the potential implications for the relevance and use of information generated?

4. How did the qualitative work in this case study inform the quantitative analysis of program impacts?

5. What limitations would have arisen in this study if the researchers had clung only to the original randomized controlled trial design in the analysis of program impacts? What knowledge or information would have been lost for the interpretation and future replication of this work?

APPLICATIONS TO YOUR OWN WORK

- Consider a program evaluation that you are involved in or would like to undertake. Who or what organizations should be invited to develop the guiding questions for your project? How will you ensure that the different stakeholders' primary issues or concerns are factored into the decision making while keeping a manageable focus for the project?

- In the project you identified for the previous question, which organizations or stakeholders will have a direct role in implementing the program and/or evaluation? What mechanisms will you develop to coordinate the activities of the partners and to allow for feedback and revisions to your plans as the program and evaluation roll out?

- For the program you are evaluating, create a diagram or flowchart—similar to the diagram in Appendix 6.7 that was constructed to summarize the Families Forward program enrollment process—to help guide your study of program processes and identify program implementation and/or evaluation challenges that should receive additional monitoring or focus in your work.

- Develop a menu of methods that could be applied in your evaluation project given the data that are available to you and your own expertise or that of other researchers involved. Which of those methods are most viable and important given the objectives and resources available to your project? How might you expect this assessment to change over the course of your project?

APPENDIX 6.1: CHILD SUPPORT ARREARS FORGIVENESS PROJECT TIMELINE

April 2004–January 2005

April 2004: Conference call to discuss project timeline, plans for focus group data collection, program design, and evaluation issues.

May/June 2004: Begin preparations for running focus groups and collecting data to inform the Child Support Arrears Forgiveness Program design (Bureau of Child Support [BCS] and Institute for Research on Poverty [IRP]).

- Update additional caseload data as necessary to select focus group site (outside of Racine County).
- Determine the appropriate county to run the focus group pre-study.
- With assistance of BCS, contact the selected county for approval and assistance in soliciting pre-study participants.
- Arrange for focus group site(s), moderator(s), and equipment for sessions.
- Select and contact focus group participants.

June/July 2004: Focus group data collection (IRP)

- Conduct focus groups.
- Analyze focus group data.
- Prepare a summary of findings from the focus group sessions.

August–early September 2004: Program design decisions (BCS, Racine County, IRP)

- Circulate focus group findings to BCS and Racine County staff (early August).
- Arrange meeting with BCS, Racine County, and IRP staff to discuss focus group pre-study findings and program design features.
- Finalize program features through additional meetings as necessary.
- Develop a plan for extracting data from existing information systems for tracking the progress of the experiment.

September–November 2004: Policy development and preparation for program implementation and evaluation (BCS, Racine County, IRP)

- Determine sample frame for participants based on finalized program features.
- Develop a random assignment plan for selecting participants and procedures for implementation.

- Develop documentation of the program terms and conditions that will be used to inform prospective program participants.
- Develop agreements and consent forms for custodial parent/noncustodial parent (CP/NCP) participation in the arrears forgiveness demonstration (between the state and the NCP and/or between both the NCP and CP).
- Determine any additional program supports or resources necessary to administer the program in Racine County.
- Finalize program outcome/performance measures.
- Prepare administrative data systems (new and/or existing) for the implementation of the program and experiment (e.g., additional data fields).

December 2004: Final preparations for program implementation (BCS, Racine County, IRP)

- Have one or more meetings (if necessary) to discuss final preparations for program implementation.
- Begin release of information about Child Support Arrears Forgiveness demonstration and/or targeted "marketing" of the program to sample frame of potential participants.

January 2005: Begin program implementation and evaluation (BCS, Racine County, IRP).

APPENDIX 6.2: CHILD SUPPORT DEBT REDUCTION PROGRAM DESIGN DECISIONS MEETING SUMMARY

August 31, 2004

Bureau of Child Support, Racine County Child Support, Institute for Research on Poverty

I. Program design decisions

a. Program features

i. Rate of arrears forgiveness:

The standard arrears forgiveness agreement will require custodial parents (CPs) to forgive 50 cents for every dollar of current support paid by the noncustodial parent (NCP). If the NCP also has state-owed arrears, the state will also forgive 50 cents for every dollar of current support paid by the NCP.

ii. Forgiveness of interest vs. principal owed

The standard agreement will allow for the forgiveness of both state- and CP-owed interest and principal. The interest owed to the CP and state will be forgiven first as the NCP pays current support. Only when there is no more interest owed to the state will the reduction of principal owed to the state begin within the 2-year agreement period. Similarly, only when there is no more interest owed to the CP will the reduction of the principal owed to the CP begin within the 2-year agreement period.

In addition, on the first day of the quarter that the agreement becomes effective, the accrual of interest on NCP-owed arrears to the state and CP will be stopped.

iii. Forgiveness of CP-owed and/or state-owed arrears

Both CP-owed and state-owed arrears will be forgiven in the program. Tax intercepts are excluded from any accounting of payments made by NCPs in this program.

If an NCP pays more than the current support owed in a quarter, all payments (for a qualifying case) will be credited as eligible to arrears forgiveness.

iv. Timing of arrears forgiveness (wait period, quarterly accounting, etc.)

The term of every NCP-CP arrears reduction agreement will be for 2 years. In general, participation will begin on the first day of a quarter following execution of an agreement. However, if the NCP-CP couple completes an agreement in the first month of a quarter, they have the option of beginning the program that quarter or waiting until the next quarter (or even a subsequent quarter within the first 9 months) to begin the program. All arrears reductions will be made quarterly according to the amount of current support paid that quarter.

v. Increasing rates of forgiveness as payment on current support increases

There will be no increasing rates of arrears forgiveness in the program.

vi. Termination of agreement and restart terms (enforcement actions, penalties, conditions)

If the NCP fails to make a single payment for two consecutive quarters of participation in the program (i.e., current support paid = $0), the agreement is terminated and cannot be restarted for the remainder of the 2-year period. (*Note:* The 6-month period discussed in the meeting has been defined here as two consecutive quarters so that the timing is more consistent with the quarterly operation of the program.)

Interest accrual will be restarted on the first day of the quarter after termination of the agreement.

There will be no changes to enforcement actions for those participating.

    vii. Credit for other program participation (e.g., Children First)

          There will be no credit allowed for other program participation.

  b. Target group for enrollment

    i. The program will include NCPs with debt owed to the CP and/or the state.

          Only cases with current support orders will be included. The maximum age of the youngest child should be 15 years to ensure that at least 2 years of current support payments are still owed.

          No foster care or kinship case types will be included in the program.

    ii. NCPs who have not recently made a current support payment or who have an inconsistent payment history will be targeted.

          The NCPs included in the target group will meet at least one of the following criteria (as well as the minimum threshold criteria, below):

      1) No payment on current support made within the last 3 months

      2) Made a payment on current support in less than 6 of the last 12 months

      3) Paid less than one half of what is owed in (annual) current support over the last 12 months

    iii. Minimum arrears threshold

          All targeted NCPs will owe at least $4,000 in total arrears (CP- and state-owed, interest and principal). In calculating the total arrears, no arrears arising from kinship care or foster care cases will be included. (*Note:* IRP staff will check to see how many cases are excluded by this criterion. This amount may be changed to $3,000 or another number.)

    iv. Minimum age of order

          All NCP-CP child support cases (in the target group) must have orders in continuous effect for at least one year. (*Note: Continuous* is defined to mean no gap larger than 1 month. This will permit cases with orders that have been modified to be included.)

    v. Simple vs. complex cases (e.g., cases with multiple CPs)

          Complex cases will be included in the program. Each NCP-CP couple—that is, court case—(for NCPs with multiple CPs) will be treated as a separate case in the program. As the NCP makes current support payments that are divided among his/her respective CPs, arrears will be reduced accordingly only for the portion of the payment that is received by the CP(s) who is/are party to the agreement.

vi. Other considerations

No interstate cases will be included in the program. The court order for the case has to be in Racine County. At least one of the parents (CP or NCP) has to reside in the state of Wisconsin.

II. Other program design considerations

Note: These other program design considerations will be deliberated after we have confirmed the program features and obtained data that indicate the size of the sample frame based on the selection criteria defined above.

a. How to make the initial offer to participate in the program (phone, mail, etc.)

b. Timing of program participation offers (at one time, sequentially)

c. How to approach NCPs with multiple CPs

d. Contract with participants: An arrears forgiveness stipulation could be used as the agreement/contract for both parties. The life of the stipulated agreement would be 2 years, regardless of the initial quarter of entry.

III. Next steps

a. Racine and BCS will draft a single form/stipulation that will act as a contract/agreement for the parties.

b. IRP will draft program design notes.

c. IRP will estimate potential size of eligible population.

d. BCS will begin work on reports, automation.

e. BCS and Racine will draft proposed outreach materials. IRP will make suggestions to ensure readability and promote interest among potential participants.

APPENDIX 6.3: RACINE COUNTY CHILD SUPPORT DEBT REDUCTION PROJECT TIMELINE

October 2004–January 2005

October–December 2004: Ongoing preparation of management information system (MIS) for data collection (Bureau of Child Support [BCS], Racine County, Institute for Research on Poverty [IRP])

- Modifications to **Kids Information Data System** (KIDS): Identify and implement changes.
- Develop standardized KIDS reports for tracking participant payments.
- Develop reports and other methods to monitor outreach, intake, and participation during first year.
- Finalize method to make and track C/E assignment in KIDS.
- Determine what information, if any, cannot be tracked in KIDS.
- Set up database for tracking participant progress and program outcomes (if separate data collection activities are necessary).
- Finalize program outcome/performance measures.
- Develop documentation and training materials for BCS, BITS, Racine, and IRP staff.

  o Goal: Data systems should be ready by mid-December.
  o Primary responsibility: MIS/data management committee

October–December 2004: Policy development and preparation for program implementation (BCS, Racine County, IRP)

- Develop documentation of the program terms and conditions that will be used to inform prospective program participants and brochures or posters for publicity of the program.

  o Finalize decisions about phone numbers, contact persons, other instructions to include on posters/pamphlets/letters.
  o Goal: Posters/pamphlets are ready for display in the Racine County office and elsewhere in the community by December to facilitate targeted "marketing" to the full sample of potential participants.
  o Primary responsibility: BCS (with Racine)—stipulations; brochure and draft of letter to noncustodial parents/custodial parents (NCPs/CPs); Racine—contact information/instructions; IRP—posters

- Complete and submit Office of Child Support Enforcement (OCSE) grant proposal for additional resources to facilitate program outreach and enrollment into the program in Racine County.

  o Identify and make initial contacts with nongovernmental organizations (NGOs), other organizations, and individuals, to assist with outreach.
  o Goal: Anticipated November submission date
  o Primary responsibility: Jan—grant proposal; Racine—initial contacts with local organizations

- Develop agreements and consent forms for CP/NCP participation in the arrears forgiveness demonstration (between the state and the NCP and between the NCP and CP).

o Submit appropriate documentation to Human Subjects Institutional Review Board (IRB).
o Goal: Consent forms and any enrollment forms should be ready by mid-November.
o Primary responsibility: IRB for human subjects research issues

- Follow up with NGOs, others, as appropriate. Develop materials, assist in training, etc.
- Hold a December orientation session in Racine to fully inform/prepare all staff about implementation and evaluation issues and to answer questions about program rollout.

o Primary responsibility: Racine, BCS, and IRP

October–December 2004: Random assignment design and preparation for evaluation activities (BCS, Racine County, IRP)

- Develop random assignment plan for selecting participants and procedures for implementation.

o Goal: Random assignment plan determined by beginning of November
o Primary responsibility: IRP

  - Estimated maximum sample frame size is 5,323 cases (see Racine County sample selection memo).
  - Recommended approach: Send rolling invitations to participate, beginning in January with a mailing to a 10% random sample (about 500 cases) with an invitation to participate in the arrears forgiveness program.
  - Monitor responses to invitations to participate and follow up with additional outreach activities monthly (increasing outreach as necessary).

o Proposed random assignment plan

  - Identify eligible cases at the start of the program and add newly eligible cases each month.
  - Randomize at point of first contact from the eligible NCP *or* CP indicating interest in the program.
  - Randomize to treatment and control groups using a 2:1 ratio (i.e., two cases to treatment for each case assigned to the control group).

- Select the first random sample of prospective participants and prepare mailings to invite them to participate.

o Goal: Mailings should be ready before the end of December and mailed on the first business day in January 2005.

       o Primary responsibility: IRP—case selection and preparation of mailing labels; BCS will mail letters.

- Develop a procedures "manual" to follow in program implementation.

       o Detail the terms of program participation for NCPs and CPs.
       o Describe procedures for tracking responses to invitations to participate in the program.
       o Document random assignment procedures.
       o Develop data entry procedures for new program participant cases.
       o Create system for filing participation agreements and recording important communications or problems during program implementation.
       o Send ongoing (rolling) offers to participate in the program.
       o Goal: Procedures manual should be ready by mid-December.
       o Primary responsibility: IRP will draft the first copy.

- Develop a reporting system for joint BCS–Racine County–IRP monitoring of program progress during the first year of implementation.

       o Primary responsibility: BCS–Racine County with input of IRP

January 2005: If OCSE grant application is successful, establish bookkeeping, budget monitoring, and check-writing systems.

- Finalize budget and plan for expending funds for outreach.

       o Primary responsibility: IRP with Racine County

January 2005: Begin program implementation and evaluation (BCS, Racine County, IRP).

- Mail letters to first 500 randomly selected participants.
- Follow procedures for intake, random assignment, and enrollment as detailed in the procedures manual.
- File participation agreements.
- Track responses to invitations to participate.
- Continue to build outreach networks and activities.
- Revise outreach materials as needed. Send revised copies to Human Subjects IRB.
- Mailing to second group of prospective participants should be ready by the end of January.
- Racine County should monitor time and resource commitments of staff to the project.
- BCS, Racine County, IRP should monitor KIDS; other MIS system should be functioning to ensure that new program cases are processed appropriately.

APPENDIX 6.4: NONCUSTODIAL PARENT FOCUS GROUP SCRIPT

Introduction

Thank you for coming here tonight. My name is ___ and I am here with *(names of other people)*. We are researchers at the University of Wisconsin–Madison. In our work, we've found that the amount of child support owed to custodial parents and overdue for payment has been going up across the country. Researchers and government officials are concerned about the hardships experienced by children and parents when fathers or mothers don't pay court-ordered child support and become increasingly in debt.

As a result, the state of Wisconsin Bureau of Child Support and the UW-Madison Institute for Research on Poverty have developed a child support debt reduction program called Families Forward, which is being implemented on a trial basis in Racine County. The program allows noncustodial parents to reduce the amount of back child support they owe, if they make regular payments to the children and the custodial parent. The state also suspends interest charges on debt if noncustodial parents continue to make regular payments.

The program is intended to benefit everyone. The goal is to develop a program in which custodial parents regularly receive child support payments; noncustodial parents are motivated to make regular payments and begin to see relief from burdensome debt and penalties; and children benefit from increased financial support. In March 2005, the first letters were sent to eligible noncustodial and custodial parents like you in Racine County, inviting them to participate in the program. We will continue to invite more parents to participate over the next few months. At this time, however, not all of those who are invited will have the chance to participate. We have set up a system that randomly selects persons who are eligible to participate; this gives everyone an equal chance of participating at this time.

Last summer, when we were designing the program, we held several focus groups like this one to get input from custodial and noncustodial parents about what kind of debt reduction program would work best. This information was very helpful to us. We've asked you to come here tonight because now that the trial program is under way, we would like to learn more about how you found out about the program, why some people choose to participate while others choose not to participate, and your opinions about how the program is working and how it has affected you and your family.

We are going to ask you as a group to answer some questions, but we're not going to ask you to sign up for the program at this time or to make any kind of commitment regarding future participation. We are hoping that the information you share with us tonight will help us better understand how the program is working and what needs to be improved.

Are there any questions?

Program Implementation Issues

Deciding Whether to Participate

As we mentioned in the introduction, we have sent out letters inviting eligible custodial and noncustodial parents in Racine to participate in the Families Forward program. Some parents have responded to the letters and signed up for the program. Others have tried to learn more about the program but decided not to participate. Still others have not responded to the letters at all. We would like to understand more about why people do or don't respond to the letters, and why they choose to participate or not to participate in the program.

- All of you should have received a letter inviting you to participate in the Families Forward program. Did you receive and read the letter to participate?

    o If you did not receive the letter, do you have any ideas about why you didn't receive it or what might have happened to it?
    o If you received the letter but did not read it, why did you choose not to read it?
    o If you did not receive a letter, but learned about the program somewhere else, how did you learn about it?

- If you did read the letter, what was your first impression of the program?

    o Were the explanation of the program and terms of eligibility clear?
    o Do you think the terms of the program are fair to you? Why or why not?
    o Did you want to participate but were in a situation that made it difficult or impossible to make regular child support payments and satisfy the terms of participation?
    o Were you worried that the invitation to participate was an enforcement trap?

- Were you willing to get involved with the CP in such a program? Why or why not?

    o Do you have other arrangements for making payments to the CP?
    o Did you want to participate, but the CP would not agree to the terms of the program?

- For those who are participating, how did you arrive at the decision to join the program?

    o Did you discuss the opportunity to participate with the CP before making a decision? How did these conversations go?
    o Did you feel any pressure to participate? If so, from whom?

Outreach Issues

We would also like to know more about how people are learning about the Families Forward program and whether we are doing enough to draw attention to the program and encourage people to participate.

- In addition to sending out letters, we have also put up posters and pamphlets about the program at several locations in Racine. Have you seen any of these posters or pamphlets? Where were they?
    - Is the message in these posters and pamphlets clear?
    - Did the message make you interested in signing up for the program? Why or why not?
    - Where else might we put posters and pamphlets to help more people learn about the program?
    - Are there other ways we might help people learn about the program?

- Did you call the Racine child support agency to learn more about the program? Did this help you decide whether to participate in the program? Explain.

Enrollment

Because this program is being run on a trial basis and researchers at IRP will be evaluating it, it is important for us to know how well the processes developed for making sure people are eligible for the program and enrolling them in the program are working.

- How much time did it take for you to get an appointment or move forward to the next stage of enrollment after you let the child support office know you were interested in participating?
- Who originally called the child support office about the program, you or the CP?
- Which one of you (NCP or CP) called the other to talk about the program?
    - How did these conversations go?
    - Would it be beneficial to have another person help make these contacts (e.g., to explain the program or help come to an agreement)?
    - In general, when talking about this program, were your interactions with the CP positive? Were there any problems?

- When discussing this program, were your interactions with the child support agency staff helpful and positive?
- At any point, did you change your mind about your decision to participate or not participate? If so, when and why, and what did you do about it?

Understanding Program Impacts and Investigating Other Impacts

Although it is still early in the trial run of the program, we would like to hear your opinions about what effects (if any) the program has had on you and your family so far.

- Have you paid more child support since enrolling in the program?

  o If so, why?
  o If not, are there any barriers that are preventing you from being able to make regular payments?
  o Has it been made clear to you how much your debt has been reduced?

- Have your ideas about or attitudes toward the program changed over the course of the program (e.g., in terms of your reason for participating, perceptions of yourself, your ideas about your obligation to your family, etc.)?
- Have your interactions with the CP, either when first considering the invitation to participate in the program and/or throughout your involvement in the program, changed any particular aspects or the nature of the relationship between you and the CP?
- Has your involvement with your child(ren) changed during your time participating in the program?

  o If so, have these changes been in any way coordinated with how often you made payments or the amount of payments you made during this time?

- By participating in this program, has your family benefited in ways other than having more money (e.g., reduced stress, more friendly contacts between parents, improved child well-being, etc.)?
- If your debt has been reduced, how has this affected other aspects of your life (e.g., reduced likelihood of enforcement actions, lower stress, improvements in relationships with persons other than the CP and the supported children, etc.)?
- Is there anything else about the program's effects on your family that you would like to share with us?

Conclusion

Are there any questions or comments that anyone would like to make? Thank you again for your participation; we greatly appreciate your coming here today to share your opinions with us.

APPENDIX 6.5: FAMILIES FORWARD 1–800 CALL FLOWCHART

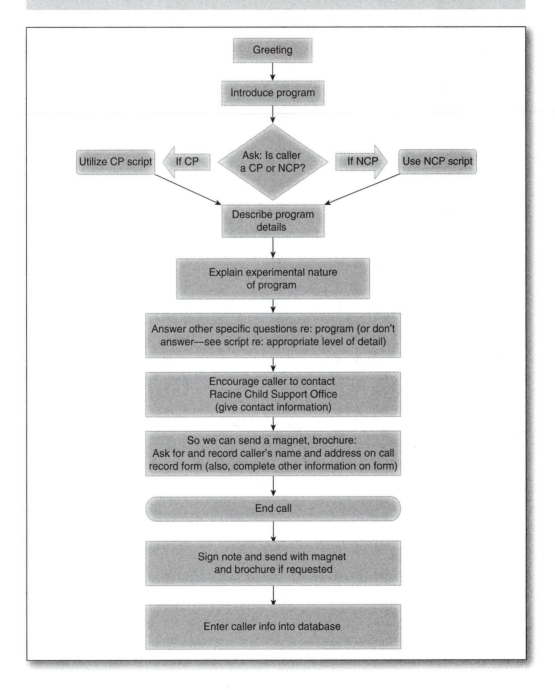

APPENDIX 6.6: RANDOM ASSIGNMENT STAFF TRAINING HANDOUT

Your help recording _every_ query about the program is critical to the success of the evaluation.

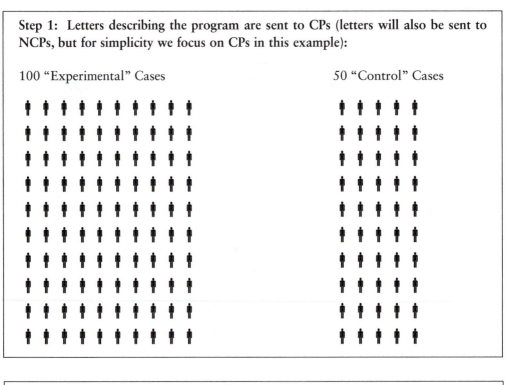

Step 1: Letters describing the program are sent to CPs (letters will also be sent to NCPs, but for simplicity we focus on CPs in this example):

100 "Experimental" Cases   50 "Control" Cases

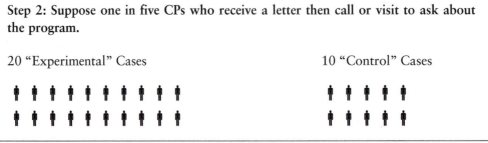

Step 2: Suppose one in five CPs who receive a letter then call or visit to ask about the program.

20 "Experimental" Cases   10 "Control" Cases

Step 3

Suppose half the CPs who call and are offered the program eventually agree to participate.

Since those in the Control group are not eligible to participate, the initial call or visit (in Step 2) is the only event that is recorded.

👤 👤 👤 👤 👤 👤 👤 👤 👤 👤

To measure the effect of the debt reduction project we need to compare the "experimental" and "control" cases from the *same* step of the process.

If every inquiry (by phone or in person) about the program is recorded as a KIDS event, we can compare all the cases that made it to Step 2 and called or visited to ask about the program.

Experimental   Control

👤 👤 👤 👤 👤 👤 👤 👤   👤 👤 👤 👤 👤

👤 👤 👤 👤 👤 👤 👤 👤   👤 👤 👤 👤 👤

Among those who make it to Step 2, half the Experimental cases and none of the Control cases participated in the debt reduction program. If the debt reduction program has an effect, we have a good chance of being able to measure it.

If some inquiries about the program are not recorded as a KIDS event, we will not have the same percentage of Experimental and Control cases moving from Step 1 (getting a letter) to Step 2 (calling or visiting). If some of the calls and visits are not recorded, we can only compare the full Experimental and Control groups in Step 1.

100 "Experimental" Cases   50 "Control" Cases

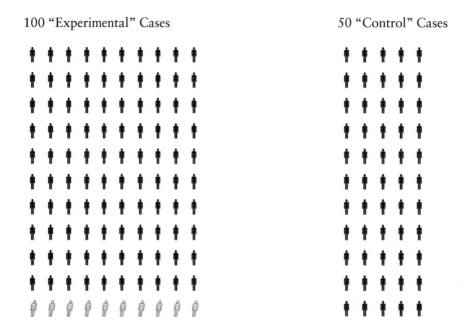

Among those who got a letter (Step 1), only 10% of the Experimental group will have participated. Even if the program has an effect, we are unlikely to be able to measure (or detect) it.

Bottom line: Unless _every_ inquiry—whether it comes from someone in the Experiment or Control group—is recorded as a KIDS event, we will not be able to evaluate the effect of the program.

APPENDIX 6.7: DIAGRAM OF ENROLLMENT PROCESS WITH EXIT POINTS

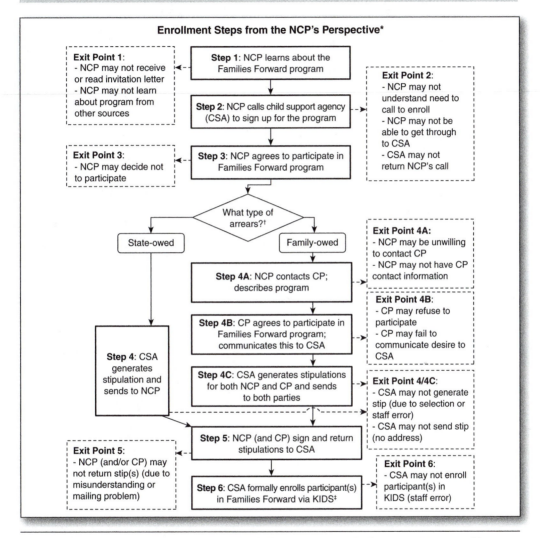

---

* It is possible for a CP to initiate contact with the child support agency. In these cases, Racine would generate a stipulation and send it to the NCP, even if s/he had not contacted the agency.

† An NCP may have both state- and family-owed debt. If the CP refuses to participate in Families Forward, the NCP cannot enroll for family-owed debt forgiveness but she or he may still enroll for state-owed debt forgiveness.

‡ After enrollment, NCPs may be dropped from the program due to failure to pay child support over a period of 6 months. CPs may also voluntarily exit the program.

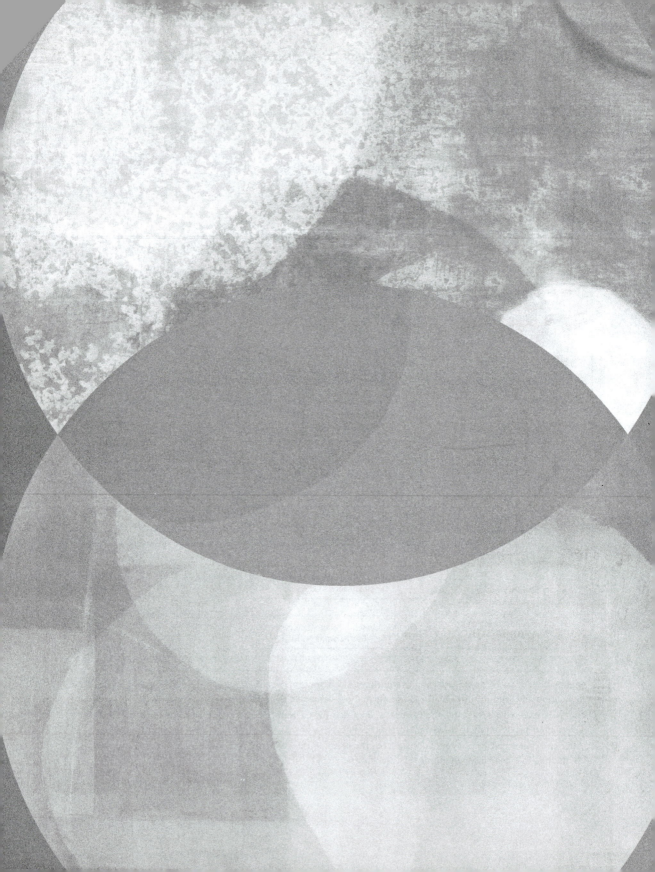

CHAPTER 7

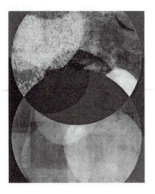

Mixed Methods Research in an International Context

INTRODUCTION

Demand for policy and program evaluation research has been rapidly expanding in international contexts, with collaborative efforts such as the International Initiative for Impact Evaluation (3ie) joining other nongovernmental organizations (e.g., the World Bank, UNICEF, Inter-American Development Bank, and International Food and Policy Research Institute, to name a few) in actively supporting and extending evaluation work across regions and sectors. There is also an increasing emphasis on the use of randomized controlled trials for identifying impacts of social programs (i.e., in education, health, and social protection sectors), although many evaluation efforts necessarily mix qualitative and quantitative methods to describe and understand program implementation and its relationship to program impacts. Moreover, there is growing recognition of the value of applying mixed methods early in the research design phase to strengthen various components of the research, such as the development of instrumentation, sampling, and data collection strategies.

It is still more common than not, however, for the quantitative and qualitative components of many evaluations to be conducted separately or side-by-side, with limited interchange between researchers in the course of their investigations. In some evaluations, the qualitative work is conducted primarily to inform the design of the intervention (in advance of the quantitative study), whereas in others, the qualitative research may be used only at the end of the study to inform the interpretation of the quantitative results. It is also a relatively frequent practice to subcontract with different organizations to carry out the qualitative and quantitative research activities, for example, employing one organization or research team to study program implementation and another to conduct the empirical evaluation of program impacts. Considerably rarer are evaluations that explicitly aim to integrate the qualitative research and the corresponding quantitative work from the beginning to the end of the evaluation.

International policy and program evaluation contexts can also pose additional challenges for researchers in the form of cultural and language barriers; onerous physical environments for conducting fieldwork; limitations of public infrastructure or capacity for supporting research efforts, such as administrative data access or availability of information on policy and process; and coordination issues in multi-institutional collaborations. In these circumstances, active management of the research process by team members committed to applying mixed methods jointly and interactively can go a long way toward easing or overcoming barriers to achieving evaluation goals. In this chapter, we draw on a case study to highlight the opportunities for enhancing policy and evaluation work in international contexts with a fully integrated, mixed methods approach, as well as to illustrate some of challenges that are encountered and the advantages that a mixed methods design can bring to meeting them head on.

The remainder of this chapter first introduces core elements of the context for this program evaluation, including its objectives, setting, research team, basic design, and timeline. The mechanisms and structures used to facilitate integration of qualitative and quantitative methods across the various stages of the research process in this case are discussed next. The chapter then turns to a focus on the benefits and results—that is, what was gained—from applying a fully integrated, mixed methods approach across the key stages of research and instrumentation design, data collection and analysis, and interpretation and dissemination of findings. The chapter concludes by revisiting important elements for successful qualitative-quantitative integration in applied research as well as acknowledging some of the limitations that are likely to be encountered in future efforts toward applying a more tightly integrated, mixed methods approach.

CHILD SUPPORT GRANT IMPACT EVALUATION IN SOUTH AFRICA

The Child Support Grant (CSG) program in South Africa commenced in 1998 as part of the national government's strategy to meet its constitutional obligation to increase access to social protection. At the time, more than one-half of South Africa's children were living in poverty. The CSG targeted the poorest one-third of families for monthly cash transfers to reduce child poverty and its associated negative outcomes. The CSG is now South Africa's largest social cash transfer program, reaching over 10 million children each month through expansions in coverage that have increased its potential to significantly improve the well-being of South African children into their adulthood.[1]

Although social cash transfers have long been an important strategy for tackling poverty and promoting human development, there is increasing demand by governments and development partners for rigorous and convincing evidence of the impacts of these programs, particularly in the context of tight budgets and fiscal conditions. They want to know whether the programs they are funding and implementing are reaching their intended goals, as well as how to improve program effectiveness.

In 2007, the Minister of Social Development in South Africa declared "Putting Children First" the Department of Social Development's (DSD's) 3-year theme, and in 2008, it called for an impact evaluation of one of its most significant national programs for fighting child poverty, the CSG.[2] As stated in the terms of reference for the evaluation: "The DSD considers impact evaluations to be operational and management tools, not academic exercises. They are undertaken to assist in showing clearly and indubitably what works and to allow the identification of the best uses of allocated budget resources." Two primary questions were taken up in the evaluation: How does early enrollment in the CSG affect the well-being and cognitive development of children compared to children who enrolled in the program later, and what is the impact of the CSG on adolescent children?

The terms of reference (TOR) stipulated five "stages" of the CSG evaluation, two of which required (separately) the conceptualization of a quantitative impact evaluation and the conceptualization and implementation of a qualitative evaluation. The other stages or components were the design of survey instruments for the evaluation, the collection and analysis of data, and the fielding of follow-up surveys and preparation of an impact evaluation report. In the original projected timeline for the evaluation (in the TOR), the quantitative and qualitative evaluation components were shown as taking place at different times (as separate stages). In addition, the TOR encouraged the use of nonexperimental methods for identifying program impacts, given a constitutional provision that precluded random assignment (i.e., the exclusion of eligible children from the CSG), and it also specified that the sampling strategy would be determined by the quantitative evaluation design.

---

[1]The South African Social Security Agency (SASSA) reported 10,789,595 beneficiaries in 2012.

[2]The study was commissioned and funded by the Department of Social Development (DSD), the South African Social Security Agency (SASSA), and the United Nations Children's Fund (UNICEF) South Africa. Carolyn Heinrich was a co-principal investigator of this study.

Although the TOR were focused primarily on details of the quantitative evaluation and appeared to treat the qualitative and quantitative components as distinct contributions to the overall impact evaluation, in practice, a fully integrated, mixed methods approach to the research process was planned from the start by the evaluation team contracted to undertake the work.[3] The evaluation team set out seven guiding objectives for implementing a tightly linked qualitative and quantitative impact evaluation design:

1. Consistency

    Alignment between quantitative and qualitative components and respective data collection efforts will be achieved for each evaluation module through the integration process.

2. Technical design in modeling

    Focus group topics for the qualitative research will be identified to specifically address key issues affecting the quantitative analysis of impacts.

3. Technical design of instruments

    Results and findings from the qualitative analysis will inform the development of each survey instrument module prior to and during pre-testing and may alter priorities for inclusion of specific items or formatting of questions.

4. Practical implementation lessons

    Lessons learned in the implementation of the qualitative research (e.g., sampling and finding respondents) will inform survey design and implementation.

5. Assumptions

    The qualitative research will be used to identify and check assumptions underlying the quantitative impact evaluation strategies.

6. Explanatory scope and capacity

    Findings from the qualitative study will be used to help interpret and explain program impact results obtained through the quantitative analysis.

---

[3]The CSG program evaluation was carried out by the Economic Policy Research Institute (EPRI) of South Africa (for which Carolyn Heinrich was a team leader), in partnership with the International Food Policy Research Institute (IFPRI), the Institute for Development Studies (IDS), Oxford Policy Management (OPM), Reform Development Consulting (RDC), and Take Note Trading (TNT).

7. Quantifying qualitative results

   Information collected in the questionnaires will be used to quantify and test qualitative results (with larger sample sizes), which should aid in distinguishing effects or relationships that were purely anecdotal versus those that represent statistically significant findings across a broader population.

As the research team members were based in six different organizations across three continents, it was particularly important to have a consensus on these objectives for the mixed methods approach at the outset of work, for purposes of research coordination as well as design. In practice, the extent of qualitative-quantitative team coordination in specific work tasks often went deeper and broader than suggested by these initial guiding principles for the evaluation.

QUALITATIVE-QUANTITATIVE INTEGRATION PROCESS IN THE CSG IMPACT EVALUATION

One of the first tasks required of the CSG impact evaluation by the DSD and the other funding partners was the development of a comprehensive theory of change for the CSG program that would explicate how the monthly cash transfers were expected to drive change and improve short-term, intermediate, and long-term outcomes for poor children and their families. Specifically, this involved the identification of the following:

- Hypotheses about the mechanisms through which the CSG would produce impacts
- A common set of evaluation questions, flowing from the hypothesized relationships, to be addressed jointly in the qualitative and quantitative studies
- Key measures or indicators of impacts, including health, education, early child development, adult and child labor, consumption, social welfare, risky behavior, and intra-household decision making, as well as unintended impacts

Figure 7.1 shows a diagram of the theory of change that was developed by the research team members in consultation with the DSD, SASSA, and UNICEF officials. The diagram begins with processes and factors that determine participation in the program, which is essential to addressing important questions about access to and coverage of benefits, as well as to the specification of empirical models used in estimating program impacts. The intervention or "treatment" is the monthly cash transfer that is received by the caregiver of the CSG-eligible child, and the outputs (generally speaking) are either the expenditures or savings and investments made by the caregiver or other family members. The diagram also describes the pathways through which the CSG was expected to effect a variety of outcomes, differentiating those more likely to be illuminated by qualitative or quantitative methods or both types of methods combined. The key indicators of program outcomes are also colored in this diagram to identify those that were measured and assessed through mainly qualitative, mainly quantitative, or both types of methods (without priority to one or the other). The theory of change suggests that as the research moved from examining more readily measured short-term outcomes, such as types of expenditures made with the cash transfers, to medium- or longer-term outcomes, the integration of the two types of methods would become increasingly important, given the greater complexity of those pathways to impacts. In effect, the value of tightly integrating the qualitative and quantitative work became apparent very early on and continued throughout the research process.

Table 7.1 elaborates on the constructs or proposed measures presented in the theory of change, describing the (planned) quantitative indicators and their corresponding qualitative dimensions for a sample of the constructs and proposed measures. For some of the constructs, such as social and risky behaviors, education, and CSG administration and receipt, there were plans for qualitative study of each of the quantitative indicators. For other constructs, such as the physical development of the child and intra-household relations and gender issues, the proposed indicators were either solely quantitative or exclusively qualitative, respectively. In reality, there were few indicators that were not informed by or operationalized through both the qualitative and quantitative investigations. One example is decision making about household expenditures, which was initially expected to be informed primarily by the qualitative research. Information gathered in the focus group discussions was used to construct a module with quantitative measures of household decision making that inquired about who in the household was involved in decision making for specific types of purchases.

An additional, more elaborate step was taken to link the theory of change and research questions to the constructs in Table 7.1 and the specific operational (empirical) measures that would be used in the estimation of program impacts. This evaluation design matrix, as it came to be known, was fleshed out as the evaluation progressed. For example, the main research questions were

Figure 7.1 Theory of Change

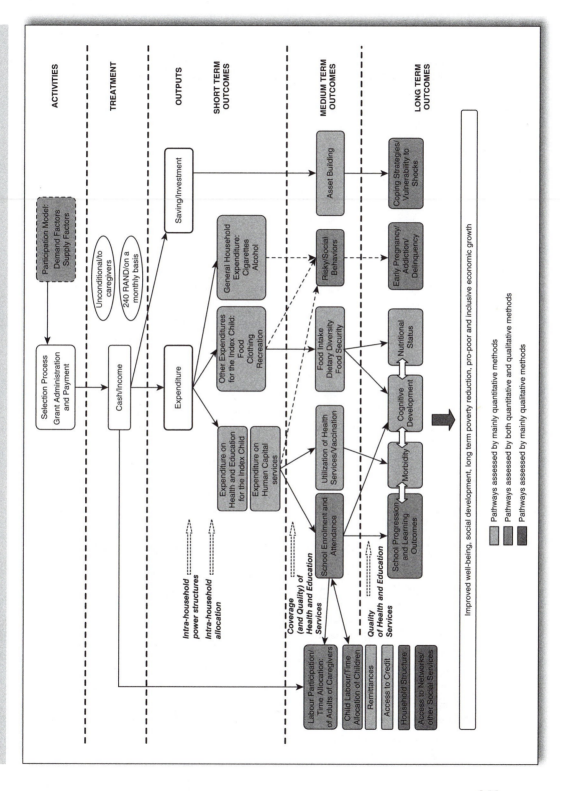

Improved well-being, social development, long term poverty reduction, pro-poor and inclusive economic growth

Pathways assessed by mainly quantitative methods

Pathways assessed by both quantitative and qualitative methods

Pathways assessed by mainly qualitative methods

Table 7.1   Quantitative Indicators and Qualitative Dimensions

Construct/Measure	Quantitative Indicators	Qualitative Dimensions
Sociodemographic characteristics of household and children	Gender (household and child)	
	Marital status	Polygamy
	Age/birth date (household and child)	Fertility choices
	Number of children	Fertility choices; decisions on fostering
	Child resides with parents (including biological vs. fostered)	Household perceptions of who is part of the household; changing household composition
	Number of wives and children in other households	Household disintegration; polygamy; household perception of who is part of the household; fertility choices
	Other household structure information	Changing household composition (including related to grant access)
	Type of area (rural dwelling/ urban formal/urban informal)	Household disintegration
	Ethnic group and language	
	Education level of caregivers	
	Migration (reasons for migration; locations)	Migration choices
Physical development	Child weight at birth	
	Child head circumference at birth	
	Child weight > 6 months (WFA)	
	Child height > 6 months (HFA)	
	Child waist > 2 years	
	Blood pressure	

Construct/Measure	Quantitative Indicators	Qualitative Dimensions
Intra-household relations and gender issues		Intra-household control/allocation of resources (particularly food)
		Decision making/control of grant (gender/generations)
		Intergenerational relationships
		Sibling rivalry (Is it gendered?)
		Fertility choices
		Women's time spent out of home
		Domestic violence
		Girls'/boys' aspirations for education and work
		Men's attitudes toward CSG
		Women's access to documents
		Women's interaction with institutions
		Tensions over who is the primary caregiver
		Treatment of biological vs. fostered children
Expenditures	Consumption composition	
	Spending and saving behaviors (Do you have savings of money earned previously/savings account?)	Perception of grant (difference with other income)
	Disaggregation of spending on different children (see categories at right)	Spending decisions for different children (boys/girls; younger/older; biological/fostered; CSG/non-CSG)

(Continued)

Table 7.1 (Continued)

Construct/Measure	Quantitative Indicators	Qualitative Dimensions
Labor force participation	Child labor (< 15) (Is the child working?)	Child labor/definitions of child labor/children's job aspirations
	Labor participation > 15 (working or not and where)	Children's job aspirations
	Wage rates (labor income)	Relation between grants and labor-seeking behavior (discouraging/increasing)
	Job turnover (of the household)	Job losses and gains/episodic work
	Work hours inside the home	Relation between grants and labor-seeking behavior (discouraging/increasing)
	Other time use (activities)	
Education	(Child) enrollment in school	Attitudes toward education; reasons for not enrolling in school; young mothers returning to school
	Child attending school (school attendance)/not attending due to cost, or working/not attending due to other reasons (pregnancy, safety, performance, distance, school quality; perceived value of education for future)	Attitudes toward education; reasons for not attending school; how grant affects participation
	Drop out	Reasons for dropping out/returning to school; young mothers returning to school
	Repetition, school progression	Young mothers returning to school; effect of being old for grade
	Cognitive ability	How parent's perceptions of ability, and children's self-perception, affect schooling decisions

Construct/Measure	Quantitative Indicators	Qualitative Dimensions
	School quality	Perceptions of school quality
	Education aspirations/plans	Attitudes toward education/ education plans/ aspirations
Social/risky behaviors	Presence and frequency of alcohol use	Substance abuse
	Substance abuse	Substance abuse
	Unprotected sex	Safe sex vs. risk-taking; reasons for taking risks; pregnancy decisions
	Contraceptives use	Safe sex vs. risk-taking; reasons for taking risks; pregnancy decisions
	Number of partners	Age-specific issues; social and economic factors that influence number of partners
	Age of partners	Age-specific issues; social and economic factors that influence age of partners
	Age of sexual debut	Age-specific issues; social and economic factors that influence age of sexual debut
Receipt of CSG and efficiency of CSG administration	Distance to Social Services office	
	Smoothness of application	Application process experience; application of means-test criteria; behavior of welfare office personnel; access to needed documents; assistance with applications
	Length of CSG receipt (dosage)	Perceptions of targeting; take-up among adolescents ages 15 to 17
	Length of time between application and first receipt	Burden on welfare office personnel

(Continued)

Table 7.1 (Continued)

Construct/Measure	Quantitative Indicators	Qualitative Dimensions
	Place of application (Welfare office? Received application at hospital at birth?)	Resources for assistance with applications and problems; access to needed documents; burden on welfare office personnel
	Where learned about grant (source of information: e.g., welfare staff, jamborees, NGO, media, friend)	How people learned about grant; grant access campaigns/information on grant
	Use of cell phones for transfers	Experience with technology
	Waiting times on paydays	Experience on paydays; burden on welfare office personnel; role of social grant (e.g., pension) committees
	Other grant receipt	Reasons for not applying to CSG
	Motivation/reason for application; reasons for not applying to CSG	Reasons for not applying to CSG; application of means-test criteria; perceptions of targeting
	Reasons for applications rejected	Reasons for applications rejected; application of means-test criteria

broken down into sub-questions for each of the major areas of expected program impacts (e.g., education/schooling, food intake/nutrition, child labor, etc.), and the specific measures (both the qualitative dimensions and the quantitative indicators) were specified, along with a description of how their integration would be facilitated and how sampling and data analysis would be conducted. An extract of several rows of the evaluation design matrix is shown in Table 7.2. The development of this matrix took place through workshops in which the qualitative and quantitative team members met in person with the evaluation funders and stakeholders (e.g., DSD, SASSA, UNICEF, etc.), as well as through ongoing technology-facilitated exchanges among the team members (e.g., e-mail, Skype conferences, etc.).

It is interesting that, in both this international project and the SESIQ² project with researchers based entirely in the United States (but in different locations), the proportion of in-person versus technology-facilitated meetings was approximately the same, even though the costs of bringing the research team members together in South Africa was considerably higher. This likely reflects two facts: (1) Where technology can be used to conserve project resources, the opportunity is almost always taken; but (2) there are often key or strategic decision-making points or junctures in project activities that benefit considerably from more intensive and sustained (in-person) exchange, for example, to realize consensus on fundamental design issues, resolve problems or respond to dynamics in the project or its environment, or disseminate preliminary or final results. Alternatively, in the local context of the Families Forward program evaluation discussed in Chapter 6, most meetings between researchers, program implementers, and other stakeholders were conducted in-person, given the low cost of travel and the project scope, which encompassed program design as well as evaluation. Researchers, whether working individually or in teams, need to appropriately budget for the costs of in-person meetings with collaborators that will be critical to project success.

Collaboration in the Design of Instrumentation for Data Collection

The many benefits of quantitative analysis in social sciences and policy research—for example, objective inference, more precise empirical distinctions, predictive power, replication and comparison of findings, and so on—are predicated on the strong assumption that we are accurately measuring what we intend to measure. To do so, we need to have a thorough understanding of the properties of the phenomena or characteristics we are trying to measure and be able to justify their correspondence with our choice and scale of measures. In this regard, the qualitative work in the CSG impact evaluation played a fundamental role in the design of the instrumentation for quantitative data collection, by both exploring issues that were complex or potentially difficult to capture empirically and informing the construction of specific empirical measures in the questionnaires.

Table 7.2 Evaluation Design Matrix (Extract)

Questions	Sub-questions	Measures	Qualitative Dimension	Quantitative Indicator	Qualitative/ Quantitative Integration	Gender Dimensions	Sample	Data Analysis	Data Sources	Data Collection Instrument
How has early versus late enrollment affected the well-being and cognitive development of children?	How has this affected cognitive ability?	Literacy and numeracy test scores		Difference in mean NIDS test numeracy scores between groups (i) and (ii)		How do boys' and girls' scores differ?	Children receiving the CSG aged 9-11 years and enrolled (i) within 15 months of birth or (ii) from 5 to 7 years of age	Propensity score matching	Young children	Anthropometry
				Difference in mean EGRA test scores between groups (i) and (ii)						

168

Questions	Sub-questions	Measures	Qualitative Dimension	Quantitative Indicator	Qualitative/ Quantitative Integration	Gender Dimensions	Sample	Data Analysis	Data Sources	Data Collection Instrument
	How has this affected educational attainment?	Enrollment, attendance, repetition, grade-for-age	How characteristics of early vs. late CSG enrollers relate to constraints on school access	Difference in mean enrollment rates between groups (i) and (ii)	The qualitative analysis will provide greater insight into the causal factors for the education-related impacts identified in the quantitative analysis, and particularly how early vs. late enrollment affects the impacts.	How do boys' and girls' educational attainment differ? How do boys' and girls' incentives to succeed in school differ? How do boys' and girls' access to education differ?		Propensity score matching	Caregivers and older children	Young child and household questionnaires
			Reasons why boys and girls (a) miss days of school; (b) drop out of school	Difference in mean non-attendance rates between groups (i) and (ii)						
			How CSG does and does not respond to these constraints on access for boys and girls	Difference in mean repetition rates between groups (i) and (ii)						
			Factors affecting girls' vs. boys' school achievement	Difference in mean grade-for-age between groups (i) and (ii)						

In approaching this central evaluation task, members of both the qualitative and quantitative teams first worked together to identify key areas that required further probing to facilitate accurate and appropriate measurement in the questionnaires. These included, for example, the following:

- How the grant (CSG) was accessed at different stages of a child's life, how caregivers or other family members learned about its availability, why they choose to apply for it or not, and their experiences in applying for the CSG
- Caregivers' and other family members' understanding of the purpose of the CSG and how they made decisions about expenditures
- Access to social welfare and health care services to support early childhood development
- Life circumstances and risks to youth at different ages

Several of these items were particularly critical to appropriate empirical modeling of individual and household decisions to access the CSG—that is, in accounting for nonrandom selection of children/families into the program—which is essential to increasing the internal validity of the impact analysis, given evidence of baseline differences between those who enrolled (vs. did not enroll) in the CSG. Accordingly, quantitative team members provided feedback on the instrumentation developed by the qualitative team for their field research to ensure the results would inform the quantitative instrument development. In addition, one member of quantitative team was directly engaged in the qualitative study (i.e., a member of the qualitative team as well).

The qualitative research team went into the field to conduct focus groups and key informant interviews approximately 1 year in advance of the full-scale survey data collection. In light of the evaluation objective to determine how early versus late enrollment in the CSG affected the well-being and cognitive development of children, the focus group discussions included the following groups:

1. *Early recipients:* primary caregivers with 8- or 9-year-old children who received the grant early in the child's life (0–18 months)

2. *Late recipients:* primary caregivers with 8- or 9-year-old children who received the grant later in the child's life (5–6 years)

3. *Non-beneficiaries:* Women with eligible children who do not receive the CSG

And to explore the impact of the CSG on adolescent children, focus groups were conducted with the following groups:

1. *Adolescent girls:* 14- to 16-year-old CSG and non-CSG girls

2. *Adolescent boys:* 14- to 16-year-old CSG and non-CSG boys

3. *Women with older children:* primary caregivers with 14- to 16-year-old children

One additional focus group was conducted with men from households with and without CSG beneficiaries to better understand intra-household decision making about use of the grant. In addition, key informant interviews were conducted with SASSA staff, education and health care workers, and community leaders.

The qualitative data gathered and recorded in these focus groups and interviews were transcribed, processed, and analyzed to produce findings that could be shared with the quantitative team and reported to the DSD. The fact that some members of the evaluation team had skills and experience with both qualitative and quantitative methods supported constructive interchanges and sharing of information between the respective teams. That said, the evaluation leaders also took concrete steps to support a more intensive stage of integration and cross-communication in using the qualitative findings to inform the development of the questionnaires and other evaluation tasks.

In structuring the discussions of the qualitative (focus group and interview) findings and their input into the questionnaire design, the evaluation team leaders first paired members of the qualitative and quantitative teams for each of the major questionnaire components (e.g., grant access, intra-household decision making, health, education, child labor, etc.). Table 7.3 shows the topics, respective team members assigned with leading those topical areas, and other contributors for each of 11 major components of the questionnaires. Other preparations for this work included sending out a first (early) draft of the qualitative field research report and information from pro forma questionnaires to help guide and coordinate the work of the various team members on their respective sections of the questionnaires. For example, a team member working on developing questions for the child labor section of the questionnaire received the information shown in Box 7.1.

BOX 7.1 INFORMATION USED IN DEVELOPING QUESTIONNAIRE ITEMS

Young Child Section 4: Labor Supply and Time Allocation

Team member with primary responsibility: [Name]
Target length: 5 minutes
Indicators from evaluation design matrix:

- Difference in the mean hours per week spent on domestic tasks between group (i) and group (ii)
- Difference in the mean hours per week of child labor (< 15) and mean wages or earnings between group (i) and group (ii)

Questions from pro forma questionnaire (covering indicators above):

Does this child work for pay outside the home?

If yes, what type of work does this child do?

Typically, how many hours per week does . . . [NAME] . . . work in this job?

[Allow for multiple jobs.]

Typically, how many hours per week does . . . [NAME] . . . spend on domestic tasks (fetching water, firewood, cleaning, cooking, and child care)?

Typically, how many hours per week does . . . [NAME] . . . spend working on businesses operated by the household (including farm work, cattle herding, and other family business)?

Changes expected due to qualitative-quantitative integration:

Qualitative analysis will help identify more specific questions with respect to child labor, intra-household decision making, and poverty status, as well as illuminate the complex relationships between the CSG and child labor.

The evaluation design matrix states: "The relationship between social grants and child labor is particularly complex, involving intra-household decision making, poverty status, and other factors."

In developing their respective questionnaire sections, the quantitative team leads consulted with the qualitative team leads and also drew on these sources:

- Existing questionnaires and initial sources: National Income Dynamics Survey (NIDS); other Statistics South Africa surveys and South African household questionnaires (GHS—KIDS); and the pro forma questionnaire
- Relevant academic research on both question development and survey implementation
- Early findings from the first phase of the qualitative research

Table 7.3 Quantitative-Qualitative Team Responsibilities

Topic	Qualitative Lead	Quantitative Lead	Other Contributors
Grant access	SD	MS	LP, CH
Pay points (grant disbursal)	SD	NR	LP, MS
Intra-household decision making	RSW	RSW	CH, MA
Use of grant	RSW	LP	SD
Health	SD	NR	LP
Education	MA	JH	NR, CH
Child labor	SD	CH	LP
Risky behavior	MA	CH	RSW
Social welfare	SD	LP	DF
Early childhood development	SD	LP	UNICEF, DSD
Unintended impacts	RSW	All	

The quantitative team leaders were responsible for the initial draft of the different sections, and then the qualitative and quantitative team leaders worked through several iterations of the questionnaires to prepare a version that would be circulated in advance of an integration workshop. Particular attention was given to the phrasing and prioritization of question items, the identification of appropriate response categories, and other additions or modifications to improve question items and increase learning from the evaluation.

Qualitative-Quantitative Integration Workshops

The evaluation team members, funders, and other stakeholders came together for numerous workshops throughout the research process to work intensively and facilitate the tight integration of qualitative and quantitative methods. Workshops took place in online forums as well as in person, given the high costs of bringing team members together in one location. Materials were prepared and circulated in advance of the workshops, and some of these documents were exceptionally detailed (such as field research reports) to support discussion and decision making. The major workshop topics reflected the key stages of the evaluation process and included the following:

- Preliminary evaluation design, theory of change, and research implementation plans at the project inception
- Qualitative and quantitative sampling strategies and evaluation design matrix
- Questionnaire design and integration of preliminary qualitative research findings
- Pilot testing of sampling strategies and pre-testing of questionnaires
- Finalizing instrumentation and training of fieldwork teams for data collection
- Preliminary fieldwork results and review and refinement of fieldwork strategies for data collection
- Data quality checks and preliminary analyses of sample coverage/representation and statistical power
- Preliminary quantitative analysis findings and qualitative findings linked to them, modifications to model specifications and estimation strategies
- Full study results, interpretation, and policy implications
- Dissemination of study findings

Each of the workshops also included discussion of the qualitative-quantitative integration process and assessment of whether the research objectives were being met or were on track to be achieved.

For example, in the workshop on questionnaire design and integration of preliminary qualitative research findings (conducted via multiple teleconferences), the qualitative team members began by providing an overview of qualitative study results and their perspectives on how they might inform the design of the quantitative instruments. This was done section by section for each of the major components shown in Table 7.3. Each overview was followed by interactive discussion between qualitative and quantitative team members to identify specific issues for further analysis or consideration of the qualitative evidence (e.g., HIV-AIDS, barriers to access to CSG for adolescents, recall of past application process, nature and incidence of risky behaviors, crowding out of informal transfers, etc.). For each section of the questionnaire where important issues for further exploration were identified, the text of the qualitative data transcription and minutes of focus groups and interviews were shared

---

BOX 7.2 DETAILED EXAMPLE OF DEVELOPMENT OF RISKY BEHAVIOR QUESTIONS

- A first draft of questionnaire items on risky behaviors was prepared by the quantitative team leader, drawing on research, established instruments, and information in the first draft of the qualitative field research report.
- This draft of risky behavior questions was circulated to the qualitative co-leader and another contributing team member prior to the integration workshop, with key issues for discussion identified in the interchange.
- The qualitative team leader presented a discussion of key issues in the integration workshop, including female adolescents dating older men, substance use and gang activity, the phrasing of questions to elicit honest responses, and prioritization and level of detail on sensitive questions such as sexual partners.
- Subsequent revisions to the risky behavior question items were made via an iterative process among qualitative and quantitative team leaders and other contributors, with input from the partner organization that conducted the pre-testing on issues of length, form of administration, etc.
- Examples of specific changes made to the questionnaire included the following:

  o A more comprehensive set of risky behaviors was identified for inclusion, and a more thorough set of codes were developed for the survey responses.
  o The format for responses to a question about risk factors was changed to capture more information.
  o Given the importance identified in qualitative research of the risks associated with girls dating older men for economic purposes, questions and code-lists were revised to better capture information on the nature of relationships with sexual partners.
  o Based on the findings of the qualitative research, the module was expanded from 14 questions to 33 questions for the initial pre-testing.

with respective qualitative-quantitative team leaders and contributors. This was followed up by further discussion and interchanges on specific question items. In Box 7.2, we present additional details for one specific survey section (on risky behaviors) to show how this process worked to significantly improve the design of the data collection instruments.

Although an overall timeline for the evaluation work was laid out in considerable detail by month and week, the number and timing of qualitative-quantitative integration workshops was scheduled more flexibly, so as to be responsive to research needs and challenges as they emerged in the design stages, fieldwork, and analyses. The qualitative-quantitative integration process developed for the CSG impact evaluation worked particularly well because the evaluation team members were highly dedicated and responsive in an intensive set of interactions, frequently conducted online, that had very critical timing elements to ensure effective functioning and progress toward evaluation goals. Having one or two organizations (or persons) of a multi-organization/multi-person evaluation team such as this one serve in the lead coordinating roles at different stages in the evaluation—providing timelines and guiding documents with frequent updates and reminders—was also essential to providing structure for the process and supporting ongoing engagement among the evaluation team members. In addition, English was the common language used among the researchers; for the field research, piloting of instrumentation and data collection, local (South African) organizations that could offer translation in many different languages were engaged as well.

BENEFITS OF A TIGHTLY INTEGRATED QUALITATIVE-QUANTITATIVE RESEARCH APPROACH

As elaborated in Chapter 2, our description of fully integrated, mixed methods research is that which is conducted "from the start and simultaneously in ways that are 'interactive and iterative,'" where "every step of the process proceeds from interaction of the two [qualitative and quantitative], with instrumentation and interpretation, for example, growing out of that interaction." The strategies employed "support a process of constant 'illumination.'" However, as described in this case study, there is also considerable time, effort, and additional resources involved in a process that fully integrates qualitative and quantitative methods. Thus, it is a fair question to ask if the benefits of this approach are likely to outweigh the additional costs in personnel and time to complete evaluation tasks. In this section, we review the benefits of this approach for the research design, instrumentation design, data collection and analysis, and the interpretation and dissemination of study findings in the context of this case study.

Research Design

The benefits of a fully integrated, mixed methods approach for the research design are more likely to be realized if the integration process begins with the initial steps of defining the goals and scope of the research or evaluation. In this regard, the intensive integration at the first project inception workshop that led to a detailed explication of the theory of change for the CSG evaluation was a critical first step (see Figure 7.1). This effort laid the groundwork for qualitative-quantitative integration at each subsequent research stage and specified in advance the various pathways to program impacts and their measures that would be investigated with both types of methods. It also formed the basis for the evaluation design matrix that was expanded over time as the integration process generated new knowledge and allowed for more detailed specification of the models and measures.

In addition, the CSG evaluation funders and research team members agreed early on that it would be valuable to examine additional levels of analysis beyond the household level, including social relations within the communities and gender and generational issues. As the primary data collection instruments were designed to capture household and focal child data, it was determined that community/social issues would be explored, beginning with qualitative methods. In this particular case, it was probably more cost-effective to pursue these additional levels of analysis in an integrated approach, where the qualitative research could first identify the most salient social and community dimensions with potential for further investigating quantitatively.

Pursuing tight linkages between the qualitative and quantitative components of the evaluation also facilitated the generation of complementary information on key topics in the evaluation, without unnecessary duplication. For example, having both qualitative and quantitative data on household survey topics such as intra-household decision making and child labor allowed for cross-checking of patterns in the data and also added depth and texture to our understanding of pathways to program impacts. At the same time, the integration process also clarified topics or areas where it would not be useful to mix methods (i.e., where value would not be added), such as in measuring children's cognitive outcomes.

The integration of qualitative and quantitative methods in the research design also supported the exploration of some of the more complex, sensitive issues such as risky behaviors among youth. The qualitative information generated early in the evaluation informed the design of both household and adolescent survey questions and the process by which they would be administered, to ensure that the questions would not be inappropriately or insensitively structured and that adolescents would be inclined to complete the surveys and provide candid responses. This was a research design issue because the study of youth risky behaviors was a major and highly sensitive undertaking in this project, particularly in light of the AIDS crisis in South Africa. It was also clearly a benefit for instrumentation design, which we turn to now.

Instrumentation Design

As described already in this chapter, the qualitative-quantitative integration process was particularly intensive in questionnaire design phase, as the lion's share of the evaluation resources were invested in the survey design and subsequent fieldwork for original data collection. If a given question was unclearly phrased or response categories were not adequate or appropriate, it could render the data collected flawed or unusable. Given the comprehensiveness of the survey, there also had to be a strict time budget for each topic or set of questions designed to extract specific information or responses. Thus, any failings in the survey design could be very costly to the evaluation, both substantively and monetarily.

Through the intensive integration process pursued in designing the instrumentation, each section of the questionnaires went through successive revisions to improve the question wording, taking into consideration issues of respondent aptitude and cultural sensitivity (as identified in the early qualitative investigation) that could affect the quality and completeness of responses. As the integration work was carried out within a strict time frame in a well-structured process (as described earlier), the evaluation team was able to complete a first full draft of the quantitative instruments in time for the first scheduled pre-testing. Keeping to the original schedule and time frames for the evaluation work also had important implications for evaluation costs, in light of seasonal weather and school calendars that could affect the availability of survey respondents and the fieldwork costs.

In addition, the lead organization conducting the pre-testing was able to consult with team members during the course of multiple rounds of pre-testing (primarily through teleconferences and electronic mail) and make rapid-time adjustments to the instruments. These included decisions about the elimination of specific items from the questionnaires to manage survey length. As both qualitative and quantitative team members had worked together in developing the theory of change for the evaluation and elaborating measures in the evaluation design matrix, they were particularly attentive to preserving key indicators that would be critical to understanding potential pathways to program impacts. The improvements attained in the efficiency and quality of the instrumentation would likely not have been possible without the high level of engagement that the intensive qualitative-quantitative integration process cultivated in the survey design process.

Data Collection and Analysis

The qualitative-quantitative integration process contributed similarly to efficiencies in data collection. The early qualitative fieldwork that involved identifying representative members of the groups that would later be surveyed—that is, households with early CSG recipients, late CSG recipients, adolescents, and non-beneficiaries—generated valuable information on some of the challenges that the data collection teams were likely to encounter in their random sampling "finding" strategies. Issues related to the languages required for survey administration, where households accessed the grant, community perceptions of the CSG program and its administration, and related issues of the grant's accessibility and coverage were also illuminated in the qualitative analysis (of focus group data and key informant interviews) and used to inform the sampling strategies and quantitative data collection procedures.

Because the fieldwork for survey data collection also had a relatively tight time schedule to follow to ensure that data on each of the sampled groups were collected within a comparable time frame, it was likewise important to facilitate rapid responses for troubleshooting difficulties in data collection. During the pilot testing, the qualitative and quantitative team members had gone into the field in "mixed methods teams" to observe first-hand how the surveys would be administered. They subsequently stayed engaged with the fieldwork team throughout the data collection process and made team decisions when issues of concern arose. For example, in administering the cognitive tests (early grade reading and math) to young children, it became apparent that the presence of a parent could be anxiety-inducing or could complicate the effort to obtain complete data, depending on the parent's attitude and relationship with the child. Some children felt additional pressure to perform well when a parent was present, and some parents worried that a child's performance could affect their access to the grant. The fieldwork team sought advice from both qualitative and quantitative team members on how best to collect consistent measures of children's cognitive achievement while minimizing stress or potential harm to the children.

Many insights were gleaned from the fieldwork undertaken in the early qualitative research as well as in the data collection process that informed the quantitative analyses of CSG benefit receipt and impacts. In a nonexperimental evaluation such as this one, it is critically important to model the process by which treatment group members select into the intervention (i.e., the CSG program), so that adjustments can be made for potential selective differences in who gets access to the benefits. In the focus groups, the qualitative research team probed the participants on topics related to how they became aware of the program, steps they took to apply, barriers they encountered in enrolling in the program, challenges in maintaining access to the grant, and other issues that would affect their receipt of the CSG. This information enabled the research team to develop a set of questionnaire items that would generate quantitative measures to use in controlling for these selective factors and processes when estimating program impacts.

The fact that the qualitative-quantitative integration process began early in detailing a theory of change for the CSG and its expected program impacts was also key to ensuring that the models for estimating impacts would be appropriately specified. As many possible areas of grant impacts were interrelated, such as health, nutrition, and early childhood development, it was important for team members to collaborate across topical areas as well as methodological approaches (as shown in Table 7.3) to ensure that data were being gathered that would allow for adequate controls for factors that might mediate the pathways of the CSG to program impacts in various areas. The qualitative-quantitative integration process facilitated a richer and deeper understanding of the potential causal pathways, which also aided in the formulation of hypotheses for testing and modeling both intended and unintended impacts of the grant program.

Findings of the qualitative field research and fieldwork for data collection also yielded some important, practical insights about household CSG receipt that led to some modifications to the quantitative impact estimation strategies. It was more difficult than expected to find households with no current or previous grant receipt for children. In households where no grant was being received at the time of the survey, it was often the case that a grant had been received in the past for the focal child or another child in the household. The qualitative research had also suggested that it was not uncommon for the grants to be expended in ways that benefitted more family members than just the targeted child. Thus, an original plan to use regression-discontinuity methods[4] with youth who had just missed the age cutoff for eligibility for the grant (over successive policy changes that raised the age of eligibility)—where those youth who were just over the age of eligibility would serve as a control group—was not feasible if the analysis took into consideration past grant receipt in the household or receipt for other children in the household. Not only was the number of households with no grant receipt a small fraction of the total sample, but the comparability with "treated" households was also limited. The quantitative research team therefore shifted the primary impact estimation strategy to one that focused on using variation in both the timing and duration of grant receipt to identify program impacts for both younger and older children.[5]

Interpretation and Dissemination of Findings

Cumulatively, the benefits of applying a tightly integrated, mixed methods approach to policy evaluation work suggest that the research findings generated by such studies are likely be viewed as more credible and relevant to policymakers and other stakeholders who are looking to use them. The objectives and foci of the evaluation were developed together with the evaluation funders and policymakers, and they participated in many of the integration workshops (in person and sometimes by conference) in order to provide input into some of the critical decisions along the way, especially those that affected the scope and focus of the evaluation when resource limitations came into play. The instrumentation for original data collection and the qualitative and quantitative analyses of the data generated were also strengthened by the intensive, mixed methods integration process, which in turn contributed to greater stakeholder confidence in the study findings. The ongoing engagement

---

[4] Regression-discontinuity methods may be used if access to treatment (i.e., to a program such as the CSG) is determined by some continuous measure (such as the child's age), where a threshold is established (i.e., age of eligibility) that determines who gets the benefit and who is excluded from treatment. The impact of the program is evaluated by comparing individuals with values just below the threshold (i.e., those who are eligible because of their age) to those just above the threshold (i.e., who missed the age cutoff and are excluded from treatment). Assuming the outcome measure is also continuous, the effect of treatment should show up as a sharp change (or discontinuity) in the outcome at the threshold value.

[5] In these analyses, children who had access to the grant earlier and for a greater number of years are compared to those who obtained access at a later age and accordingly received the grant for a shorter time.

with policymakers and program stakeholders throughout the research process likewise increased their understanding of how and why program impacts might be observed (or not) and reduced the likelihood that they would be taken by surprise with any of the evaluation findings.

Similarly, the qualitative research, in combination with the quantitative analyses, helped to draw out some of the nuances and context for interpreting the evaluation findings (as also discussed in Chapter 3). For example, in exploring through focus groups how grant recipients expended the cash transfers, the qualitative research team found that some of the grant money was shared with adolescents and that some female adolescents used it to purchase beauty supplies and services. The media and some community members initially described these purchases as a misuse of the grant funds; however, the qualitative and quantitative analyses together shed a different light on these findings. The qualitative research had also shown that it was not uncommon for female adolescents to have older boyfriends, who would provide them with money to purchase personal items and/or food or other basic needs for the household in exchange for a sexual relationship. Stories of these relationships came not only from the adolescents but also from family and community members. The qualitative researchers suggested in their report that "the CSG could potentially serve as a substitute for the resources that this relationship brings into the household, and a pathway by which the CSG can lead to reduced adolescent risk." The quantitative analysis, in turn, found statistically significant impacts of the CSG in reducing sexual activity (or "transactional sex") and other risky behaviors among female adolescents. Thus, the qualitative research offered a plausible, alternative interpretation of these findings to policymakers and program administrators, and one that contradicted a popular view that these expenditures represented a misuse of the grant.

The use of both qualitative and quantitative methods—without strong priority given to one or the other in the dissemination of findings—likely increased the interest and appeal of the results to broader academic and policymaking audiences. In the South African context in which the CSG evaluation findings were first released, there was generally less trust in quantitative evaluation methods, which made the tight integration of the qualitative and quantitative in this research particularly important to stakeholders' openness in receiving the findings and perceptions of the study's credibility. The workshops also compelled detailed documentation of the research process and decisions made throughout its execution, which contributed to transparency in the evaluation as well as the potential for replication of this model for conducting research in future projects.

CONCLUSION

We chose to present this case study of a tightly integrated, mixed methods program evaluation in an international context because of the growing need and demand for this type of mixed methods evaluation in a rapidly expanding area of applied research. In addition, we intended to underscore some of the challenges that may be encountered in contexts where the collaboration may be multinational as well as multidisciplinary. In our own work, we have found the processes and challenges of conducting mixed methods research in international contexts to be less distinctive than one might expect. In this particular study, the internationally oriented obstacles were likely more readily circumvented or overcome through the involvement of local organizations and their staff in the research design processes as well as in the "on-the-ground" evaluation tasks such as instrument pilot-testing and data collection. Evaluation projects undertaken without the benefit of local involvement might encounter more cultural and capacity constraints in conducting the project activities.

More generally, this chapter has highlighted structures and processes by which the mixed methods work was facilitated, as well as the different functional areas where research may be strengthened by this approach. The examples presented to illustrate key points or arguments in support of this research approach were a select few among many that could have been featured. At the same time, there were limitations encountered in conducting this work that also bear further discussion or revisiting as this chapter concludes.

First, there are additional time and monetary costs to fully engaging qualitative and quantitative researchers as well as other project stakeholders over the course of the research process. In the CSG evaluation, when resources became limited because of funder budget constraints and escalating fieldwork costs for data collection, difficult decisions had to be made regarding how to preserve important elements of the evaluation plan, particularly the intended research sample sizes and the integrity of the data collection. Ultimately, the research partners contributed more time and resources than could be compensated to ensure that sufficient data could be collected (without compromising quality) and allow for adequate statistical power for detecting program impacts. This is probably not an attractive solution to this problem that other research or evaluation efforts would want to, or be in a position to, emulate.

Another consequence of the high-resource needs of this tightly integrated, mixed methods research process is that the more rapid (than expected) spend-down of resources left the integration process lacking in the analysis and interpretation of findings. There were simply not enough resources to maintain the same level of engagement of all partners that had been achieved in earlier phases of the research, such as in the design of the instrumentation. In future efforts, evaluation designers and funders may want to identify, in advance, functional areas that would be prioritized for the highest possible levels of mixed methods engagement and plan and budget for this accordingly. The particular phase of the research process where it may be more or less limiting to economize on integration and personnel resources is likely to vary from one project to another.

The mixed methods integration process is also likely to proceed more smoothly if one or more members of the research team have knowledge and experience in applying both quantitative and qualitative methods or, at a minimum, prior experience working closely with researchers applying methodologies different from their own. Although there is growing appreciation in both academic and practitioner audiences for the value of mixed methods research, it is still typical for researchers to orient their training and skills development toward one main approach or the other. Thus, if researchers skilled in applying both major types of methods are not available for a given project, it may be worthwhile to invest in training for some or all members of the research team in advance or at the outset of the project work. Some of this type of training could be built into qualitative-quantitative integration workshops (of the types that were conducted in the CSG evaluation), with more emphasis on training in the functional areas where integration is expected to be most important. It is our hope that this book will serve as a resource for mixed methods training efforts and a guide to applying fully integrated mixed methods in future policy and evaluation research.

DISCUSSION QUESTIONS

1. The Child Support Grant (CSG) evaluation team identified seven principles or objectives to guide their implementation of an integrated mixed methods approach. Which of these do you think was most important for enhancing the quality of the research? Is this a helpful or workable set of principles for most studies? What other principles or objectives might have been identified or prioritized instead?

2. The theory of change developed in this study in collaboration with program stakeholders was intentionally comprehensive but also (as a result) fairly elaborate. What are the potential advantages and disadvantages of a more concise versus a more comprehensive model for guiding the research process?

3. This study had the luxury of designing new instrumentation for data collection. In situations where original data collection is not possible and researchers instead rely on existing resources, could a similar process of joint qualitative-quantitative review and discussion of measures used be beneficial? How might this process change the approach pursued in modeling, analyzing, and interpreting data?

4. In this particular case, the project funders and stakeholders (in particular government and nongovernmental officials) were intentionally closely involved in the research design process and at various stages as the research was executed. In situations where stakeholders are less engaged or interested in the research process, what steps can researchers take to ensure that the work is still relevant, responsive, and transparent to stakeholders?

5. The qualitative and quantitative research teams in this study made substantial efforts to coordinate and integrate their work throughout the research design and execution process. What constraints did they encounter in their efforts at full integration, and what opportunities for improving the research may have been missed as a consequence?

APPLICATIONS TO YOUR OWN WORK

- Consider a policy or program evaluation that you have been involved in domestically or internationally. You would like to replicate it in an international context (or in a different country than first undertaken). Describe the research and program partners you would attempt to bring together to define the project objectives and what they would contribute to the project.

- For the project you described in the previous question or for another area of research (in an international context) that interests you, search for possible existing data resources that could be utilized in the research. Identify the strengths and limitations of the data source(s) you find. For which constructs or variables would you need to develop your own measures and collect original data?

- Assess your own training and experience in research methodologies (quantitative and/or qualitative) and describe the strengths that you would bring to an international research effort. What type of research partner(s) would you seek (in terms of qualifications and expertise) to complement your contributions to the project?

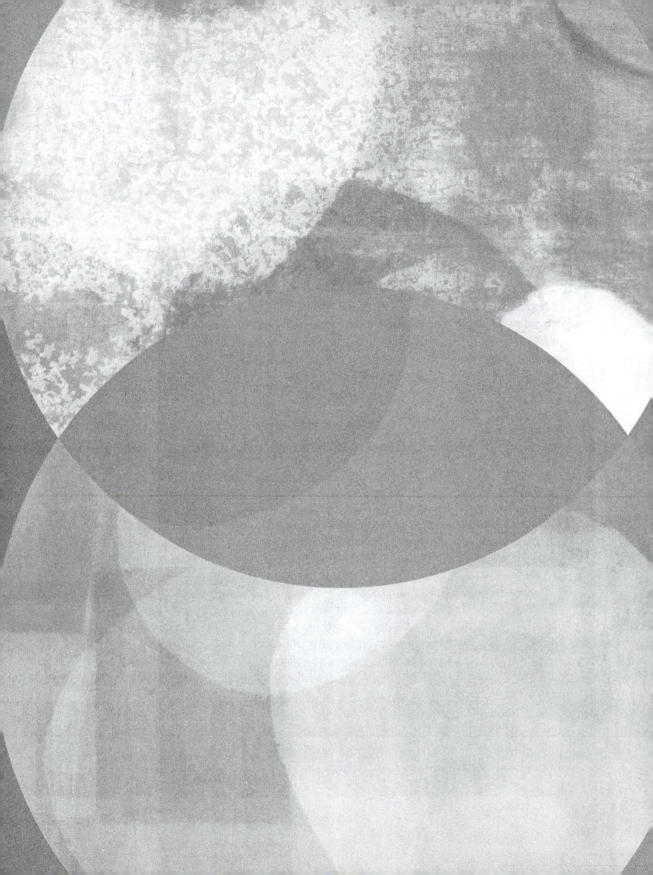

CHAPTER 8

On the Future of Fully Integrated Mixed Methods Research: Context and Common Lessons From the Cases for the Field

We recognize that some of our readers may come to this concluding chapter feeling as though we have not delivered a prescription or a series of steps for how to conduct mixed methods research. In fact, we intentionally steered clear of a stance that would have suggested there is a single best approach to undertaking mixed methods research. This book began from the broader question of not only what mixed methods research is but also how to execute it and for what ends. In Chapter 2, we presented a conceptual model for understanding what striving toward full integration of mixed methods for policy research and program evaluation might look like. Chapter 3 delved into the mechanics and logistics of integrating qualitative and quantitative methods in four main areas: research design, instrumentation design and data collection, data analysis and interpretation, and dissemination of findings. The intent of following with cases that illustrate applications of this general approach was to provide convincing accounts of how fully mixed methods research can be conducted in a variety of policy and practice settings, what they can achieve, and how the methods and tools can generate richer, more rigorous findings and insights to inform policy and program development and improvement. Although the cases foreground fundamental principles and techniques that can be used in any setting, we also fully recognize the role of broader political and organizational dynamics and other aspects of context as additional influences on the design of mixed methods research and how it unfolds "on the ground."

This chapter goes further in situating integrated mixed methods studies as an active and changing practice conducted in complex policy and political environments. We argue that context will often play a key role in shaping how a given mixed methods research design develops and that there are opportunities to be grasped when the methodological approach is allowed to be malleable in a changing environment. We begin with a synthesis of the ways in which context mattered in our mixed methods study of Supplemental Education Services (SESIQ^2), first introduced in Chapter 2, and how we managed changes in context in ways that leveraged opportunities, while taking care not to compromise study objectives. As part of this discussion, we consider the broader set of economic and political developments driving these challenges. We then turn to a summary of cross-cutting patterns across the various cases and what they teach us about the power of fully integrated mixed methods research in applied policy research and program evaluation. We conclude by raising questions about how methods training at universities might be restructured to support the strengthening and application of fully integrated mixed methods work.

HOW CONTEXT MATTERS

There are fundamental principles of integrated mixed methods research that can be applied productively in diverse settings. That said, as in policy implementation, context matters in fully integrated mixed methods work. The contexts in which a study is conducted can have a mediating influence on *how* and how well research is conducted. We can try to control for aspects of that context in our sampling and modeling, while being alert to the broader picture of how our methodological choices in a given context influence the research we undertake, the findings we derive, and how we can best communicate them.

In this section, we look specifically at three contextual features (policy and institutional history, formal and informal governance, and inter- and intra-organizational context for implementation) that created particular challenges and opportunities for our work in studying Supplemental Educational Services. We argue that recognizing and taking aspects of this context into our research strengthened rather than detracted from our study objectives and accomplishments.

Policy and Institutional History

The institutional context for a policy study can be characterized across a number of dimensions—political, social, historical, as well as the interaction of these forces in a policy space. We focus here on the "environment of ideas" surrounding our work—embedded in policy and institutional history—and how they shape expectations about the implementation of a program or policy, the "problem" that it is intended to solve, and how policy and program impacts will be measured. We also examine the big poles around which policy outcomes are debated—in our case, the relative importance of equity and efficiency—and how lines in the debate can move together or apart over time. For example, Title I of the Elementary and Secondary Education Act (ESEA) was enacted into law in 1965 as part of a new chapter in federal programming known as the War on Poverty programs. In this historically important era, accompanied by major civil rights legislation, these programs converged around the idea that the federal government could play a significant role in influencing educational outcomes for disadvantaged students (in the case of ESEA, through the distribution of federal dollars to schools serving high concentrations of students in poverty).

Accordingly, in the context of discussions about equal opportunities and rights for all and a more ambitious role for federal policymaking in promoting these goals, early national studies of Title I programs reflected the movement that tied new federal money to *input* metrics of policy success, such as the number of low-income students served by the program and evidence that program funds were being used to serve these students. At the same time, the massive new outlays of federal spending on education and social welfare programs were compelling calls for greater public accountability for program outcomes and efficiency, and the field of public administration was advocating new forms of technical and systems analysis for evaluating the efficiency of public programs (e.g., the Planning, Programming, and Budgeting System; zero-based budgeting; and management by objectives). The discourse on accountability correspondingly shifted more toward efficiency and metrics of policy results based on individual as well as organizational levels of performance.

The "new public management" reforms of the 1990s took these administrative developments a step further, aiming to change both organizational incentives and individual motives in ways that mimicked the private sector. The impetus for these reforms included increasing public demands for a more efficient or business-like government; the corresponding development of new public-private partnerships through devolution and contracting out of public service responsibilities to local quasi-public and private partners; and rising expectations for a more responsive, customer-oriented service delivery approach and for more information on government performance. The U.S. No Child Left Behind (NCLB) Act of 2001, following in the wake of these reforms, sought to "close the achievement gap [in public education] with accountability, flexibility, and choice." In a White House report, President George W. Bush (2002) described the priorities of the Act as "based on the fundamental notion that an enterprise works best when responsibility is placed closest to the most important activity of the enterprise, when those responsible are given greatest latitude and support, and when those responsible are held accountable for producing results" (p. 2).

The NCLB Act accordingly required annual testing of public school students in Grades 3 through 8 and tied individual student test scores to a progressive and significant series of sanctions and incentives for schools identified as not making adequate yearly progress (based on those scores). Concern for equity was now embodied in measures that assessed gaps in student achievement between subgroups of students based on race and economic disadvantage. This shift in education policy continued when President Barack Obama took office for a first (and then second) term and championed a policy agenda that assessed the value of educational institutions based on student test scores and graduation rates and stepped up their incentives to perform through the Race to the Top federal funding initiative.

Simultaneously, far-reaching, high-stakes discussions (within and outside of policymaking circles and academia) were taking place about the need for common principles in education research that were based on scientific "gold" standards. This was reflected in the request for research proposals that we responded to in 2009, which specifically called for experimental and quasi-experimental designs that were sufficiently powered to identify program impacts. We therefore intentionally sought in our study the participation of large urban districts with sizable numbers of students eligible for Supplemental Educational Services, which would allow us to construct comparison groups of eligible, nonparticipating students and give power to our estimates of program effects. Although in our proposal we described in detail how our mixed methods research design would unfold in multiple phases, we were aware that external review criteria would be focused primarily on our ability to establish the rigor of our quasi-experimental methods. Had we been responding to a call for federally funded research at a different historical and political moment, we may have given equal or more priority to other measures of the policy's valued added or sought participation from a broader range of educational institutions (e.g., small to medium-sized districts as well).

Over the course of our study, our research funders and stakeholders came to more fully appreciate how the tight integration of qualitative and quantitative work in our study enabled us to build depth and texture into our understanding of student participation (and implications for equity), as well as to generate rich insights about program effectiveness and efficiency and the factors that aided or limited program impacts. For example, the fieldwork provided a lens for us to see which students (already registered in the program) were getting significant "doses" of the intervention and what was driving variation in their treatment levels. As such, the institutional and organizational factors that might typically be viewed as outside of our control, or as something merely to control, moved to the center of our research focus. Our tightly integrated, mixed methods design enabled us to respond to what we were observing in the policy and practice environment (i.e., in the implementation of the intervention) in methodologically rich and rigorous ways that ultimately generated more useful and impactful research findings for a diverse range of research stakeholders.

Formal and Informal Governance Context

In policy research, the governance context—separate from but not necessarily unrelated to the policy and institutional context discussed earlier—has implications for the design of a fully mixed methods study, in terms of both formal (e.g., centralized or decentralized) and emergent or informal (e.g., lateral or networked) structures of governance arrangements that may shape the policy or program implementation landscape. For example, the public education governance structure in the United States is a highly decentralized and fragmented system, with funding and authority over instructional programming devolved by the federal government to state educational agencies and in turn transferred by state law to the local level.

This context engendered both challenges and opportunities in our use of mixed methods. Although in accordance with the law (NCLB Act), evidence of policy impact was sought at the level of *student* (achievement) outcomes, we recognized (and therefore designed our research to capture) how students' receipt of the tutoring intervention was mediated by overlapping state and local governance contexts. For example, although federal policy set the stage for the reform, states, school districts, and the schools within them filtered and shaped how the policy was implemented. Indeed, implementation of the intervention varied widely on both formal dimensions (i.e., where authority for decision making was situated within a state and/or school district) and informal ones, the latter depending on how state and local educational agencies attempted to guide or discipline the private market of tutoring providers.

The design of our mixed methods study of the implementation and impact of Supplemental Educational Services reflected this formal and informal governance context in several ways. For example, to explore how (and to what extent) program and policy characteristics were linked to student outcomes, we mapped back from the individual student level to decisions made and policy actions taken at the provider, school, district, state, and federal levels. The system in this case consisted of a labyrinth of interrelationships across decentralized levels of governance. In addition, conducting our research across five school districts—the core cases that defined the basic structure of our research project—we were able to look both within and across each case to attend to how state and district policy context mattered in implementation. In interviews with state-level administrators, we were able to grasp their aims and intent in regulating the work of districts and monitoring providers, and this, in turn, contributed to our understanding of district-level policy actions and their interactions with tutoring providers. Using our mixed methods approach to zoom in on key aspects of these relationships, we also learned from interviews with district staff that they had little capacity to assess vendors' quality of instruction. This suggested to our team that state- and provider-level decisions were key to understanding instructional quality in the intervention, and we adjusted our research design to build more robust tools (e.g., the observation instrument) and empirical methods for understanding not only provider effectiveness but also the leverage points through which the system could influence instructional quality.

Rising interest in this type of mixed methods work has come in the context of political change, including mounting criticism of public agencies and calls for more accountability and transparency, as well as growing support for greater involvement of for-profit entities in the design and delivery of social programs, including public education. For example, if public schools were failing to increase student learning, it was argued that nongovernmental agencies might be able to do better and that traditional government functions should be outsourced in order to test this theory. These ideas were "baked" into the design of the policy that we were studying, where, by law, districts were required to contract with for-profit and nonprofit providers of out-of-school-time tutoring rather than providing these services themselves. School districts and state departments of education were strictly limited in regulating these providers in the sense that they could not restrict rate-setting or require providers to design their programming in ways that complemented the day-school curriculum.

This legislated hands-off role for government entities in program implementation also posed challenges for the fieldwork component of our study, particularly in negotiating access to provider sites where tutoring services were delivered. For example, providers were hesitant to participate in research that would offer a 360-degree view of their program's characteristics and potentially expose their business model (i.e., how program characteristics were linked to outcomes). The production of information in our study on provider effects on student achievement also posed challenges for providers who conducted their own internal product evaluations and were concerned about how the dissemination of our study findings might affect their competitiveness. Our study findings also at times confronted information collected from providers and released by state educational agencies or the conclusions of studies commissioned by states. In an environment where it was assumed that low-quality services would be weeded out by competition and parental choice (and that the market would govern itself), having reliable information on provider effectiveness that was accessible to parents was key, yet an in-depth, independent evaluation of instructional quality and program effectiveness was not equally appreciated by all program stakeholders.

At the same time, we also saw opportunities in this context, given that provider actions mediated student-level outcomes in very substantive ways. In a context in which nongovernmental agencies had significant influence over program design, the audience for our dissemination had to include these for-profit and nonprofit providers of Supplemental Educational Services. We made sure that providers knew when we would be making our study findings public and scheduled separate webinars for providers to discuss the findings. We also responded to providers' individual requests for explanations of findings via personal phone calls and emails. Over time, these strategies had the effect of strengthening providers' confidence in our methods, building trust in the Research-to-Practice Collaborative, and opening up more opportunities for us to see and measure provider practices. In several instances, apprehensive providers that might otherwise have declined to engage with the study reported that their concerns were allayed after conversations during which we described our mixed methods approach and our interest in understanding implementation as well as impact.

Intra- and Inter-Organizational Context for Implementation

In designing our study, consistent with organizational theory, we predicted that organizational context would be a mediating influence on program implementation and effectiveness. The school districts participating in our study had varying degrees of human, financial, and political capital to support our shared research objectives, and the ebb and flow of these resources exerted a dynamic influence on what we were able to do.

For example, all districts experienced some degree of staff turnover, which at times made it difficult for us to secure administrative and student data that were essential to the analysis in a timely manner. Time and personnel resources that might have been spent conducting research were instead expended in making calls to districts to establish new connections, to determine who was in charge (or who had left), and to decide who could assist in providing access to the data. We also encountered varying levels of knowledge and experience with research methods among district staff, which affected our interactions in all phases of the study and some of our methodological choices as well. Some district staff understood our standards for qualitative research (and one was even in the midst of a Ph.D. program using qualitative methods), whereas other staff within the same district viewed the qualitative work as an add-on, referring to it as anecdotal and "soft" data. In another example, our early efforts to apply a regression-discontinuity approach for identifying program impacts depended on district staff's consistently following an established assignment rule (of their choice) for prioritizing students for access to Supplemental Educational Services. Because the districts employed different strategies for enrolling students (some of which allowed providers to directly enroll students as well) and frequently faced last-minute funding and administrative constraints, the necessary level of control (and understanding of the importance of fidelity to the assignment rules) was not attained, precluding the use of this method.

Over time, we learned more about how to work with differing degrees of capacity and resources in the districts, without compromising our own standards for mixed methods research. This was essential if we were to achieve our goals of identifying district-level actions and key leverage points for improving programs, while simultaneously translating our research findings for stakeholders in ways that they could immediately put them into practice. As described in Chapter 4, we developed research tools that fully explained our methods in a user-friendly manner, and the discussion of methods became part and parcel of every research briefing and public webinar that we conducted. We defined what we meant by mixed methods research, how we conducted it, and how our methods contributed to the project's objectives and the aims of the intervention itself.

These conversations also created a space where the project stakeholders felt comfortable talking about their own research experiences, either in doing research or as a consumer of research. Doing research became part of a shared conversation—not something we were doing to them, but a principle or interest we held in common. The outcomes of these efforts included direct investments by some districts in extending the work (beyond the planned study), allowance for additional longitudinal data or better comparison data, and offers to take the research in new directions. It also meant that districts increasingly felt comfortable turning to us for help in obtaining or understanding other kinds of research, other studies being conducted on similar kinds of programs, or others' research on Supplemental Educational Services. In effect, their knowledge base for evaluating their own programs was expanded through our joint research efforts.

In summary, three specific dimensions of context—institutional, governance, and organizational—created specific challenges to our integration of qualitative and quantitative methods in the research, as well as for communication among researchers and policymakers (critical to the success of this approach). These challenges also often had implications for our research budget and the allocation of personnel resources, both of which required adjustments over time. For example, the delays in obtaining access to the district test score data ultimately placed considerable pressure on quantitative research team members to work intensively in the short time between data arrival and the start of the next school year (when districts needed results on provider effects for decision making). If a research appointment had to be extended to complete work, as a result of these delays, the costs had to be shifted from another area of the budget. Research team members went to considerable lengths to conserve resources wherever possible—reducing travel costs, minimizing the outsourcing of services such as transcription, and offering uncompensated principal investigator time—while leveraging other sources of funding to support additional research assistance and research dissemination at conferences.

The examples offered here were also intended to provide guidance on how one might design and conduct mixed methods research within volatile (and sometimes political) environments and to do so in a way that strengthens rather than detracts from the goals of mixed methods policy research and program evaluation. The tensions and opportunities that we have described in this chapter (illustrated through our joint work) were also threaded throughout the other case studies included in this book. We now turn to another purpose of this book, which is to draw out some of the larger principles that guide mixed methods work and encapsulate a few of the collective lessons that these different cases offer.

BROADER LESSONS FOR THE FIELD

Researcher Credibility and Stakeholder Confidence

The cases discussed in this book illustrate how mixed methods research can enhance research credibility and stakeholder confidence. Existing research and conventional wisdom suggest that much policy research has been largely ineffective in conveying findings to policymakers in ways that they will be trusted and used. Although there is limited research examining the practices that contribute to credibility and usefulness of mixed methods findings for policymakers, there is a growing understanding that practitioners are more likely to use research where researchers act strategically to make it relevant for the real-time problems they face. For example, in the study of child support in Wisconsin, profiled in Chapter 6, state and county administrators were fully engaged with the research team in the design and planning for the program to reduce child support debt and for the mixed methods evaluation of the program. The entire effort was motivated by the state's need to reduce growing child support debt levels, as tracked by federal performance measures, and careful attention was given to existing policy efforts in other states so as to devise a solution to this problem that was both innovative and viable as well as a good fit with the state's particular political context. In the study of class size reduction described in Chapter 5, there were partisan battles over reauthorization of the program. Republicans argued that state funds would be better spent on programs with more of a proven track record, whereas Democrats argued in support of the value added of the program for the state's economically disadvantaged students. In this high-stakes climate, policymakers appeared to have little patience for qualitative data and were hungry for numbers that they could use to bolster their arguments. Yet the tight integration in methods generated knowledge that deepened the debate, reframing the problem from "What works?" to "Under what conditions are gains most likely?"

Besides helping to frame the research questions at hand in ways that will generate the kinds of results that policymakers can act on, researchers also need to choose tools of dissemination that make it easy for research stakeholders to consume the findings. In our study of the implementation and impact of Supplemental Educational Services, we disseminated the research findings in short, colorful briefs for parents (to help them choose providers); in booklets used by the districts at the start of the school year to share information on provider performance to parents and school-based staff (e.g., principals); in in-person briefings and cross-district webinars for our district partners, as well as public webinars for a broader audience; and in policy briefs for federal, state, and local officials. In the case of the child support debt reduction program, the evaluation findings were disseminated at professional conferences for county child support officials, as well as at the National Child Support Enforcement Association conference and in invited presentations for other state child support agencies. Tight integration in the study of class size reduction meant that researchers could easily translate findings into a suite of products (e.g., two-page policy briefs, professional development materials, journal articles) that were accessible to various stakeholders with varying degrees of expertise. For a given project, the tools and venues for dissemination will necessarily have to take into consideration the different contexts for mixed methods research that we've discussed, as well as timing for important program or policy decision making (e.g., program funding decisions, legislative reauthorizations, etc.).

Sometimes, for reasons beyond the control of the researchers or other stakeholders, the availability of new findings may be at odds with the optimal timing for their use. In these circumstances, researchers need to attend to how their products can be made relevant and enduring beyond their release date. In the South African Child Support Grant program evaluation, the research findings were conveyed in a national press conference, but this was at a time when the country was experiencing labor strikes and discord. They resurfaced in national policy debates almost 2 years later when the federal government was in a position to consider their implications for extending and expanding the program funding. We argue, as seen in patterns of practice across our cases, that employing a fully integrated, mixed methods approach contributes to the durability and usefulness of the research findings. For example, we have described how school districts that are under state or other waivers from the provisions of the NCLB Act and are no longer required to operate Supplemental Educational Services programs are actively using the research evidence from our study to inform the design of new interventions for the same populations of disadvantaged students.

In future work and in training users of fully integrated mixed methods approaches, there needs to be explicit attention as to how mixed methods studies can be designed to support policy impact. Currently, this type of training is rarely offered in a classroom and is more likely to come through experience with policy and program research. Research investigators need to make a priority of the use of mixed methods to enhance communication with policymakers and other research stakeholders and develop strategies (as described in this book) to support stakeholder collaboration in interpreting and using research findings.

Transparency and Replication

The cases also illustrate how the processes of fully integrating mixed methods in research can contribute to greater transparency in how evidence is generated and validated. This, in turn, can support replication of a given research or program model by other researchers and stakeholders. For example, in the Child Support Grant evaluation, researchers held methods workshops (with program stakeholders) that required detailed documentation of the research process and decisions made throughout its execution. Tight and systematic communication (via workshops and meetings) aided stakeholders and researchers in laying out strategies for conducting and sequencing the qualitative and quantitative research (and for addressing challenges confronted along the way), making it easier for future research efforts to replicate this model. Likewise, in the mixed methods study of transfer and completion rates in Latino-serving community colleges, tight integration of methods (in particular, integration of qualitative and quantitative work in data collection and dissemination) enabled researchers to develop an interactive website where research participants could see how their organization's equity score compared to those of other institutions participating in the study, and then look behind these numbers at vignettes that brought the experiences and voices of students into close view. Rather than having to call or schedule a briefing with study directors in order to access up-to-date study findings, study participants could look on the website and, in that interactive space, download and provide feedback on the external validity of instrumentation (e.g., survey measures) among other instrumentation.

Efforts to make research methods and tools used in research transparent can also contribute to their wider use after a study's end. For example, we made available the observation instrument employed in our study of Supplemental Educational Services to school districts (and to the broader public via our project website) and provided support to district staff for using this tool in future district monitoring of out-of-school time services. And in the development of a child support debt reduction program, the state of Texas was able to directly use documentation and evaluation products from the Wisconsin demonstration program—which included an operations manual, monitoring tools, reports, and other rich descriptions of program processes, as well as analyses of their implications for program impacts—to launch its own arrears payment incentive program (and an accompanying evaluation) in a small fraction of the time that Wisconsin stakeholders spent developing the program. In this particular case, the state of Wisconsin had delayed expansion of the pilot program, and state administrators and researchers were eager to share their work and to see if another state would replicate the pilot program's results.

The examples discussed in the previous paragraph show how these types of investments made by research teams to promote transparency and support replication can contribute to stakeholders' engagement in and use of the research, as well as their capacity for program improvement both during and after a research project has concluded. In future work and training of mixed methods researchers, a strong emphasis should be placed on ensuring that mechanisms (e.g., public websites for research dissemination) and strategies (e.g., careful documentation of research processes and design/methodological decisions) are adopted to support transparency in all phases of the research. In principle, transparency is a necessary but not sufficient condition for replication. Future work might also consider what tools for promoting transparency in mixed methods research are most conducive to replication, and what other factors—such as dissemination of research at the right times or to the right people or in specific contexts—would make replication more feasible. For research projects with tight finances, future research might also explore what low-budget options (technological and other) are most effective in facilitating transparency and broad dissemination of findings, without compromising research integrity or jeopardizing research relationships while the work is in progress.

Effective Use of Research Resources

Indeed, at a time when state and local budgets for education and social programs are being cut by 20% or more, the use of fully integrated mixed methods research can contribute to more effective use of research resources. Since the deep economic recession of 2007, researchers and policymakers have been under even greater pressure to demonstrate the cost-effectiveness and returns on investment of their research endeavors and policy initiatives. For example, in the case of the child support debt reduction program (see Chapter 6), state program administrators and researchers intentionally chose a pilot program site where they expected implementation to be challenging, and where demographics and debt levels resembled those of other high-need counties. The research effort carefully documented challenges and problems encountered in program implementation and engaged with policymakers to develop solutions to them (e.g., new strategies for outreach and communication with eligible noncustodial parents), so that the research resources were contributing to better returns on the public investment in program resources, as well as knowledge of program impacts. In effect, evaluation was employed as an operational and management tool that could point to what was working (or not) and inform ongoing policy development and use of budgetary resources.

More generally, the fully integrated mixed methods approach, as applied in this case and others, facilitated the types of formative and targeted feedback that are critical to program improvement and valued by policymakers and program funders. Integration of methods at every step of the research process was also important to minimizing duplication of research effort or disjointedness that can limit opportunities for feedback or leveraging of knowledge and insights across methods. For example, the pooling of qualitative and quantitative expertise in the design of survey instruments in the Child Support Grant program evaluation was key to ensuring that essential data on program processes and outcomes were collected, while simultaneously staying with time budgets and still allowing opportunities for cross-checking patterns in the data. And tight integration of qualitative and quantitative approaches in the design and development phase of the class size reduction study freed up resources that enabled the team to expand the number and depth of exemplary case studies over time and thereby build greater understanding of the conditions supporting what works. As information was acquired in one aspect of this study, it became part of the integrated design, so that the doing and learning from research became inseparable. Thus, across the cases, integration of methods in various stages of the research process became integral to efficient deployment of research resources. This realization is important, because qualitative methods have at times been criticized as labor and resource intensive and thus have been more likely to be cut from a design in the face of budget constraints. Although more work is needed in this area, the cases in our book suggest that the priorities and practices of fully integrated mixed methods can align (as opposed to conflict) with institutional and societal emphasis on efficiency and productivity.

CONCLUDING THOUGHTS

We fully expect the demand for mixed methods research to grow as government agencies are being asked to do more with less and to justify ongoing investments in established programs or to outsource their activities. Much research has focused on whether outsourcing of government functions saves money. Mixed methods research can help us look more systematically and deeply at the practices of public-private partnerships and third-party vendors and their management by government. A continuing need for capacity building within governing bodies to bring about policy and program improvement and implement reforms that promote equity and efficiency in social programs is also placing additional calls on mixed methods research. Tight integration of methods can help to shed light on whether and how these policy reforms and developments further the public purposes of social programs and broader societal goals (such as the equitable distribution of resources), while also striving for efficiency. At the same time, government funding of research—at sufficient levels for the type of high-quality mixed methods research that we have described here—has been lagging behind the demand for policy and program evaluations. Too often, expectations for what can be achieved in these research efforts far exceed the resources allocated, or more is asked of the research team during the study period without the provision of additional financial support.

By examining the application of tightly integrated mixed methods research across a range of settings, this book has aimed to identify practices around which these studies converge, and to consider (1) how integration of methods across multiple stages of the research process provides a robust methodological foundation for future applied policy and evaluation research, and (2) how communication and collaboration among researchers and policymakers throughout the research process strengthens the application of these methods and furthers the broader aims of relevance and impact. In addition, we sought to show how various dimensions of context play a role in shaping our choices in the design and execution of mixed methods research, and how this context could be drawn into the research design and leveraged to generate insights about how and why program implementation and impacts vary systematically across settings.

The future utility of a fully integrated mixed methods approach and its potential for broader use in policy and evaluation research also depends, however, on the institutional context in which our work is situated, that is, of the academic institutions and philanthropic organizations that host and support our work. If mixed methods research is to gain additional traction, a shift in thinking may be required about the value of qualitative work in policy research and methods training and its connection to the dominant quantitative methods. From our vantage point and those of many others, qualitative analysis has a valued place on its own, and it is also increasingly seen as an equal contributor in mixed methods research designs. As demonstrated by the cases in this book, tight integration of methods can be associated with highly efficient use of research resources, increased reliability and validity of inferences from research, and greater credibility, relevance, and use of research findings in policy and practice settings. At the same time, the polarization of methods is still powerfully embedded in the culture of academic institutions, as reflected in graduate training programs across the disciplines that specialize in either quantitative or qualitative methods. To continue to make advances in the application of mixed methods work, we need training programs that will build capacity among the next generation of policy researchers in both qualitative and quantitative methods and the strategies described here for facilitating their tight integration. We have yet to identify exemplars for such a methodological training model in academia, but we are hoping this book will help to spur and guide their development.

References

Bartfeld, J. (2003). *Forgiveness of state-owed child support arrears* (Special Report No. 84). Madison, WI: Institute for Research on Poverty.

Baum, F. (1995). Researching public health: Behind the qualitative-quantitative methodological debate. *Social Science and Medicine, 40*(4), 459–468.

Bazeley, P. (2003). "Computerized Data Analysis for Mixed Methods Research" in Tashakkori and Teddlie Eds. Handbook of Mixed Methods in Social and Behavioral Research. SAGE Publications.

Bazeley, P., & Jackson, K (Eds.). (2013) Qualitative data analysis with NVivo, Sage Publications.

Bensimon, E. M. (2007). The underestimated significance of practitioner knowledge in the scholarship on student success. *Review of Higher Education, 30*(4), 441–469.

Bensimon, E. M., & Dowd, A. C. (2009, Winter). Dimensions of the transfer choice gap: Experiences of Latina and Latino students who navigated transfer pathways. *Harvard Educational Review,* pp. 632–658.

Bensimon, E. M., & Dowd, A. C. (2012). *Developing the capacity of faculty to become institutional agents for Latinos in STEM.* Los Angeles: University of Southern California.

Bensimon, E. M., Dowd, A. C., Alford, H., & Trapp, F. (2007). *Missing 87: A study of the "transfer gap" and "choice gap."* Long Beach, CA: Long Beach City College; Los Angeles: University of Southern California, Center for Urban Education.

Bensimon, E. M., & Malcom, L. E. (2012). *Confronting equity issues on campus: Implementing the Equity Scorecard in theory and practice.* Sterling, VA: Stylus.

Bensimon, E. M., Polkinghorne, D., Bauman, G., & Vallejo, E. (2004). Doing research that makes a difference. *Journal of Higher Education, 75*(1), 104–126.

Bryman, A. (2006). Integrating quantitative and qualitative research: How is it done? *Qualitative Research, 6*(1), 97–113.

Burch, P., Theoharis, G., & Rauscher, E. (2010). Class size reduction in practice investigating the influence of the elementary school principal. *Educational Policy, 24*(2), 330–358.

Bush, G. W. (2002). *No Child Left Behind* (White House report). Retrieved from http://www .rethinkingschools.org/static/special_reports/bushplan/no-child-left-behind.pdf

Cancian, M., & Meyer, D. R. (2005). *Child support in the United States: An uncertain and irregular income source?* (Discussion Paper No. 1298–05). Madison, WI: Institute for Research on Poverty.

Caracelli, V. J., & Greene, J. C. (1997). Crafting mixed-method evaluation designs. *New Directions for Evaluation, 1997*(74), 19–32.

Chase, M. M., Bensimon, E. M., Shieh, L. T., Jones, T., & Dowd, A. C. (2013). Constraints and opportunities for practitioner agency in STEM programs in Hispanic serving community colleges. In R. T. Palmer & J. L. Wood (Eds.), *Community colleges and STEM: Examining underrepresented racial and ethnic minorities* (pp. 172–192). New York, NY: Routledge.

Clandinin, J. D., & Connelly, M. (2004). Knowledge, narrative and self-study. In J. J. Loughran, M. L. Hamilton, V. K. LaBoskey, & T. Russell (Eds.), *International handbook of self-study of teaching and teacher education practices* (pp. 575–600). Dordrecht, Netherlands: Springer.

Clarke, P. N., & Yaros, P. S. (1988). Research blenders: Commentary and response. Commentary: Transitions to new methodologies in nursing sciences. *Nursing Science Quarterly, 1*(4), 147–149.

Collins, K. M. T., Onwuegbuzie, A. J., & Sutton, I. L. (2006). A model incorporating the rationale and purpose for conducting mixed methods research in special education and beyond. *Learning Disabilities: A Contemporary Journal, 4*(1), 67–100.

Cook, P. J., & Ludwig, J. (2006). Aiming for evidence-based gun policy. *Journal of Policy Analysis and Management, 25,* 691–735.

Creswell, J. W. (1999). Mixed-method research: Introduction and application. In G. J. Cizek (Ed.), *Handbook of educational policy* (pp. 455–472). San Diego, CA: Academic Press.

Creswell, J. W., & Plano Clark, V. L. (2011). *Designing and conducting mixed methods research.* (2nd ed.) Thousand Oaks, CA: Sage.

Creswell, J. W., Plano Clark, V. L., Guttman, M., & Hanson, W. (2003). Advanced mixed methods research designs. In A. Tashakkori & C. Teddlie (Eds.), *Handbook of mixed methods in social & behavioral research* (pp. 209–240). Thousand Oaks, CA: Sage.

Dowd, A. C. (2010). Improving transfer access for low-income community college students. In A. Kezar (Ed.), *Recognizing and serving low-income students in postsecondary education: An examination of institutional policies, practices, and culture* (pp. 217–231). New York, NY: Routledge.

Dowd, A. C. (2012). Developing supportive STEM community college to four-year college and university transfer ecosystems. In S. Olson & J. B. Labov (Eds.), *Community college in the evolving STEM education landscape: Summary of a summit.* Washington, DC: National Academies Press.

Dowd, A. C., Bensimon, E. M., Gabbard, G., et al. (2006). *Transfer access to elite colleges and universities in the United States: Threading the needle of the American dream.* Lansdowne, VA: Jack Kent Cooke Foundation.

Dowd, A. C., Bishop, R., Bensimon, E. M., & Witham, K. (2012). Accountability for equity in post-secondary education. In K. S. Gallagher, R. Goodyear, D. J. Brewer, & R. Rueda (Eds.), *Urban education: A model for leadership and policy* (pp. 170–185). New York, NY: Routledge.

Dowd, A. C., Cheslock, J. J., & Melguizo, T. (2008). Transfer access from community colleges and the distribution of elite higher education. *Journal of Higher Education, 79*(4), 442–472.

Dowd, A. C., & Malcom, L. E. (2012). *Reducing undergraduate debt to increase Latina and Latino participation in STEM professions.* Los Angeles: University of Southern California.

Dowd, A. C., Malcom, L. E., & Bensimon, E. M. (2009). *Benchmarking the success of Latino and Latina students in STEM to achieve national graduation goals.* Los Angeles: University of Southern California.

Dowd, A. C., Malcom, L. E., & Macias, E. E. (2010). *Improving transfer access to STEM bachelor's degrees at Hispanic-serving institutions through the America COMPETES Act.* Los Angeles: University of Southern California.

Dowd, A. C., & Melguizo, T. (2008). Socioeconomic stratification of community college transfer access in the 1980s and 1990s: Evidence from HS&B and NELS. *Review of Higher Education, 31*(4), 377–400.

Dowd, A. C., Pak, J. H., & Bensimon, E. M. (2013). The role of institutional agents in promoting transfer. *Education Policy Analysis Archives, 21*(15), 1–44.

Dowd, A. C., Sawatzky, M., Rall, R. M., & Bensimon, E. M. (2013). Action research: An essential practice for 21st century assessment. In R. T. Palmer, D. C. Maramba, & M. Gasman (Eds.), *Fostering success of ethnic and racial minorities in STEM: The role of minority serving institutions* (pp. 149–167). New York, NY: Routledge.

Driscoll, D. L., Appiah-Yeboah, A., Salib, P., & Rupert, D. J. (2007). Merging qualitative and quantitative data in mixed methods research: How to and why not. *Ecological and Environmental Anthropology, 3*(1), 18–28.

Fry, G., Chantavanich, S., & Chantavanich, A. (1981). Merging quantitative and qualitative research techniques: Toward a new research paradigm. *Anthropology & Education Quarterly, 12*(2), 145–158.

Grall, T. S. (2009). *Custodial mothers and fathers and their child support: 2007* (Current Population Report No. P60–237). Washington, DC: U.S. Census Bureau.

Graue, E., Rauscher, E., & Sherfinski, M. (2009). The synergy of class size reduction and classroom quality. *Elementary School Journal, 110*(2), 178–201.

Graue, M. E., & Sherfinski, M. (2011). The view from the lighted schoolhouse: Conceptualizing home-school relations within a class size reduction reform. *American Journal of Education, 117*(2), 267–297.

Greene, J. C. (2007). *Mixed methods in social inquiry.* San Francisco, CA: Jossey-Bass.

Greene, J. C., & Caracelli, V. J. (Eds.). (1997). Advances in mixed-method evaluation: The challenges and benefits of integrating diverse paradigms. *New Directions for Evaluation, 1997*(74).

Greene, J. C., Caracelli, V. J., & Graham, W. F. (1989). Toward a conceptual framework for mixed-method evaluation designs. *Educational Evaluation and Policy Analysis, 11*(3), 255–274.

Gueron, J. M., & Rolston, H. (2013). *Fighting for reliable evidence.* New York, NY: Russell Sage Foundation.

Happ, M. B. (2009). Mixed methods in gerontological research: Do the qualitative and quantitative data "touch"? *Research in Gerontological Nursing, 2*(2), 122–127.

Heinrich, C. J. (2007). Evidence-based policy and performance management: Challenges and prospects in two parallel movements. *American Review of Public Administration, 37*(3), 255–277.

Heinrich, C. J., & Brill, R. (2014). *Stopped in the name of the law: Administrative burden and its implications for cash transfer program effectiveness* (Working paper). University of Texas at Austin.

Heinrich, C. J., Burkhardt, B., & Shager, H. (2011). Reducing child support debt and its consequences: Can forgiveness benefit all? *Journal of Policy Analysis and Management, 30*(4), 755–774.

Heinrich, C.J., Shager, H., Rothe, I., & Cancian, M. (2005, December). *Families Forward: Child Support Arrears Forgiveness Program and evaluation: Implementation report.* Madison, WI: Institute for Research on Poverty.

Hennessey, J. A., & Venohr, J. (2000). *Exploring options: Child support arrears forgiveness and passthrough of payments to custodial families* (Report to the Minnesota Department of Human Services Child Support Enforcement Division). Denver, CO: Policy Studies, Inc.

Hesse-Biber, S., & Johnson, R. B. (2013). Coming at things differently: Future directions of possible engagement with mixed methods research. *Journal of Mixed Methods Research, 7*(2), 103–109.

Honig, M. I. (2005). *New directions in educational policy implementation: Confronting complexity.* Albany: State University of New York Press.

Jang, E. E., McDougall, D. E., Pollon, D., Herbert, M., & Russell, P. (2008). Integrative mixed methods data analytic strategies in research on school success in challenging circumstances. *Journal of Mixed Methods Research, 2*(3), 221–247.

Johnson, B. R., & Onwuegbuzie, A. J. (2004). Mixed methods research: A research paradigm whose time has come. *Educational Researcher, 33*(7), 14–26.

Kowalski, T. (2009). Need to address evidence-based practice in educational administration. *Education Administration Quarterly, 45*(3), 351–374.

Madey, D. L. (1982). Some benefits of integrating qualitative and quantitative methods in program evaluation, with illustrations. *Educational Evaluation and Policy Analysis, 4*(2), 223–236.

Malcom, L. E., Dowd, A. C., & Yu, T. (2010). *Tapping HSI-STEM funds to improve Latina and Latino access to the STEM professions.* Los Angeles: University of Southern California.

Melguizo, T., & Dowd, A. C. (2009). Baccalaureate success of transfers and rising four-year college juniors. *Teachers College Record, 111*(1), 55–89.

Morgan, D. L. (2014). *Integrating qualitative & quantitative methods: A pragmatic approach.* Thousand Oaks, CA: Sage.

Morgan, D. L. (1998). Practical strategies for combining qualitative and quantitative methods: Applications to health research. *Qualitative Health Research, 8*(3), 362–376.

(Not sure if these are the same author, though, I imagine it is.)

No Child Left Behind (NCLB) Act of 2001, Pub. L. No. 107-110, § 115, Stat. 1425 (2002).

Office of Child Support Enforcement (2000). *State IV-D program flexibility with respect to low income obligors* (PIQ-00–03). Washington, DC: Author.

Onwuegbuzie, A. J., & Leech, N. L. (2005). On becoming a pragmatic researcher: The importance of combining quantitative and qualitative research methodologies. *International Journal of Social Research Methodology, 8*(5), 375–387.

Ovwigho, P. C., Saunders, C., & Born, C. E. (2007). Arrears forgiveness: A strategy for child support's $100 billion problem? *Journal of Policy Practice, 6*, 23–44.

Pate, D. (2002). An ethnographic inquiry into the life experiences of African American fathers with children on W-2. In D. R. Meyer & M. Cancian (Eds.), *W-2 child support demonstration evaluation: Report on nonexperimental analyses* (pp. 29–118). Madison, WI: Institute for Research on Poverty.

Pearson, J., & Griswold, E. A. (2001). *New approaches to child support arrears: A survey of state policies and practices.* Denver, CO: Center for Policy Research.

Plowright, D. (2011). *Using mixed methods: Frameworks for an integrated methodology.* Thousand Oaks, CA: Sage.

Rivlin, A. M. (1971). *Systematic thinking for social action.* Washington, DC: Brookings Institution Press.

Rossman, G. B., & Wilson, B. L. (1985). Numbers and words: Combining quantitative and qualitative methods in a single large-scale evaluation study. *Evaluation Review, 9*(5), 627–643.

Saldaña, J. (2013). *The coding manual for qualitative researchers* (2nd ed.). Thousand Oaks, CA: Sage.

Sale, J. E. M., Lohfeld, L. H., & Brazil, K. (2002). Revisiting the quantitative-qualitative debate: Implications for mixed-methods research. *Quality and Quantity, 36*(1), 43–53.

Sanderson, I. (2002). Evaluation, policy learning, and evidence-based policy making. *Public Administration, 80*, 1–22.

Sorensen, E., Sousa, L., & Schaner, S. (2007). *Assessing child support arrears in nine large states and the nation.* Retrieved from http://aspe.hhs.gov/hsp/07/assessing-CS-debt/

Sorensen, E., & Zibman, C. (2001). *Poor dads who don't pay child support: Deadbeats or disadvantaged? Assessing the New Federalism* (Policy Brief B-30). Washington, DC: Urban Institute.

Spillane, J. P. (1998). State policy and the non-monolithic nature of the local school district: organizational and professional considerations. *American Educational Research Journal, 35*(1), 33–63.

Stake, R. E. (2012). Qualitative case studies. *Handbook of qualitative research* (pp. 443–466). Thousand Oaks, CA: Sage.

Steckler, A., McLeroy, K. R., Goodman, R. M., Bird, S. T., & McCormick, L. (1992). Toward integrating qualitative and quantitative methods: An introduction. *Health Education Quarterly, 19*(1), 1–8.

Strauss, A. (2003). *Qualitative analysis for social scientists.* Cambridge, UK: Cambridge University Press.

Strauss, A. (1987). *Qualitative analysis for social scientists.* Cambridge, UK: Cambridge University Press.

Sundra, D. L., Scherer, J., & Anderson, L. (2003). *A guide on logic model development for CDC's Prevention Research Centers.* Atlanta, GA: Centers for Disease Control and Prevention, Prevention Research Centers Program Office.

Tashakkori, A., & Teddlie, C. (1998). *Mixed methodology: Combining qualitative and quantitative approaches.* Thousand Oaks, CA: Sage.

Tashakkori, A., & Teddlie, C. (2003). The past and future of mixed methods research: From data triangulation to mixed model designs. In A. Tashakkori & C. Teddlie (Eds.), *Handbook of mixed methods in social & behavioral research* (pp. 671–701). Thousand Oaks, CA: Sage.

Tashakkori, A., & Teddlie, A. (2009). *Foundations of mixed methods research: Integrating quantitative and qualitative approaches in the social and behavioral sciences.* Thousand Oaks, CA: Sage.

Teddlie, C., & Tashakkori, A. (2006). A general typology of research designs featuring mixed methods. *Research in the Schools, 13*(1), 12–28.

Tseng, V. (2012). The uses of research in policy and practice. *Social Policy Report, 26*(2), 3–16. Retrieved from http://www.srcd.org/

Woolley, C. M. (2009). Meeting the mixed methods challenge of integration in a sociological study of structure and agency. *Journal of Mixed Methods Research, 3*(1), 7–25.

Index

⑤SAGE research**methods**

The essential online tool for researchers from the world's leading methods publisher

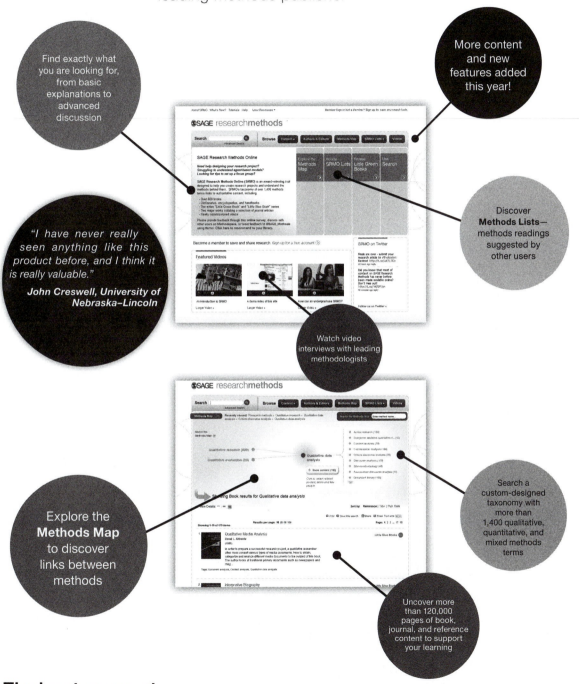

Find exactly what you are looking for, from basic explanations to advanced discussion

More content and new features added this year!

"I have never really seen anything like this product before, and I think it is really valuable."

John Creswell, University of Nebraska–Lincoln

Discover **Methods Lists**— methods readings suggested by other users

Watch video interviews with leading methodologists

Explore the **Methods Map** to discover links between methods

Search a custom-designed taxonomy with more than 1,400 qualitative, quantitative, and mixed methods terms

Uncover more than 120,000 pages of book, journal, and reference content to support your learning

Find out more at
www.sageresearchmethods.com